From Philanthropy
to Activism

HOLOCAUST SERIES

The Holocaust Series publishes original, interdisciplinary research centering on Jewish life and the Holocaust. Drawing on history, theology, art, philosophy, psychology and other fields of the social sciences, the series covers hitherto unexplored areas of Holocaust Studies shedding light on the human and social conditions of the period.

Titles published in the Series

AMISHAI-MAISELS, Z.
Depiction and Interpretation: The Influence of the Holocaust on the Visual Arts

ECKARDT, A. (ed.)
Burning Memory: Times of Testing and Reckoning

SHIMONI, G. (ed.)
The Holocaust in University Teaching

A related title

BAUER, Y.
Out of the Ashes: The Impact of American Jews on Post-Holocaust European Jewry

A related Pergamon journal

European Judaism

From Philanthropy
to Activism

*The Political Transformation of American
Zionism
in the Holocaust Years 1933–1945*

by

DAVID H. SHPIRO

PERGAMON PRESS

OXFORD · NEW YORK · SEOUL · TOKYO

UK	Pergamon Press Ltd, Headington Hill Hall, Oxford OX3 0BW, England
USA	Pergamon Press Inc., 660 White Plains Road, Tarrytown, New York 10591, USA
KOREA	Pergamon Press Korea, KPO Box 315, Seoul 110–603, Korea
JAPAN	Pergamon Press Japan, Tsunashima Building Annex, 3–20–12 Yushima, Bunkyo-ku, Tokyo 113, Japan

First edition **1994**

Library of Congress Cataloging in Publication Data
Shpiro, David H.
From philanthropy to activism: the political transformation of American Zionism in the Holocaust years, 1933–1945/by David H. Shpiro.—1st ed.
p.   cm.—(Holocaust series)
Includes bibliographical references.
1. American Emergency Committee for Zionist Affairs.
2. Zionism—United States—History.   3. Jews—United States—Politics and government.   4. Holocaust, Jewish (1939–1945)—Influence.   5. United States—Ethnic relations.   6. American Zionist Emergency Council.
I. Title.   II. Series.
DS149.A1A4728   1993   973'.04924—dc20   93-25532

British Library Cataloguing in Publication Data
A catalogue record for this book is available from the British Library

ISBN 0 08 041378 1 (hardcover)

Printed in Great Britain by Galliard (Printers) Ltd, Great Yarmouth

In memory of my dear mother

LILIAN (LEA RACHEL) GOLD-SHPIRO

an American Zionist pioneer

whose life was dedicated to the Zionist ideal.

Contents

Preface

"Never before has a single Jewish community been placed in such a position of responsibility . . . It is the blindness of inertia, the paralysis of habit, that permits some American Jews to think that in the years ahead of us our organizations can go on moving in their separate orbits without regard to world events."

DR. S. GOLDMAN, 1940

EARLY in May, 1939, the American ambassador in London, Joseph P. Kennedy, assured the British government that it need not worry about the American Jewish reaction to publication of the projected "White Paper" on Palestine: "The Jews would make some noise, but it would not be serious." Just eight years later, the President of the United States complained that the White House had never before been under such pressure or subjected to such intensive propaganda as has been set in motion over American policy on Palestine. What brought about this drastic change?

In the course of just a few years American Zionism underwent a radical transformation. The Zionist movement had been peripheral to the American Jewish community which, on the whole, set its sights on rapid integration within the non-Jewish environment. But this community, with its gamut of social and fund-raising bodies, was transformed into the determined standard-bearer of a Zionist political solution to the Jewish problem, and the major ally of the Jewish community in Palestine. Moreover, American Zionism had been converted from an apolitical, philanthropic entity into a powerful, well-organized political influence group that had adopted many of the methods inherent in the American democratic process and had learned to manipulate the diverse forces at play on the American scene.

To identify and interpret the factors instrumental in bringing this change about, the following pages concentrate on the story of the Zionist Emergency Committee (later known as the American Zionist Emergency Council). Between 1938 and 1945 the Emergency Committee came to organize and direct

American Jewry's struggle for the formation of a Jewish state in Palestine. It became the primary address for the American government, Palestine's Jewish community, American Jewry and the Zionist movement with respect to all plans for Palestine in the postwar world.

On the basis of material gleaned from memoirs, personal interviews and reminiscences, correspondence, minutes and documents (many of which were not made available to the public until recently), three major spheres of the Emergency Committee's work are analyzed:

a) The internal Zionist sphere, with particular emphasis on how American Zionism, although totally unprepared, nevertheless met the organizational, political and ideological challenges with which the war and the annihilation of European Jewry confronted it.

b) The internal Jewish sphere as shown in the light of the Emergency Committee's success in popularizing the idea of the establishment of a Jewish state in Palestine as a postwar solution for Jewry, and in activating the Jews of America to work toward that objective.

c) The sphere of American Jewry's relations with American society and the extent to which the Emergency Committee adopted methods and instruments characteristic of the American political scene to influence the governmental establishment and rally favorable public opinion.

A far-reaching study of this hitherto untold chapter in the history of American Zionism is of utmost importance for an understanding of the central and sometimes decisive role of the Jews of the United States in the establishment and support of the Jewish State.

The idea for this book originated in a conversation with the late Professor Jacob Talmon at the Hebrew University. When I remarked to him that the great political influence of American Zionism had come about as a reaction to the Holocaust, he replied: "The matter is not so simple—and should be thoroughly studied." This challenge inspired the writing of my doctoral dissertation, which was carried out with Professor Yehuda Bauer as my adviser. To the latter I express my gratitude for guiding me through all the stages of my study at the Institute of Contemporary Jewry of the Hebrew University. I also extend particular gratitude to Professor Ben Halpern of Brandeis University—a friend and scholar who accompanied this work from its inception.

So many people gave me their time and assistance that I cannot hope to acknowledge all of them. But I particularly want to thank Dr. Michael Heymann and his successor Mr. Yoran Mayorek, director of the Central Zionist Archives in Jerusalem, and the members of his staff who were all exceptionally helpful. The same is true of Ms. Sylvia Landress and Ms. Esther Togman at the Zionist Archives and Library in New York; Dr. Gustafson and Ms. Nicastro of the Diplomatic Branch and Mr. J. Taylor of the Modern Military Records Branch at the National Archives in Washington D.C.; the Franklin D. Roosevelt Library, Hyde Park; the A.H. Silver Papers (The Temple, Cleveland); the Weizmann Archives, Rehovot; the Ben-Gurion Archives, Sde-Boker; Palestine Statehood

Committee Papers, Yale University Library; the Public Records Office, London; and the National and Hebrew University Library, Jerusalem.

I am indebted to many individuals who were active in the Zionist movement during the period covered by this study and who granted me extremely interesting oral history interviews. Their names appear in the bibliography.

Special mention must be made of the assistance given me by the late Dr. Emanuel Neumann who, as one of the leaders of American Zionism, planned and carried out the political Zionist struggle in the United States; his constant encouragement and help during this book's earliest stages were invaluable.

I wish to thank the Franklin D. Roosevelt Library of Hyde Park, New York, for permission to quote from President Roosevelt's memorandum to Cordell Hull dated May 17, 1939; HarperCollins Publishers for the use of a quote from *Palestine Land of Promise* (copyright 1944 by Walter C. Lowdermilk; reprinted by permission of HarperCollins Publishers); and the director of the Central Zionist Archives in Jerusalem for permission to include a number of quotations from documents in the files.

I wish to express my gratitude to Shirley Shpira for her work on the English version of this manuscript.

Last but not least, I thank my wife Carmela and my five sons who patiently encouraged me on the long way toward completion of this book, for which they sacrificed a great deal.

PLATE 1. The Provisional Emergency Committee for Zionist Affairs, New York, 1915. At far right, Judge Louis D. Brandeis.

Introduction: Antecedents

THE outstanding characteristic of American Jewry in the early decades of this century was its extraordinary diversity, from the standpoint of country of origin, time of immigration, extent and nature of religious observance, social and economic status, vocation, ideological belief, and organizational affiliation.[1] Moreover, Jewish organizational life was marked by total decentralization. The American Jewish scene had turned into a competitive arena in which countless ideologies and interests ran at counter currents.[2] If Zionism hoped to make substantial inroads within such a heterogeneous community, it would have to seek out and exploit any existing common denominators, and unite motley factions around a single overriding issue.

Two major factors underlying the extreme diversity of this Jewry were the origin and timing of each wave of immigration.[3] The first group that came to America, the "Spanish-Portuguese" Jews, was so small that by the third decade of the twentieth century almost no trace of it remained; the second wave of immigrants came from Central Europe and were known as "Germans" because they tended to speak German regardless of their country of origin. They numbered about 250,000 and arrived between 1840 and 1880.[4] They acclimatized quickly and by the second quarter of the nineteenth century had founded religious and welfare institutions based on patterns similar to those they had known in Europe. By the 1930s many of the descendants of these immigrants were wealthy—bankers, businessmen and professionals.[5] They tended to affiliate with Reform Jewry, that had its roots in the West European emancipation.[6] Organizationally, they formed charitable societies based on patterns similar to those they had known in Europe, belonged to Bnai Brith, and a particularly distinguished group of them organized the American Jewish Committee. Integrated into the American scene, these people considered themselves the most enlightened Jews in America, an elite qualified to lead and represent American Jewry as a whole. Most of those who belonged in this category defined Jewry as a religious entity and rejected national or ethnic identification.

The largest wave of immigration came between 1880 and 1924—over two million Jews from Russia, divided Poland, Romania and the eastern parts of the

Austro-Hungarian Empire. This group formed two distinct blocs, which can be termed "labor" and "central." The "labor" bloc stood at the extreme opposite of the Jewish spectrum vis-a-vis the "German" bloc. These newcomers to America were strongly felt at the beginning of the twentieth century, when large numbers of Jewish immigrants labored in the sweatshops of the garment industry. Their ideology, steeped in a working-class ethos, was an amalgam of socialism imported from the East European Pale of Settlement and American trade-unionism—which they helped to establish. Anti-Zionist groups such as the Bund-oriented Workingmen's Circle functioned alongside Socialist-Zionist groups such as the Farband. The far left was represented by the Stalinist Jewish People's Fraternal Order. By the 1930s and 1940s, although still a force to be reckoned with, this category was rapidly thinning out as more and more Jews rose to higher occupational levels.

The "central" bloc comprised the majority of American Jewry, either immigrants from Eastern Europe or their offspring. They were artisans, industrial workers, owners of small or medium-sized businesses, and some—relatively few—were professionals. Many were still Yiddish speakers. They were either altogether uninterested in any religious affiliation or leaned toward the Conservatives, with a small minority retaining their Orthodox practices. Jewry was defined by them in national-ethnic, cultural and religious terms. Although in the 1940s this group was undergoing the process of assimilation into the mainstream of American life, it was the prime reservoir of strength of Jewish organizational life, including the Zionist movement.

The strongest ties of all the above groups were those forged in America with other immigrants from the same town or region in Europe. As a result *Landsmanshaften*—organizations that combined a social and religious framework with mutual aid for the membership—were formed. A more generalized kind of group identification also had a regional-geographical base: the "Litvak" versus the "Galitzianer"; the "Bessarabian" versus the "Rumanian"; the "Aleppan" versus the "Damascan."

This multiplicity was reflected in the community's organizational structure, which was decentralized and nearly "anarchic," combining organizational forms transplanted from European Jewish life with those prevalent in America. The chaotic nature of organizational life may be attributable to the sudden freedom from repression that found expression in almost irresponsible disorganization. Another possible explanation is the breakdown of traditions and disintegration of communities engendered by the philosophy that lauded individualism and laissez-faire as the epitome of the American way of life.[7] Without a delimiting framework, with no obligatory norms, the Jews in America felt free to choose the institutions and organizations that seemed best to represent Jewish interests.[8]

In 1924 the United States immigration quotas put an end to mass immigration from Central and Eastern Europe, so that by 1940, ninety percent of the Jews in America had been in the country a minimum of fifteen years, and

most much longer.[9] They had become Americanized rapidly, while simultaneously becoming more involved in the social and political scene. Unlike other
immigrants to the United States, the Jews did not look upon their country of
origin as "home." Fleeing poverty and persecution, the Jew came to America
with his whole family to settle permanently, retaining little nostalgia for the
land he had left. Nonetheless, his strong sentimental attachment to, and concern
for the Jews who had remained behind—in fact for all Jews less fortunate than
himself, and for all things Jewish in the widest sense of the word—remained
unchanged.

The influence of the community far exceeded its actual numbers. In the
period just before the Second World War, American Jewry had attained a
relatively high status, having advanced more quickly than other groups that
had come to the country at about the same time.[10] Their social standing,
however, while somewhat higher than that of most immigrant societies, fell
below their economic position. Whereas only some 45 percent of the American
population were employed in industry, commerce and the free professions, 70
percent of the Jews worked in these occupations.[11] Jews were conspicuously
absent from agriculture—with only about one-half of one percent engaged in
farming, as compared with 18 percent of the general population. Better
economic conditions and the educational and cultural facilities located in the
urban areas where Jews were concentrated provided an ideal outlet for the
traditional love of learning. Consequently, the educational level was extremely
high,[12] and the number of Jewish authors in literary and scientific journals
proliferated.

The Jews' political leverage was reinforced by the fact that, between the
wars, 78 percent of American Jewry (who numbered almost five million) was
concentrated in fourteen large cities, some two million of them in New York
City. Although they could be found scattered throughout the entire country,
the Jews, approximately three percent of America's total population, comprised
eleven percent of the population in cities with over 100,000 residents. Their
concentration in certain states (California, Connecticut, Maryland, Michigan,
Minnesota, Missouri, Texas—not to mention New York) also facilitated the
organization of Zionist activities in relatively few but highly important areas.
Wherever they were, Jews were involved in economic life and therefore in
contact with the non-Jewish community, which enabled them to exert an
influence on local policy-makers.[13]

While some Jews sought a panacea in socialism and communism, most of
them, sharing the middle-class values to which the various "isms" and radical
ideologies were anathema, gave their unbridled allegiance to Roosevelt and the
New Deal. For them, the New Deal was not just pragmatic policy but a social,
even quasi-messianic cause, whose prophet could turn democratic capitalism
into a framework allowing them to lead prosperous lives as both Jews and
Americans.

Roosevelt, keenly aware of this trend among American immigrant, urban communities, encouraged Jews and other minorities to assume key positions in his administration and the Democratic Party. Henry Morgenthau, Jr.,[14] Felix Frankfurter,[15] and Samuel Rosenman were among his chief advisers. The exciting prospect of rebuilding American society attracted countless Jews from assorted backgrounds to the new agencies and departments set up under the New Deal.[16]

Political activism alone would not have sufficed to turn the Jewish community into fertile ground for the Zionist message were it not for the existence of another quality which served to bind the fragmented community: concern for *Klal Yisrael*—for all of Jewry. The precept of mutual aid that is so deeply rooted in Jewry kept the Jews in America keenly aware of the conditions in which their kinfolk abroad lived. In the "New Country," the willingness to aid their coreligionists abroad spawned numerous welfare organizations prepared to proffer economic, social, medical and professional assistance. The activities of the American Jewish Committee and the founding of the American Jewish Joint Distribution Committee during the First World War are outstanding examples of this.[17] And for many Jews, the concept of *Klal Yisrael* also encompassed the Zionist movement.

The Beginnings of Zionism in America

The first outposts of the Zionist movement in America were the Hoveve Zion societies, founded in the 1880s by immigrants from Eastern Europe. These failed to attract any appreciable following since the abolition of the Diaspora—one of the basic tenets of political Zionism—was in direct contradiction to the almost messianic belief harbored by the vast majority of American Jews in their community's future existence and prosperity. In the face of the apathy—and downright hostility—of the Jewish community, whether Orthodox or Reform, newly arrived or veteran, Conservative or assimilationist, the Hoveve Zion movement foundered and, by the mid-1880s, had virtually disappeared.

An upsurge of interest in Zionism was triggered off by the First Zionist Congress and led to the establishment of the Federation of American Zionists (FAZ) in 1898.[18] Up to 1914, the FAZ was mainly active in relief work and its influence on the Jewish community was marginal.[19] In the political arena it confined itself to the dispatch of memoranda to the State Department, none of which received more than an official acknowledgement. The members of the FAZ (some 12,000 by 1914, out of a total Jewish population of three million)[20] were culled chiefly from the ranks of immigrants from Eastern Europe, who had been fired with enthusiasm by a leading Zionist activist, Shmaryahu Levin. From 1906 to 1914, Levin visited America frequently and preached the Zionist doctrine in hundreds of speeches. Small numbers of both foreign-born and native American Jews began to be attracted by the movement. At the same time, the new American Zionist leadership began developing a uniquely American understanding of Zionism, attuned to the pluralistic society in

America.[21] The outbreak of hostilities in August 1914 prevented Levin from returning to Europe, whereupon he directed his efforts toward transforming the American Zionist movement into the center of world Zionism. The first important step was taken with the establishment of the Provisional Executive Committee for General Zionist Affairs, headed by the well-known jurist, Louis Dembitz Brandeis.

Brandeis, whose membership of the Zionist movement dated back scarcely a year, was an ardent liberal whose creed combined European liberalism with American faith in democracy.[22] Leaving a successful law practice to fight social issues through litigation, he became one of the pillars of American progressivism, earning himself the nickname, "the people's attorney." Brandeis's first significant contact with Jewish issues occurred in 1910 when he negotiated the settlement of the cloakmakers' strike in New York and became involved for the first time with the masses of Jewish immigrants from Eastern Europe. Soon afterward, he came under the influence of an early disciple of Herzl, Jacob De Haas, who won him over to the Zionist cause.[23]

While this "conversion," well into his middle years, signified an awakening of Brandeis's ethnic consciousness, it did not stem from identification with the history and cultural heritage of East European Jewry. Brandeis did not grasp their ideological differences and had no patience for hairsplitting theoretical polemics. Instead, he redefined Zionism in accordance with his liberal, reformist American creed. To Brandeis, Zionism was American and progressive as much as it was Jewish. In his view, the endeavors of the Palestinian pioneers were equal to American reformist ventures. He based the compatibility of Zionism with Americanism on his new definition of Americanism. Abandoning the prevailing melting-pot theory, he adopted the cultural pluralistic view which saw in true democracy the recognition of differentiation versus uniformity. American civilization would be enriched if each national or cultural group contributed from its own heritage. Thus, Brandeis set the Zionist movement in America firmly within its American context, and refused to accept for the United States the Herzlian premise of perpetuating universal antisemitism.[24]

Brandeis's brand of Zionism was fresh and original: "It became clear to me that to be good Americans, we must be better Jews, and to be better Jews, we must become Zionists."[25] This approach not only ruled out the possibility of dual loyalty, but postulated that since Zionism was synonymous with American ideals of democracy, the Jews, as loyal Americans, were actually duty-bound to join the Zionist movement.

In his first speech as chairman of the Provisional Executive Committee, Brandeis set forth his goals clearly: ". . . the Jewish people have something which should be saved for the world; . . . the Jewish people should be preserved, and . . . it is our duty to pursue that method of saving which most promises success."[26] Zionism was the method he chose to pursue.

Determining to reorganize American Zionism, Brandeis's first symbolic step was to move the Zionist offices from the old ramshackle building in the Lower

East Side into the mainstream Fifth Avenue and 18th Street. To further his aims, he drew on all the professional, social and political connections he had. The invigorated activity drew ambitious young men. Harvard law professor Felix Frankfurter, Reform rabbi Stephen S. Wise,[27] and Circuit Court judge Julian Mack were only a few who followed Brandeis.

A combination of factors led to a steep rise in FAZ membership during the war: the prestigiousness of the Zionist leadership, which had easy access to the Wilson administration—including the President himself; President Wilson's ideals of self-determination for every nation, as against the prevailing mania for Americanization; the publication by Britain of the Balfour Declaration; and the horrors of the war in Europe and Palestine. By 1919, the FAZ and its affiliates numbered 144,820 members.[28] There was a corresponding rise in membership of Mizrachi and the Labor Zionist organizations.

During the war years, the Provisional Executive Committee raised substantial sums for the Jews in Palestine. The Emergency Committee, which had been established in 1914, was now renamed the Palestine Restoration Fund. Brandeis's target figure of 100,000 dollars was doubled several times during the ensuing years, and in 1918, over 3 million dollars were raised[29] (an extraordinary achievement, given the total of 14,000 dollars contributed by American Zionists only four years earlier).

By the end of the war, American public opinion had swung to some extent in favor of the Zionists. The leaders of the Provisional Committee, and Brandeis in particular, continued to exert pressure on Wilson. As a Presbyterian, Wilson was sympathetic to Zionist aims, which tied in with his ideals of self-determination, and he approved Brandeis's proposals for a democratic Palestine.[30] It may be assumed that the domestic implications of an increasingly powerful Zionist movement were not lost upon the government. A letter circulated in June 1918 among the members of Congress, requesting their reactions to the Balfour Declaration, elicited 300 positive responses by the end of the year, including some which advocated American assistance in implementing the Declaration.[31]

From 1914 to 1918, the Provisional Committee concentrated on two principal objectives: to protect and assist the Jewish community in Palestine, and to obtain American support for the Balfour Declaration. With respect to the first of these goals, the Committee succeeded in obtaining an official American protest to the Ottoman authorities regarding the deportation of Jews of foreign nationality from Palestine. Through separate negotiations with the Allies and the Central Powers, the shipment of food and medication to the Jews in Palestine across the war zone was made available (as long as the United States remained neutral). The government was so sympathetic to this venture that it agreed to reserve space for the consignments aboard US Navy ships, since private shipping could not be used. The American Treasury also aided the Committee by permitting funds raised in America to be transferred to the near-starving Jews in Palestine. These funds provided the sole source of support for both veteran and newly-established Jewish settlements during one of the most harrowing periods in their history.

As for the second goal—obtaining support for the Balfour Declaration—Brandeis attempted repeatedly to obtain Wilson's endorsement of the Declaration, but failed to secure more than indirect approval.[32] The State Department objected to any support for Zionist claims on the grounds that since America was not at war with Turkey, it had no right to determine the fate of Turkish territory after the war. Secretary of State Lansing advised the President to refrain from any official statement regarding the future of Palestine. Zionist pressure on the President did not slacken, however, and on August 31, 1918, Wilson came closer than ever before to an official declaration of support. In a New Year's greeting to Rabbi Stephen Wise, which was intended as a public message to American Zionists, Wilson expressed satisfaction at the growth of the Zionist movement in America and in the Allied countries, following the British government's publication of the Balfour Declaration.[33]

Realizing the importance of suitable representation of Zionist claims to the American administration, the Provisional Committee determined to establish a democratically elected body which could speak for American Jewry as a whole. The project was bitterly opposed, however, by the "German" elements of the community, headed by the American Jewish Committee. Brandeis then initiated a pro-American Jewish Congress campaign which, after many months of open dispute and major concessions on both sides, came into being in December 1918.[34] In the name of America's three million Jews, the Congress passed a resolution approving the Balfour Declaration and demanding that Britain accept the mandate over Palestine. The year 1918 also saw the establishment of the ZOA—the Zionist Organization of America— which superseded the FAZ in line with Brandeis's proposal that a single organization be set up to which every American Zionist would belong directly.

Zionism in Crisis

After the cessation of hostilities, a deep rift between the ZOA and its European counterparts became apparent and came to a head at the World Zionist Conference in London in 1920. Brandeis's Zionism was strictly practical. His visit to Palestine in 1919 had convinced him that the country's problems were first and foremost economic, and his efforts as leader of the ZOA were aimed principally at encouraging Palestine's economic growth, so that the country would be in a position to absorb large numbers of Jewish immigrants. He had no time for the endless debates on niggling points of ideology which were so characteristic of the European Zionist organizations. Neither did he understand the *shtetl* mentality of the East European Jews with which Weizmann—who sprang from that background himself—was so familiar. While appreciating Brandeis's emphasis on economic revival, the European Zionists deplored his preoccupation with discipline, professional competence and efficiency. In the eyes of Weizmann and his camp, Brandeis's Zionism stood aloof from the spiritual and cultural revival of the Jewish heritage. Moreover, Brandeis stirred up resentment by offhand dismissal of men like Leo Motzkin and Yehiel Tchlenow, who had devoted themselves to the movement.[35] When Brandeis called for experts, non-Zionist if need be, to create a viable economy in Palestine, the European old-timers were deeply offended. Brandeis, for his part, blamed the Zionist leadership in Palestine for inefficiency, factional power struggles, local hierarchies and personal prerogatives. A new administration, with Louis Lipsky as president, was elected.

In an attempt to bridge the gulf between the two poles, it was proposed to set up an Executive Committee of European and American Zionists, with Brandeis as chairman. Brandeis refused the position, and barred the other members of his delegation from accepting any post other than that of honorary president. This left the ZOA isolated from the world Zionist movement, and bereft of any clear sense of purpose.

Brandeis's high-handed and sometimes patronizing methods had already come under criticism in the past, and opposition to his leadership by the pro-World Zionist Organization faction in the ZOA crystallized in the wake of Weizmann's visit to the United States in 1921.[36] At the ZOA convention in Cleveland in June of that year, the delegates refused to vote their confidence in the administration and Brandeis resigned, together with the chief members of his staff.

The Brandeis–Weizmann dispute, which culminated in a total rift in the movement, dealt a severe blow to American Zionism. To some extent the two leaders epitomized in their personalities the characteristics which American Zionism needed to succeed. Brandeis's Americanized framework would, ideologically and practically speaking, prove acceptable to the American Jewish public, while Weizmann's messianic, all-pervading sense of Jewishness would provide the link to the age-old yearning for Zion—a longing that transcended the bounds of logic. In the event, the Zionist movement labored—with little success—for the next two decades to heal the wound opened at Cleveland. It took the severe threat posed by the Arabs and British to the national home in Palestine, coupled with the horrors of Hitler's "Final Solution," to reunite American Jewry in the cause of Zion.[37]

The Brandeis faction, now outside the organized Zionist movement, limited its activities mainly to economic endeavors. It formed a body for practical work in Palestine—The Palestine Development Council—to collect funds and distribute them as investments in Palestine development projects or as donations to the Palestine Endowment Fund. In the years to come, many of the members, disillusioned with the limited scope of their strictly economic programs, started drifting back to the active leadership in the reconstituted American Jewish Congress, the Keren Hayesod and the ZOA.[38] The ZOA's new administration, led by Louis Lipsky, now found itself in a difficult position. After campaigning for a return to true Zionism, with an emphasis on Zionist ideology, Jewish culture and diaspora work, it gradually abandoned its policy during the course of the 1920s. Instead, it concentrated all its efforts on securing money for the upbuilding of the National Home—a proceeding it had formerly censured its opponents for undertaking. For this the Keren Hayesod (Foundation Fund) was set up and Weizmann came personally to America.

The pledges Weizmann succeeded in raising in 1921 and 1923 fell ludicrously short of what had been expected by the WZO in its initial five-year planned development. The JDC collected much larger sums for non-Zionist philanthropic causes overseas. It was clear now to Weizmann and his followers that the key to success was non-Zionist support.[39] As Keren Hayesod receipts failed year after year to meet anticipated requirements in Palestine, Weizmann worked toward an agreement with Louis Marshall, leader of the "German" element in American Jewry. Six long years of negotiations finally brought about the establishment of the United Jewish Agency. To the non-Zionists, the main obstacles to agreement were "Diaspora nationalism" on the one hand, and, on the other, Zionist ideology in general and the end goal of an independent Jewish state in particular. To the Zionists, the main obstacle was the plan initiated by Julius Rosenwald, the anti-Zionist millionaire from Chicago who was head of Sears Roebuck, to resettle millions of Jews on Soviet soil (particularly in the Crimea). The Joint set up the Agro-Joint for this purpose, while Rosenwald set up his own organization. The Zionists saw in this undertaking not only a diversion of millions to resettle Jews in a country which they loathed at the expense of the upbuilding of Palestine, but a negation of the basic concept of Zionism—Palestine as the Jewish national homeland.

The two sides compromised.[40] Weizmann played down political Zionism as irrelevant to the Jewish Agency. He understood that his original "purist" Zionist cultural and political stand with which he had opposed the Brandeis faction, denouncing their program as assimilationist and anti-Zionist, would not interest the wealthier American Jews, and in substance, if not in form, he adopted most, if not all, of the Brandeis program. The non-Zionists played down somewhat the Agro-Joint propaganda, and for various internal reasons in the Soviet Union the project came to a standstill at the beginning of the 1930s.[41]

By creating the Jewish Agency, the WZO undercut the possibility of the ZOA regaining the dominant role it had held during the war years, not only vis-a-vis the WZO but toward American Jewry in general and the American Zionist movement in particular. The weakness of American Zionism in the wake of the Brandeis–Weizmann rift enabled the non-Zionist American Jewish Committee to resume its dominance in the community.[42] The Weizmann-headed WZO and the Brandeis faction alike found it necessary for funding their Palestine projects to appeal for assistance to Louis Marshall and Felix Warburg of the "German" leadership.

Internally the ZOA in the 1920s concentrated virtually all its efforts on raising money and, by the end of the decade, all other activities were at a standstill. There was no development of membership and organization, and district chapters did little educational work.[43] As the American Zionist leadership became increasingly involved in the creation of the Jewish Agency and the activities of Keren Hayesod and the United Palestine Appeal, it tended to neglect those problems of administration and membership that afflicted the ZOA. This resulted in further decline in membership and revenues.[44] In an editorial in the *New Palestine*, the ZOA admitted that Zionism in America, practically speaking, was synonymous with assisting Jewish Palestine.[45]

In general, American Zionism—weakened and disjointed—started to disintegrate. Hadassah, the Zionist women's organization of America, had been allowed by the Brandeis administration to hold a semi-autonomous status, although remaining officially part of the ZOA. As progressives, the ZOA recognized Hadassah's indispensibility and function and admired the genius and drive of its leader, Henrietta Szold. Lipsky tried to force Hadassah back to ZOA rule and to induce it to participate in the Keren Hayesod campaign. Hadassah, which was led by a leadership accepting the Brandeis line, became the most successful Zionist organization in America.

When the JDC gave up its part in the American Zionist medical unit, Hadassah took it over as its full and exclusive responsibility. Hadassah conducted an open battle against Lipsky and his administration and succeeded in having all the funds its members raised expended by its own bodies in Palestine (not including membership dues, which covered organizational expenses). Hadassah also won from the Lipsky administration full autonomy as a separate organization with representation on the ZOA bodies.[46]

The two ideological parties in American Zionism, Mizrachi and the Labor Zionists, went their own separate ways, devoting their efforts to their own special concerns. The Mizrachi worked for its modern orthodox educational system and religious institutions in Palestine. Its adherents in America were active in similar projects, such as New York University.[47] The Labor Zionists, under the apocalyptic influence of the Soviet revolution, split when a considerable part joined Communist or pro-Communist groups. The Poale Zion in America shared the ideology of its sister party in Palestine, which saw in the achievements of labor Zionism in Palestine "the nucleus of an organically developing socialist or cooperativist Jewish commonwealth."[48] Its fund-raising was devoted mainly to labor projects in Palestine.

In this way, American Zionism in the 1920s diverted most of its energy and creativity into separate channels detached from the main united effort of the movement. By 1922, Zionist membership had dropped to just under 18,500. The movement was torn by internal factionalism and neutralized by public apathy. Nevertheless, the new administration, headed by Louis Lipsky, achieved a significant victory for political Zionism in the enactment on June 30, 1922, of the Lodge-Fish Congressional Resolution, which approved the concept of a Jewish homeland in Palestine.[49] Thereafter, the Zionist movement suspended its political activities and, tailoring its approach to the temper of the decade, became de facto a fund-raising body. As a philanthropic venture,

Zionism was a respectable cause for Jews and gentiles alike. Philanthropy, after all, was a revered American virtue.[50]

Dr. Weizmann, visiting the United States in 1928, confessed to the great sin of which all heads of the Zionist movement were guilty: "We have abused America as a money-making machine. Under the pressure to which America has been subject it has not developed an adequate, healthy, vigorous Zionism."[51]

Under such conditions, most American Jews viewed the political program of Zionism as passé. The distant goal of Zionism took on a religious-cultural overtone. Some of the spokesmen for this outlook (understandably, mainly rabbis), viewed the political phase of Zionism—the securing by international recognition of a Jewish homeland—as having definitely ended. Rabbi Abba Hillel Silver, who would later lead the Zionist political struggle vis-à-vis the American administration and the world community, concluded in 1929: "It is well that the political phase of Jewish messianism is coming to a close in the upbuilding of the National Homeland."[52]

For the majority of American Zionists, Zionism had come to mean not self-fulfillment but a sort of identification, a link to Jewish heritage, a buffer against gentile hostility. There was no question of dual loyalty: American Jews were Americans first. Paradoxically, many of them viewed Zionism as a movement toward normalization of their own position in America. Zionism, it was believed would give them an equal status with other ethnic immigrant groups, as well as providing the pride and dignity so urgently needed to cope with the discrimination and other forms of social antisemitism then on the increase in America.

Antisemitism, Depression and Decline

The postwar years had brought with them a recoil from the social idealism of the Wilson era. The wartime one-hundred-percent Americanism deteriorated into nativism and racism, and the concepts of pluralism were eclipsed by a monolithic conformity. With the upsurge of the Red Scare in the early 1920s, American Jews fell under the suspicion of a majority bent upon an undiluted Americanism. Jews were accused of Bolshevism, which, for many Americans, constituted the epitome of all evil. Henry Ford "discovered" the menace of the "international Jew" and set the stage for the popular reception of *The Protocols of the Elders of Zion*. Despite its exposure as a tissue of lies, the work was used by Ford until 1927 as the basis for an antisemitic campaign in his newspaper, *The Dearborn Independent*.[53] On its pages, the Jews were accused of plotting the subjugation of the whole world and of being the source of almost every American affliction including high rents, the shortage of farm labor, gambling, alcoholism, loose morals, and even short skirts! The Ford attack, absurd though it was, was merely an exaggerated manifestation of widespread antisemitism.

Prejudice became pervasive. Jews encountered economic discrimination in commercial banks, industrial corporations, insurance companies and public utilities. Landlords grew less disposed to rent to Jews. Colleges and universities, including Harvard, Dartmouth, Columbia, New York University and Rutgers, instituted quotas on Jewish enrolment. In the South the Ku Klux Klan instigated boycotts of Jewish merchants, vandalized Jewish-owned stores, burned crosses outside synagogues, and terrorized prominent Jews. Social discrimination became widespread, and all over the country Jews felt that a barrier had come down between them and the Gentiles.[54]

The Jewish reaction took different forms. Some refused to dignify their attackers by defending themselves; others, at the opposite pole, sought to negate their Jewishness. The majority followed a rational approach in refuting the antisemitic charges and showing how they negated the American democratic tradition. Despite the prevailing antisemitic climate, however, the American Zionists, in common with American Jewry as a whole, were not shaken in their belief that Jews and Judaism could survive in America. Zionists did not cite antisemitism as an argument against the future of the Jews in America; neither did they issue any serious call for emigration to Palestine.

The Great Depression at the end of 1929 came as a hard blow to American Zionism. Not only did economic woes rapidly overshadow all other concerns in life, but the very viability of capitalism as an economic system and of democracy as a political system were thrown into question. Burdened by such critical issues, most Jews declined to pay even minimal membership fees to Zionist organizations. Furthermore, since a great many Jews devoted their skills and talents to newly opened government services rather than to Jewish affairs, Zionist organizations were left with leaders of only mediocre calibre.[55]

However, despite the economic hardships and the dearth of outstanding leaders willing to work for Jewish and Zionist causes, the Zionist youth groups did manage to expand. The American-born and English-speaking youngsters in these youth groups, most of which were under the auspices of the general, labor and religious Zionist organizations, began to outnumber their European-born counterparts. These groups served as a social and cultural outlet and focused on Jewish identity, national awareness, and anti-war and anti-totalitarian principles. Those affiliated with labor or religious parties espoused the doctrine of *halutziut*, or pioneering. Hashomer Hatzair went so far as to make a commitment to move to Palestine a prerequisite for membership.

Like the New deal, *halutziut* seemed to offer a solution to the problems which had surfaced in the wake of the Depression and the rise of Hitler. A social vision incorporating the ideals of agricultural labor and cooperative living seemed a viable alternative to the capitalism which was tottering.[56] Those who took the challenge of *halutziut* seriously trained for a life of pioneering at summer camps and cooperative farms designed for this purpose. Special emissaries were sent from Palestine to serve as counselors. The number of Jews who actually realized a pioneering way of life, however, was minimal. Rabbi Stephen Wise mourned publicly that "there is a complete lull in things Zionistic in America."[57]

The Zionist Revival

Yet Zionism in America was not doomed. Cracks in the original position of the Reform movement—which held that Judaism was a religion that could thrive anywhere and denied the national component of the religion—began to appear in the 1920s, when Reform leaders participated in the economic development of Palestine. In 1935, the Central Conference of American Rabbis officially altered an earlier platform negating Jewish peoplehood, and individual rabbis were allowed to stake out their own position with regard to Zionism. Two years later, this same body affirmed the obligation of all Jews to cooperate in restoring Palestine as the Jewish homeland, and a similar commitment was undertaken by the organization of Reform lay leaders.[58] This "Zionization" of the Reform movement was largely precipitated by a shift in its membership from those of German origin to descendants of East European families. And in general, world events tended to shake its faith in the rational and enlightened progress of the human race.

Modern Orthodox and Conservative congregations were traditionally more receptive to Zionist ideals. The diverse facets of religious life—from prayer services and sermons to curriculum in the schools—gave expression to Zionism. In 1938, the ZOA accepted the Rabbinical Assembly, a Conservative body, as an affiliate with the right to send delegates to Zionist conventions. Orthodox Jews joined both the ZOA and Mizrachi, the religious Zionist party.

As the vision of universal brotherhood began to recede, Zionism made inroads among labor unions as well. A growing number of unions made contributions on behalf of labor in Palestine. In 1934, the Jewish Labor Committee was founded in order to fight Nazism and antisemitism in the United States, and many of its constituent units worked in concert with Zionist groups.

The gamut of Jewish publications—whether in English, Hebrew or Yiddish—grew increasingly pro-Zionist. Hebrew schools abounded in response to the revival of the biblical language in Palestine. The founders of Zionism figured prominently in the songs, stories and plays presented in the schools, and Jewish National Fund boxes for coins contributed by the children could be found at nearly every Jewish school. Zionist themes were transmitted, inter alia, via the Hebrew Youth Cultural Federation's dramatic group, exhibits at the Century of Progress Exhibition of 1934 and the Palestine pavilion at the New York World's Fair of 1939, and a popular film entitled *Land of Promise*.

Between 1932 and 1938, the ZOA increased its membership from 8,484 to 27,732, and then almost doubled that figure in 1939. The registered membership of Hadassah, the women's Zionist organization, grew from 27,144 in 1925 to 66,000 in 1939.[59] Like other organized Jewish bodies, however, the Zionist movement functioned mainly on a social level. Activities centered on bridge and tea parties, concerts and luncheons, usually for purposes of fund-raising. Hadassah, by far the largest and most effective of the Zionist groups, excelled in the organization of such functions. Offering opportunities for socializing while serving a "good cause," it also attracted many new members.[60]

The rise of the Nazi regime in Germany became a vitalizing challenge to the Zionists of America. It was a crisis situation which infused the dormant Zionist organizations in America with a new cause. Morris Rothenberg, president of the ZOA, described the situation in 1933 as "a new day in the history of the movement."[61] In a harrowing way, Zionist thinking on the Diaspora, at least in Europe, was reaffirmed. Many Jews felt the need to "do something" in reaction to Hitlerism. For many, Zionism was the answer.

The continuing dynamic growth of the Jewish national home in Palestine and the need to absorb fleeing German Jews were twin causes for a new upsurge in Zionist membership. There may have been another, submerged, cause which it is almost impossible to document but was felt at the time. Some of American Jewry's pro-Zionist activities originated from fear of large numbers of Jewish refugees immigrating to America. In the midst of a national economic crisis, this could only aggravate the antisemitism at home. Palestine was doing wonders as a refugee haven. Why not support it as such on a philanthropic basis?

In general, for many American Jews, supporting the Zionist cause in Palestine served as a meaningful, non-religious, cultural or political way to actively identify as Jews, enabling them to feel part of their people and assist their suffering brethren abroad.[62] Zionist activity in America was reviving from its Depression doldrums. Despite the true state of the movement, the *New Palestine* could proudly declare in January 1936 that "seldom in recent years has there been so much Zionist activity." Old Zionists seemed to have been imbued with new life and many new recruits were joining the ranks.[63] Certain Zionist leaders, however, were less enthusiastic about the recent upsurge, as they felt its basis was "refugeeism" rather than political Zionism. Addressing the National Conference for Palestine held in 1936, Dr. Abba Hillel Silver warned eloquently of the dangers of such an approach: American Zionism's emphasis on Palestine only as a haven for persecuted Jews, he maintained, diverted attention from the movement's fundamental precepts and aspirations.

Louis Lipsky, the veteran Zionist leader, analyzed the movement's position as reacting to events that took place in Europe and Palestine, rather than functioning in accordance with a pre-arranged, systematic plan. The American Zionist movement was permitting itself to be led on by catastrophic emergencies, rather than working to overcome the root cause of those emergencies—the nation's homelessness.[64]

In actual fact, the leadership of the World Zionist Organization found the passivity of the Zionists in America, the largest and wealthiest Jewish diaspora, quite convenient. Engrossed in its own internal struggles, the world leadership asked little more of American Zionism than that it fill a philanthropic role commensurate with its wealth and power, and continue to play a marginal role in the Zionist political arena. The tenuous relationship of American Zionism to the world movement became increasingly obvious after 1933, when the

Palestine Labor Movement became the dominant element in the Zionist Executive. The General Zionists in the United States felt "left out," and were becoming more and more alienated from the world leadership. As of 1934, they even stopped sending a representative to the Jewish Agency Executive in Jerusalem, their only form of representation being a non-resident delegate to the Executive in London.

The political files of the Zionist Executive in London require extensive shelf-space, but only one-quarter of one folder is needed to hold the entire political correspondence with the American Zionists from 1933 to 1938. Remote from the centers of action, with no permanent representation on the movement's central bodies, American Zionism became so fragmented internally that its various branches hardly seemed to be part of the same organization. During the debate over the Partition plan submitted by the Peel Commission, the cleavages among individuals and groups were so severe that the movement in the United States was unable to take a unified stand.

Early in 1938, convinced that the deteriorating situation in Europe and Palestine called for a unified political front, Weizmann convened the Zionist Actions Committee. Meeting in London, the Committee decided to establish an office in the United States and empower it to act in the name of the Jewish Agency Executive; it therefore had to include non-Zionist Jewish Agency members as well as Zionists. An irreconcilable disagreement arose in America over the non-Zionist member: each interested party put forward its own candidate, compromise was out of the question, and the entire plan fell through.[65]

The various branches of the American movement, however, continued to grow. In 1938, on the eve of the 21st Zionist Congress, the 245,928 shekel-holders in America represented the largest Zionist movement in the world.[66] Inevitably, the sense of importance that accompanies size fomented unrest in the movement, the membership beginning to demand representation commensurate with its numbers. The "double vote" accorded to the Palestinian Zionists, by virtue of which they had the dominant vote in the world movement, was challenged.

This unrest was largely responsible for the election of Dr. Solomon Goldman to the presidency of the ZOA at the convention held in Detroit in 1938. A veteran Zionist and a rabbi—first in Cleveland and then in Chicago—Dr. Goldman was an energetic man who became an outstanding spokesman for American Zionism. He led the growing demand for greater unity within the movement in the United States and for greater participation of the American contingent in the decisions taken by the World Zionist Organization. Before Dr. Goldman's incumbency, the Midwestern Jewish communities had been somewhat neglected by the Zionist leaders who, coming from the Eastern Seaboard region, considered New York's Jews as their prime target and major support. The new president, deeply involved as he was with the Jewry of the "hinterland," enhanced the importance of those communities.

The Zionist Response to Nazism

The rise of Nazism posed an unprecedented challenge to American Jewry. While many discounted Hitler's antisemitic demagoguery as the ravings of a lunatic, a few were disposed to take him seriously. Among the most farsighted was Rabbi Stephen Wise, who recognized the Nazi threat as early as 1931.[67] At his behest, the American Jewish Congress, together with the American Federation of Labor, sponsored a mass rally at Madison Square Garden in 1934 to present "The Case of Civilization versus Hitlerism" in the form of a mock courtroom scene. Spurred on by Wise, the AJC also threw its weight behind a public boycott of German products, rejecting warnings that such action might engender increased antisemitism. Later it became the cornerstone for the founding of the World Jewish Congress as a national Jewish response to the Nazi peril.

The Nuremburg Laws of 1935, which ejected the Jews from German society on "racial" grounds and made many forms of contact between Jew and non-Jew illegal, signalled to many not only the destruction of German Jewish emancipation, but a bad omen for Jewish emancipation everywhere. The American Jewish community could not remain complacent in the face of this onslaught. Moreover, the fact that the German Jews' high cultural level and rate of assimilation offered them no immunity against the ravages of this insane form of hatred had far-reaching implications for American Jews. New ground rules were being laid for Jewish survival.

Exacerbating the issue was the effect of Nazi propaganda in the United States. The German embassy and consulates, which were part of Dr. Goebbels' propaganda ministry, spearheaded a campaign by organizations sympathetic to the Nazi cause to propagate the doctrine of hatred within the American public. Nazi operatives wooed potential American supporters, and did not recoil from offering monetary inducements for cooperation. Politicians and Christian leaders were prime targets for these efforts.

Antisemitic groups proliferated, with the encouragement of the Nazis and their sympathizers. According to a 1939 estimate by the American Jewish Committee, over 500 antisemitic groups were active in the United States. Among them were the German-American Bund, the Order of '76, the Knights of the White Camellia, the Silver Shirts and others. Under hatemongers such as William Dudley Pelly, Joe McWilliams and Gerald K. Smith, they led the "Buy Christian" campaigns. Their technique was to exploit the anxieties bred by the Depression. It was not unusual for distributors of Father Coughlin's incendiary newspaper *Social Justice* to incite brawls with Jews and organize anti-Jewish rallies and boycotts. The "Zionist connection" was not overlooked when attacking F. D. Roosevelt's "Jewish-Zionist-Communist conspiracy," as they called the New Deal.

Alongside such overtly antisemitic groups there were those which made an attempt at respectability by cloaking their Jew-hatred in a guise of patriotism.

Their core message, however, was identical to that of the other groups. This wave of propaganda began to take its toll on American public opinion. Various polls indicated that the image of the Jews had become associated with a host of negative character traits and suspect political leanings.[68]

The surge in antisemitism served to strengthen Zionist groups. The Jews began to wonder whether life among the Gentiles was really as secure as they had believed. Neither assimilation nor separatism could guarantee their safety. Some of them saw Zionism as a solution. The opportunity to identify with a Jewish activist movement instilled the community with a sense of solidarity and pride in light of the growing hostility and discrimination.[69]

Palestine as a Refuge for Persecuted Jews

Even non-Zionists concurred with regard to the need for Palestine to serve as a refuge. In 1935 a special conference of Jewish organizations, Zionist and non-Zionist alike, representing a combined membership of over a million, affirmed its backing for the efforts being made to rehabilitate the land. Controversial issues, such as the primacy of independence and diaspora nationalism, were abandoned for the sake of unity, at least on the practical level.

Parallel with general fundraising efforts, a number of special projects were undertaken. For example, the Hadassah hospital in Jerusalem absorbed German Jewish physicians; Pioneer Women provided the funding for an agricultural school for German girls; Mizrachi women raised special funds for religious refugees. Youth Aliyah, one of the most notable of the relief projects, brought over 13,000 refugee youngsters from Hitler's Europe to safety in Palestine. All these projects combined rescue activities with the development of the Jewish national home.

And yet, the Jews stopped short of equating Zionism with a commitment to move to Palestine. They wished to combat antisemitism, but in an American way. Although their confidence in the American way of life had been shaken, they retained their fundamental faith in America as a land of promise. Nor were they even willing to admit that Germany was an unfit place for Jews to live—at least not until 1938. Any declaration to the effect that German Jews should leave Germany would have been tantamount to acquiescence in the German vision of a *judenrein* land. And if Jews could be dispossessed from one Western nation, then what would this imply for Jews in other parts of the Western world?

Consequently, there was no major revision in Zionist thinking in America. The movement remained a philanthropic endeavor to build up Palestine as a refuge for persecuted Jews. While American Jews contributed ever more willingly to Zionist causes as the crisis worsened, they maintained a low profile. Wary of fanning the sparks of antisemitism around them, American Jews, including the Zionists, grew increasingly cautious and apologetic. A delicate balance had to be maintained between concern for their brethren in Europe and apprehension over antisemitic manifestations at home. Especially sensitive was the issue of absorbing Jewish refugees in the United States, and too vocal a stand might easily play into the hands of the Jew-baiters. Anti-immigration sentiment based on both chauvinistic and economic arguments had led to legislation in the 1920s severely curtailing immigration quotas, and the Depression served to reinforce the Americans' desire to keep the number of immigrants to a minimum. American consuls abroad were instructed to make administrative procedures more difficult, and as a result only a small percentage of the quotas were filled. Both Zionist and non-Zionist organizations, intimidated by the explosive nature of this issue, refrained on the whole from pressing for a modification of the immigration laws. Instead, they settled for a holding action: unobtrusive lobbying for an easing of consular procedure, and opposition to congressional bills proposing further reductions in quotas.[70]

It was far more prudent to call on Britain to allow for mass immigration to Palestine, and the American Jewish Congress (AJC) joined the Zionist groups in pressing this demand. The British, however, were loath to cooperate. In 1936, Arab opposition to Jewish immigration—which Nazi funding and propaganda had served to catalyze—took the form of general strikes, riots and an armed uprising. The dominant tendency of the British was to appease the Arabs by restricting immigration and purchase of land by Jews.

The restrictions on Jewish immigration to Palestine spurred American Zionists to step up their pressure. Jewish groups were joined by senators and congressmen in publicly demanding that these restrictions be eased, and the ZOA beckoned the League of Nations to intervene. Various Christian groups such as the Pro-Palestine Federation and the American Christian Conference on Palestine added their voices to the demand for continued immigration. The State Department, however, maintained silence on the issue, disclaiming any responsibility.

Communiques sent by Zionist groups to the British Peel Commission, which had been set up to investigate the situation in Palestine, urged the British to responsibly fulfill their duties as a mandatory power. The Zionist memoranda cited the fact that enormous sums of American capital had already been invested in Palestine. In 1937, the Peel Commission published its recommendation for the partition of Palestine into two separate states, one Arab and one Jewish. American Zionists felt betrayed by the report, which reneged on the Balfour Declaration's pledge to have Palestine become a Jewish national home. A state comprising only twenty percent of the area of Palestine would only serve to make the Jews an insecure minority engulfed by hostile enemies. The non-Zionists opposed the very concept of statehood, claiming that it would divide world Jewry and siphon off vital resources from the battle against Nazism.

The Zionist groups prevailed upon Congress to introduce bills against partition. The ZOA asserted that according to the treaty signed in 1924, the status of Palestine could not be altered without American approval. The British took exception to this interpretation, and the American government declined to press the issue. Eventually, American Zionists reconciled themselves to the idea of partition, especially in light of the World Zionist Congress's decision not to reject partition outright but to use the proposal as a basis for continuing negotiations with the British and Arabs. The Arabs, however, were even more adamant than the Jews in their opposition to the plan, and the British were compelled to backtrack.[71]

Prologue to War

As the plight of European Jewry deteriorated steadily, Western governments did little more than pontificate on their desire to be of assistance. In Evian, France, an international conference on refugees convened by President Roosevelt refused to discuss the possibility of Palestine serving as a place of refuge for masses of immigrants. *Kristallnacht* was followed by new, more severe anti-Jewish measures. And despite the internationalist platforms they had run on, Roosevelt and Secretary of State Cordell Hull tailored their policy to the largely isolationist mood of the country. This public sentiment stemmed both from the Depression and from the sense that America had been duped by financiers and armaments manufacturers into participating in World War I. Both Congress and the administration steered a neutral course, and therefore the Nazi treatment of the Jews was regarded as an internal matter not subject to outside interference. Various resolutions in Congress for executive action died in committees. The pleas by Jewish groups for urgent action on humanitarian grounds did not daunt the powers that be.

The burgeoning antisemitism induced the diverse Jewish organizations to make periodic attempts at unity, but in the main they worked separately, all of them operating on multiple fronts. American Jewry became a competitive arena in which innumerable interests and ideas figuratively crossed swords. This, then, was the Jewish community that the rise of the Nazis and the systematic destruction of Jewish life in the Third Reich unexpectedly catapulted to center stage, forcing it to assume the burden of leadership.

Notes to Antecedents

1. A. G. Duker, *The American Jewish Community: Its History and Development*, New York, 1953, p. 17; also *Forum for the Problems of Zionism, Jewry and Israel*, vol. IV, Jerusalem, 1959, pp. 281–303.
2. For a contemporary account of the variegated trends in American Jewish life, see M. J. Karpf, *Jewish Community Organization in the United States*, New York, 1938, pp. 42–50.
3. See D. J. Elazar, *Community and Policy. The Organizational Dynamics of American Jewry*, Philadelphia, 1976, table 2, p. 38.
4. On German-Jewish immigrants, see M. I. Urofsky, *American Zionism from Herzl to the Holocaust*, New York, 1976, p. 51; B. W. Korn, *Eventful Years of Experience*, Cincinnati, 1954; R. Glanz, *Studies in Judaica Americana*, New York, 1950.

5. For a detailed study of Jewish organizational patterns, see Elazar, *op. cit.*, pp. 34f.

6. Urofsky, *op. cit.*, pp. 57ff.

7. J. B. Agus, *Guideposts in Modern Judaism: An Analysis of Current Trends in Jewish Thought*, New York, 1954, p. 11.

8. See E. Ginzburg, *Agenda for American Jews*, New York, 1950, pp. 13f.; Elazar, *op. cit.*, pp. 32–69.

9. H. Essrig, "Jewish American," in F. J. Brown, J. S. Roncek (eds.), *One America*, New York, 1952, p. 262.

10. Essrig, *ibid.*, pp. 269–73; also J. Bernard, *American Community Behavior*, New York, 1949, p. 198.

11. B. Edidin, *Jewish Community Life in America*, New York, 1947, pp. 235f.; N. Glazer, *Social Characteristics of American Jews, 1654–1954*, New York, 1955, pp. 27f.; W. Herberg, *Protestant–Catholic–Jew*, New York, 1956, pp. 241f.; Elazar, *op. cit.*, pp. 32–69.

12. Bernard, *op. cit.*, p. 198.

13. S. Halperin, *The Political World of American Zionism*, Detroit, 1961, p. 47f.

14. On Morgenthau, see H. L. Feingold, " 'Courage First and Intelligence Second': The American Jewish Secular Elite, Roosevelt and the Failure to Resist," *American Jewish History* (hereafter: *AJH*), vol. LXXII, June 1983, pp. 443–8.

15. On Frankfurter, see L. Dinnerstein, "Jews and the New Deal," *AJH*, vol. LXXII, June 1983, p. 467f.; also Feingold, " 'Courage First and Intelligence Second,' " pp. 435–43.

16. J. L. Teller, *Strangers and Natives*, New York, 1968, pp. 170f. A somewhat less favorable description of this trend is given by the veteran Washington correspondent, W. M. Kiplinger: "Jews are 'New Dealers' like non-Jews within the New Deal, but they are probably a little more 'New-Dealish' or 'leftish' than the average New Dealers" (*Washington is Like That*, New York–London, 1942, p. 373). See also Dinnerstein, "Jews and the New Deal," pp. 463f.; *idem, Uneasy at Home. Antisemitism and the American Experience*, New York, 1987, pp. 61–3.

17. See J. S. Woocher, *Sacred Survival. The Civil Religion of American Jews*, Bloomington-Indianapolis, 1986, p. 29; also Urofsky, *American Zionism, op. cit.*, pp. 70–2.

18. *Die Welt*, 1913, no. 35, p. 1146. The Zionist Congress report of 1921 mentions an even lower figure.

19. On the beginnings of Zionism in America, see M. Feinstein, *American Zionism 1884–1904*, New York, 1965; E. Friesel, *The Zionist Movement in America 1892–1914*, Tel Aviv, 1970 (Hebrew); I. S. Meyer (ed.), *Early History of Zionism in America*, New York, 1958. On the ideology and activities of the FAZ, see N. W. Cohen, "The Maccabean Message: A Study in American Zionism until World War I," *The Jewish Social Studies Quarterly* (hereafter: *JSS*), 1956, pp. 163–78.

20. A. S. Waldstein of Poale Zion wrote in 1910: "Political Zionism in America began more as a charity movement than a nationalist concept." See *Yidisher Kempfer*, June 17, 1910, vol. 13, nos. 1–2.

21. See Friesel, *op. cit.*, pp. 77–123.

22. On Brandeis's Liberalism-Zionism, see M. I. Urofsky, *Louis D. Brandeis and the Progressive Tradition*, Boston–Toronto, 1981, pp. 87–103.

23. Brandeis's biographers disagree as to the motivation for his act. At least five different explanations are given by historians. For a short, comprehensive list of the studies and their theses, see J. Gurock, *American Jewish History—A Bibliographical Guide*, New York, 1983, pp. 80f.

24. On the Zionist ideas and activities of Brandeis, see M. I. Urofsky, *A Mind of One Piece, Brandeis and American Reform*, New York, 1971; also A. Gal, *Brandeis of Boston*, Cambridge, Mass., 1980; E. Rabinowitz, *Justice Louis D. Brandeis: The Zionist Chapter of his Life*, New York, 1968; B. Halpern, *A Clash of Heroes. Brandeis, Weizmann, and American Zionism*, New York–Oxford, 1987; E. Friesel, *Zionist Policy After the Balfour Declaration, 1917–1922*, Tel

Aviv, 1977, pp. 226–46 (Hebrew); *idem,* "Brandeis' Role in American Zionism Historically Reconsidered," *AJH,* September 1979, pp. 34–65.

25. L. D. Brandeis, *The Jewish Problem—How to Solve It,* New York, n.d., p. 12.
26. From Brandeis's address at the extraordinary conference in Hotel Marseilles, New York, on August 30, 1914; *ibid.*
27. The career of Stephen S. Wise—the single most influential American Jew of his time—and his public activities both within and outside the Jewish community, is described in detail in M. I. Urofsky, *A Voice that Spoke for Justice: The Life and Times of Stephen S. Wise,* Albany, 1982, and Wise's own autobiography, *Challenging Years: The Autobiography of Stephen Wise,* New York, 1949. See also a collection of Wise's speeches and letters in C. H. Voss (ed.), *Stephen S. Wise: Servant of the People,* Philadelphia, 1969.
28. *American Jewish Year Book,* vol. 19 (1917–1918), p. 196; vol. 21 (1919–1920), pp. 329, 601.
29. *Annual Financial Reports of the Provisional Executive Committee for General Zionist Affairs,* Pittsburgh, 1918, pp. 4–6.
30. S. Adler, "The Palestine Question in the Wilson Era," *JSS,* vol. x, October 1948, p. 304.
31. The responses were later incorporated in R. Fink, (ed.), *The American War Congress and Zionism: Statements by Members of the American War Congress on the Jewish National Movement,* New York, 1919.
32. Adler, "The Palestine Question in the Wilson Era," pp. 306f.
33. F. E. Manuel, *The Realities of American–Palestine Relations,* Washington, 1949, p. 176.
34. On the confrontation and its outcome, see Halpern, *op. cit.,* pp. 118–26.
35. On the Brandeis–Weizmann dispute, see Urofsky, *American Zionism, op. cit.,* p. 260, n. 49; Halpern, *ibid.,* pp. 171–232; G. Berlin, "The Brandeis–Weizmann Dispute," *AJH,* September 1970, pp. 37–66; D. Lipstadt, "Louis Lipsky and the Emergence of Opposition to Brandeis," in M. Urofsky (ed.), *Herzl Year Book,* vol. 8, 1978, pp. 37–60; E. Panitz, "Washington versus Pinsk," *ibid.,* pp. 77–131.
36. Halpern, *ibid.,* p. 266.
37. Urofsky, *American Zionism, op. cit.,* pp. 297f.
38. Halpern, *op cit.,* pp. 256f. On Wise's return, see Urofsky, *A Voice that Spoke for Justice, op. cit.,* pp. 211f.
39. Halpern, *ibid.,* pp. 254–8.
40. Urofsky, *American Zionism, op. cit.,* pp. 323–8.
41. Y. Bauer, *My Brother's Keeper: A History of the American Jewish Joint Distribution Committee 1929–1939,* Philadelphia, 1974, pp. 76–104.
42. Halpern, *op. cit.,* pp. 254–8.
43. Urofsky, *American Zionism, op. cit.,* pp. 311f.
44. *Ibid.,* pp. 341f.
45. *New Palestine,* January 8, 1926, p. 29.
46. On the history of Hadassah during this period, see D. H. Miller, *A History of Hadassah 1912–1935,* Ph.D. dissertation, New York University, 1968; C. B. Kutscher, *The Role of Hadassah in the American Zionist Movement 1912–1922.* unpublished Ph.D. dissertation, Brandeis University, 1975; Urofsky, *American Zionism, op. cit.,* pp. 344–6.
47. Only scanty information exists on the Mizrachi movement during this period. See S. Rosenblatt, *The History of the Mizrachi Movement,* New York, 1951; also G. Klapperman, *The Story of Yeshiva University,* London, 1969, pp. 141–5.
48. Halpern, *op. cit.,* p. 253.
49. See I. Oder, *The United States and the Palestine Mandate, 1920–1948: A Study of the Impact of Interest Groups on Foreign Policy,* unpublished Ph.D. dissertation, Columbia University, 1956, pp. 26–87; H. Parzen, "The Lodge–Fish Resolution," *AJH,* vol. IX, September 1970, pp. 69–82; P. L. Hanna, *British Policy in Palestine,* Washington D.C., 1942, pp. 60–8.
50. Halperin, *op. cit.,* pp. 202–04.
51. *New Palestine,* February 21, 1936, p. 3.

52. "Herzl and Jewish Messianism. Nationalism as a Means to a Greater Goal," *New Palestine*, "Theodor Herzl Edition," 1929, pp. 254–6.

53. See P. Grose, *Israel in the Mind of America*, New York, 1983, p. 96. On Henry Ford and the publication of this infamous antisemitic forgery, see L. B. Ribuffo, "Henry Ford and *The International Jew*," *AJH*, June 1980, pp. 497–505; A. Lee, *Henry Ford and the Jews*, New York, 1980; R. Singerman, "The American Career of 'The Protocols of the Elders of Zion,' " *AJH*, September, 1981, pp. 48–78.

54. A. Lawrence Lowell, president of Harvard University, advocated a *numerous clausus* for Jews in American universities. N. W. Cohen, *Not Free to Desist: The American Jewish Committee 1906–1966*, Philadelphia, 1972, p. 143. See also D. A. Gerber (ed.), *Anti-Semitism in American History*, Urbana, Chicago, 1986, pp. 25f.

55. N. W. Cohen, *American Jews and the Zionist Idea*, New York, 1975, pp. 37–9.

56. S. Grand, *A History of Zionist Youth Organizations in the U.S. from their Inception to 1940*, unpublished Ph.D. dissertation, Columbia University, 1958.

57. Voss, *op. cit.*, pp. 167f.

58. Halperin, *op. cit.*, pp. 61–109.

59. *Ibid.*, p. 327.

60. S. Koenig, in I. Graeber, S. H. Britt (eds.), *Jews in a Gentile World*, New York, 1942, p. 224.

61. *New Palestine*, June 16, 1933, p. 1.

62. See Halperin, *op. cit.*, pp. 22f.; R. Gordis, *Judaism for the Modern Age*, New York, 1955, p. 32; E. Ginzberg, *Agenda for Modern Jewry*, *op. cit.*, pp. 57ff.

63. *New Palestine*, January 17, 1936, p. 1.

64. *Ibid.*, February 21, 1936.

65. Letter from Lipsky to Weizmann of June 24, 1938, Central Zionist Archives (hereafter: CZA), file Z4/17055.

66. See stenographic report of 21st Zionist Congress, Jerusalem, 1939, p. 20.

67. Urofsky, *American Zionism, op. cit.*, p. 265 and n. 34.

68. On American public opinion concerning Jews as reflected in public opinion polls, see C. H. Stember et al. (eds.), *Jews in the Mind of America*, New York, 1966, especially pp. 156–70.

69. On antisemitism during this period, see D. S. Strong, *Organized Anti-Semitism in America. The Rise of Group Prejudice During the Decade 1930–1940*, Washington D.C., 1941; also C. J. Tull, *Father Coughlin and the New Deal*, Syracuse, 1965; J. Higham, "American Anti-Semitism Historically Reconsidered," in *Jews in the Mind of America, op. cit.*; S. Marcus, *Father Coughlin: The Tumultuous Life of the Priest of the Little Flower*, Boston, 1973; A. Brinkly, *Voices of Protest: Huey Long, Father Coughlin and the Great Depression*, New York, 1983, pp. 82–218, 271f. On antisemitism among the Protestant clergy, see R. Stork et al., *Wayward Shepherds, Prejudice and the Protestant Clergy*, New York, 1971.

70. For American Jewry's demands on the administration and American diplomatic inactivity, see D. S. Wyman, *The Abandonment of the Jews*, New York, 1984; H. L. Feingold, *The Politics of Rescue*, New Brunswick, 1970; M. N. Penkower, *The Jews were Expendable. Free World Diplomacy and the Holocaust*, Urbana–Chicago, 1983.

71. For American Zionist reactions to the Royal Commission and its report, see Urofsky, *American Zionism, op. cit.*, pp. 150–94.

1

On the Threshold of a New Era

> Will American Jewry, I ask, rise to its full stature or will this giant among
> the Jewries of the world fetter its own hands and feet? A timid Jewry in
> America is no asset to world Jewry.

SOLOMON GOLDMAN, 1939

Darkening Political Horizons

AMERICAN JEWRY was profoundly affected by the failure of the Evian
Conference on Refugees, where Palestine was almost completely ignored as a
solution for Jewish victims of persecution and oppression. There was also
profound concern over the capitulation of the Western democracies to Hitler at
Munich which meant, among other things, exposing Czechoslovakia's Jewish
community to the Nazi tyranny. Rumors of the imminent publication of the
Woodhead Commission's Report, which in essence eliminated the possibility of
establishing a Jewish state even in the partitioned Palestine proposed by the
Peel Commission, further alarmed the Jews of America, as did indications that
the British were about to repudiate the Balfour Declaration and lock the gates of
Palestine to Jewish refugees (the number of those permitted entry had already
been drastically reduced twice since 1936).[1]

On the 15th of July, 1938, Weizmann wrote a long letter to Dr. Solomon
Goldman. After congratulating him on his election to head the ZOA,
Weizmann suggested calling a conference in America "to deal exclusively with
Palestine and its relation to the Jewish position in general . . ." (the letter was
written before the decision to convene the 21st Zionist Congress). The
participants would be the Jewish Agency, American and British Zionists and
certain outstanding Jewish individuals "such as Einstein, Blum, Freud, Brandeis,"
who would be asked to give public support, as would the American Jewish
community as a whole. The agenda would deal with both political and practical
matters, including "the raising of a large loan for development and constructive
work in Palestine."[2]

Events on the world stage were moving too quickly, however. Before such a conference could be called, Chamberlain had gone to Munich. Weizmann met with Malcolm MacDonald, the British Colonial Secretary, who frequently referred to the "Arab danger," the need to "go slow," and the difficulties of implementing partition as it "might upset the Arab world."[3] Three days later, on the 6th of October, 1938, Weizmann sent an urgent wire to the leaders of the American Zionist movement expressing his fear that a far-reaching change was about to take place in British policy with respect to the national home in Palestine. In view of the threat that Jewish immigration would be stopped altogether and that an Arab government would be formed, he asked that all friends be mobilized to petition the British ambassador in Washington and to demand that the American ambassador in London be instructed to take immediate action.[4]

Goldman at once contacted the heads of the other Zionist organizations and of the largest general Jewish organizations in America. They decided to join forces and form a National Emergency Committee for Palestine.[5]

Establishment of the National Emergency Committee

The committee was formed by the heads of the ZOA, Hadassah, Mizrachi and Poale Zion, who then co-opted representatives of the American Jewish Congress, the American Jewish Committee, the Jewish Labor Committee (which described itself as "cooperating with" rather than "joining"), and other non-Zionist groups. The Emergency Committee's declared objective was to counteract the readiness of certain British governmental circles to repudiate the Balfour Declaration's promise of a national home for Jews in Palestine, and to fight against limiting Jewish immigration. For the first time in many years not only did the Zionist organizations undertake joint action—they even joined forces with non-Zionist organizations.

In a transatlantic phone call on the 10th of October, Dr. Goldman was able to report to Weizmann that the members of the newly-formed committee were working day and night. Louis Brandeis, Felix Frankfurter and other Zionists had scheduled meetings with President Roosevelt; non-Zionists, among them Bernard Baruch, were also to meet with the President and try to persuade him to exert pressure on the British government. Bernard Baruch had even sent a cable to his personal friend, Winston Churchill, urging him to try to convince his government not to reverse its stand with respect to Palestine.[6]

The Emergency Committee sought to bring American governmental pressure to bear on the British. Attempts were made to influence the Administration to object strongly to any changes Great Britain might try to introduce in the terms of the Palestine mandate. The right of America to express such objection was based on interpreting the Anglo-American Treaty of 1924 as meaning that no changes could be made in the provisions of the mandate without the approval of the United States. Influence was to be exerted through personal diplomacy and by rousing public opinion. People with access to the President were recruited to undertake the diplomatic approach—among them Supreme Court Justices Brandeis and Frankfurter, presidential advisers Ben Cohen and Bernard Baruch, and Labor union leaders William Green and Philip Murray. Efforts to influence public opinion centered on the press, members of Congress, outstanding religious leaders, trades union heads, writers and intellectuals.

On the 13th of October representatives of the Emergency Committee met with the British ambassador in Washington; they presented him with a memorandum expressing American Jewry's objection to any change in British policy for Palestine. On the same day the delegation was received by Cordell Hull, Secretary of State. He was asked to comply with the Treaty of 1924: in other words, to insist upon America's right to validate or invalidate changes in Britain's Palestine policy.

Opening a temporary Emergency Committee office in New York, Dr. Goldman maintained round-the-clock contact with Zionist leaders throughout the United States and with Dr. Weizmann in London. Intensive activity resulted in the formation within one week of 450 local Emergency Committees throughout the United States.[7] The State Department and White House were inundated with telegrams sent at the rate of 10,000 a day.[8] Congressmen, governors and mayors also received thousands of wires and letters requesting their intervention with the President and State Department. University presidents, judges and non-Jewish liberals were urged to make public statements about the need for democratic countries to honor international obligations, in contradistinction to the European dictators.

A week after this concentrated drive was initiated, Cordell Hull declared publicly, in the name of the State Department, that Point 7 of the Anglo-American Palestine Mandate Convention had been clarified the previous year. Nothing in that agreement gave the United States the right to prevent changes in the mandate, although America could refuse to recognize the legality of any act that changed the situation with respect to American interests. The only American interests referred to concerned commerce, property ownership and missionary activities; the agreement also guaranteed America's right to enjoy the same relationships entertained by all other powers. The State Department's position was reinforced when Roosevelt publicly repeated the facts as outlined in Point 7.[9]

These public utterances by the Secretary of State and the President made it impossible for the Zionists to continue following this line of pressure on American officialdom. On the 23rd of October, 1938, Wise, Lipsky and Goldman sent the following cable to Weizmann in London:

PUBLIC UTTERANCES SKIPPER [Pres. Roosevelt] VERY FRIENDLY. DIFFICULT THEREFORE TO CONTINUE SAME PUBLIC PRESSURE. CAMPAIGN REACHING ITS MAXIMUM THIS WEEK. OUR

FUTURE PROCEDURE MUST DEPEND THAT YOU MAKE A VALUATION PRESENT SITUATION. CABLE EXPLICITLY.[10]

"Maximum" meant protests in the press by religious and social groups; letters to congressmen, the President of the United States and the Prime Minister of Great Britain; and mass meetings scheduled for the 2nd of November, the anniversary of the Balfour Declaration. On 26 October, Dr. Goldman sent a detailed report to Dr. Weizmann that included the following revealing statement:

> ... thus far we have continually emphasized that there must be no criticism of Great Britain. Our tone has been one of reasonableness and one of hope that the great liberal and sympathetic traditions of the British people would be manifested once again in the reassurance that the Balfour Declaration would be observed intact.[11]

It is ironical that the Woodhead Commission's Report published on the 9th of November, recommending an Arab–Jewish–British conference, lulled the fears of American Jewry. This report made the Partition Plan—which for different reasons both Zionists and non-Zionists rejected—a meaningless document. The feeling was widespread that the recommended conference (later known as the St. James Conference) offered practical prospects for improving the situation in Palestine. It seemed reasonable to expect some sort of rapprochement between Arabs and Jews that would facilitate implementation of the policies implicit in the Balfour Declaration and the mandate.[12]

Such optimistic prognoses, however, were hardly compatible with information the Zionist Executive sent to America. In a confidential report on the political situation, Ben-Gurion wrote that in a certain way a recent meeting with the Colonial Secretary might be considered reassuring,

> ... since it seems clear that immigration, although restricted, is not to be suspended. From another point of view, however, the conversation is very alarming: I am afraid that what is in his mind is to have some sort of partition, but without a Jewish State. It seems they want to have another Transjordan—a large part of Western Palestine into which Jews will not be allowed to immigrate, while in the Jewish area a restricted Jewish immigration only would be allowed. . . . I believe the real crisis may come about February or March, after the 'discussions' between H.M. Government and the Arabs and Jews. H.M. Government will then be trying to make up their own minds . . . and will probably be preparing new *gezeroth* [the Hebrew term for "harsh edicts" used in both English and Hebrew correspondence between Zionist leaders in England and America—author] for us.[13]

At this point the Emergency Committee suspended activities. Even the most critical issues were dropped; the conference about to be held in London, with the participation of a delegation of American Zionists, seemed to offer new possibilities. Two other elements prompted American Jewry to withdraw the public pressure it had set in motion: one was the fear of undermining British prestige at a time when England was in the forefront of the struggle against Hitler; the other was the dread of rousing latent antisemitism in the United States, where pro-Nazi organizations were finding fertile ground for their activities.[14]

The dilemma of the Jews was further compounded by their fear of exposing themselves to the accusation that they were trying to propel America into war. The men responsible for formulating British policy were not unaware of this dilemma; it may even have led them to minimize the importance of the protests originating in the United States. At the same time, however, MacDonald himself was confronted by almost as painful a dilemma: should war break out—an eventuality that could not be ignored—did American Jewry's support outweigh the friendship of the Arab world? He formulated this dilemma in a memorandum he submitted to the Cabinet in preparation for discussion of the Palestine problem.

MacDonald, architect of the White Paper policy, declared that it was hard to conceive of anything more damaging to Great Britain than loss of the support and friendship of the Moslem world. He therefore recommended that the White Paper policy be implemented as quickly as possible, adding that it would also help the government face pressure from the Jews and criticism from other sources. He stressed the undesirability of rousing strong anti-British sentiment in the United States. Should war break out, America's sympathy and support would be more important, in the final analysis, than any help England could expect from the Arab countries. He also noted that Roosevelt displayed interest in Palestine and had attempted to influence British policy.[15] All things considered, however, MacDonald's conclusion was clear: the best way to counteract Jewish pressure in matters involving Great Britain's security would be to implement the new restrictive policies in Palestine with all possible speed.

Early in February 1939, Stephen Wise, Louis Lipsky and Robert Szold left for England to represent the American Zionists at the round table conference at the Court of St. James. Not long after they arrived in London, Lipsky cabled the following message to Goldman: "RESTRAIN AMERICAN ACTIVITIES PENDING FUTURE ADVICES STOP ALL REPORTS PREMATURE TENDENTIOUS STOP . . ."[16]

Solomon Goldman, who had opposed cessation of the Emergency Committee's public activities, had grave doubts about what could be expected from the conference in London. The reports he received of the proceedings, primarily from Ben-Gurion,[17] reinforced his pessimism. He was convinced of the need to concentrate on strengthening the organization and establishing a Zionist political office in Washington. On the basis of his experience with the Emergency Committee, Goldman knew that it would no longer be sufficient to send people to Washington sporadically, to deal with urgent issues as they cropped up. Constant Zionist political action was called for, based on direct contact with various governmental offices. In other words, Zionism had to begin to "lobby" in the best American political tradition. He proposed the establishment of an office that could initiate and centralize nationwide action and simultaneously maintain personal contact with the policy-makers in the national government.

The American delegation returned after the dismal failure of the St. James Conference—which had served, essentially, to convince the British to continue with plans to appease the Arabs and limit Jewish immigration. In the name of the ZOA, Dr. Wise and Louis Lipsky gave their approval to Goldman's plan.[18] The other major Zionist parties agreed to participate, and Goldman set about making practical arrangements. He had been receiving encouragement from an unexpected source: David Ben-Gurion, in despair over British policy, had arrived in the United States early in January 1939 to mobilize American Jewry for protest activities. He enthusiastically supported Goldman's efforts to form a united political-Zionist front, and helped secure the support of other Zionist leaders. Ben-Gurion and Goldman shared a common approach to the salient issues of the time; both were more extreme in their opposition to Britain than either Weizmann or Wise, and on matters of policy Goldman turned to Ben-Gurion more and more frequently.

On the 20th of January Ben-Gurion had received a confidential cable from Weizmann warning of the imminence of war. He described the attempts being made by the British War Office to appease the Arabs and noted the British government's increasing concern with America's stand, should war break out. The cable concluded with the importance of following events in Washington as closely as possible.[19] Thereupon Ben-Gurion had called Wise, Lipsky and Szold to a confidential meeting where it was decided to open an office in Washington at once.[20] When Ben-Gurion left for the St. James Conference, Dr. Goldman determined to carry on the work they had started together.

On 3 March, 1939, the heads of the four Zionist organizations announced the formation of the "American Zionist Bureau" in Washington, declaring that it would henceforth represent the Zionist movement to the government. The Bureau's purposes were delineated as follows: to strengthen the position of Zionism in America; to keep Zionist issues before influential individuals and groups at all times; to make sure that non-Jews were informed of the accomplishments of the Jewish community in Palestine and to impress the public with Jewry's historic and political right to Palestine.[21]

These were urgent and significant tasks, but the means available for their implementation were hardly commensurate with their importance. Goldman himself had to find the funds to pay for the services of a director and a part-time secretary. His hopes and those of Isidore Breslau, a dynamic young Washington rabbi who was hired to direct the "Zionist Bureau," were soon dashed. Because of a constant lack of funds, irreconcilable differences over matters of policy and inter-organizational conflicts, the office soon became little more than a postbox for the Zionist parties.[22] Chaim Weizmann, who had visualized a progaganda and information bureau in Washington to which the London Executive could direct all its requests and correspondence, was deeply disappointed. The Emergency Committee closed the Bureau at the end of 1940, declaring it an "unnecessary expense."[23]

Putting the Emergency Committee to Work

Ben-Gurion had brought to the United States a three-point agenda for a conference to take place (after the St. James Conference) that would represent all of American Jewry. The projected agenda would include a report on the Conference in London, ways and means of defending Jewish rights in Palestine, and Jewish–Arab relations.[24] On 27 February an urgent cable came from London, outlining the provisions of a White Paper the British government was planning to issue. It provided for the establishment of an Arab state with a permanent Jewish minority, drastic reduction of Jewish immigration until, at the end of five years, it would cease entirely, and prohibition or severe limitation of land purchases in most parts of Palestine. The cable concluded with a call for help, stating that Palestine was now a matter of concern to all Jews; the Zionist leaders were asked to pool their efforts with those of Brandeis and his friends and special stress was placed on the importance of convening a representative conference of all the Jews of America.[25]

Influential Jews who had access to the President were asked to arrange a meeting with him. Ben-Gurion cabled a request that Brandeis "urge" Roosevelt to influence the British Prime Minister to allow large-scale Jewish immigration into Palestine. The President was also asked to try to persuade the British government to defer final decision on the Palestine question.[26] At the beginning of March, when the failure of the St. James Conference had become public knowledge and it was clear that the British government was about to publish the White Paper, the Emergency Committee was revitalized. There was much work to be done, a great deal of it on the level of behind-the-scenes diplomacy.

On 9 March, the American Zionist leadership received word that a reliable source[27] had informed the Zionist Executive in London that the American government had decided not to oppose the new policy the British proposed to implement in Palestine.[28] The following day Weizmann sent a cable to Goldman and the Zionist Organization declaring that the time had come for American intervention: a) to prevent a decision with respect to the final status of Palestine; b) to prevent the establishment of immigration quotas designed to keep Jews a permanent minority in Palestine; and c) to ensure large-scale Jewish immigration to Palestine during the next few years, as a solution to the refugee problem. He asked that Brandeis, Frankfurter and Ben Cohen be informed of his request for immediate action.[29]

Goldman, Wise, Frankfurter, Ben Cohen and Brandeis met to prepare for a session with Roosevelt. It was Brandeis' contention that the President would be unable to consider any action at all until he had been able to study the final text of the British declaration. Nevertheless, the following steps were decided upon: 1. A statement would be prepared at once clarifying the reaction of world Jewry to Britain's projected policy; and 2. Ben-Gurion would be asked to declare immediate implementation of a policy of non-cooperation on the part of Palestinian Jews, who would be organized into a disciplined force prepared to oppose any change in the Balfour Declaration or in the provisions of the mandate. These directives, it was stressed, were to be couched in terms the world "would recognize as fitting spiritual appeal . . ."[30]

When informed of these decisions, the Executive in London sent a long cable outlining the restrictive measures the government was planning to impose upon Palestine's Jewish community. Concluding with the declaration that "this is the final hour," the Executive asked to be informed of whatever action was undertaken.[31] In the hope that changes might still be made in the British proposals, the Zionist Executive in London had not yet issued any public statement; it suggested, however, that the American movement inform the press that it totally rejected the British proposals.[32]

The White House connections seemed to be yielding results. On March 19, Goldman informed the Executive that Brandeis was expecting the President to make a decisive move. On the 21st of March, Goldman and Wise were invited to meet the President, on which occasion Roosevelt declared his "sympathy for the Jews."[33] Pursuant to this meeting Roosevelt instructed Joseph Kennedy, America's ambassador to Great Britain, to try to persuade the British government to postpone public announcement of its new policy. The following day, at a British cabinet meeting called to discuss the Palestine issue, MacDonald reported the President's request. He interpreted the appeal from the White House to mean that American officialdom believed that immediate announcement of the new British policy—some time before that policy would go into effect—would give the Jews time to prepare anti-British demonstrations which might affect the outcome of attempts to amend America's Neutrality Act.[34] But MacDonald was not convinced. Nothing could alter his conviction that to avoid further pressure, the change in policy should be made public at once.

Goldman and Wise felt that they had achieved some measure of success, as the President had indeed instructed his ambassador to intervene. Needless to say, all they had gained was time, and very little at that. In mid-April Brandeis, Frankfurter and Ben Cohen, aware that the British were about to make their new policy public, again asked Roosevelt to use his good offices to request further postponement.

As Great Britain's betrayal in Palestine became increasingly apparent, Zionists in both America and England demanded a sharp escalation of anti-British action. In the spring of 1939, however, war in Europe seemed imminent and America was discussing amending the Neutrality Act to enable the United

States to aid its allies. Strong isolationist forces were mobilizing in the United States to oppose any such amendment. With Hitler acquiring greater strength every day and showing himself fully capable of fulfilling his promise to purge Europe of Jews, American Jewry—and American Zionists above all—certainly could not side with the isolationists. In actual fact, they had little choice as to which side to support in case of war. Dr. Wise, in explaining his position to those Zionists who demanded all-out anti-British action, expressed what became in essence the position of the American Zionist movement. Although willing to protest British policy in Palestine and to castigate MacDonald's betrayal, Wise declared it impossible to ignore Hitler and Nazism. He felt that the American Zionist movement would place itself in an untenable position if it tried to foster anti-British sentiment in the American public. In the event of war, he believed, the Zionist movement would have to extend unstinting aid to Britain as England's victory was the only hope of saving what had been created in Palestine.

On the 18th of March, three days after Prague was crushed under the Nazi heel and Chamberlain had announced the end of the British appeasement policy, Dr. Wise spoke at a public gathering in New York. State Department personnel noted that he seemed unexpectedly restrained and friendly toward the British.[35] This course was not an easy one for Zionists to follow but essentially, as American Jews, they saw no alternative: many of the anti-British groups functioning in the United States at the time were not only antisemitic, but out-and-out pro-Nazi.[36]

Rousing Public Opinion

American Zionism nevertheless sought ways of expressing its protest over British policy in Palestine, while steering clear of the rabid anti-British rhetoric of the isolationists. During the two months prior to the actual publication of the White Paper, there was a great surge of protest activity on the part of the public. The President and State Department were bombarded with requests to intercede with the British government, many of them coming from non-Jewish organizations and individuals, including more than a hundred congressmen.[37]

The Emergency Committee circulated a petition quoting the biblical phrase "If I forget thee, O Jerusalem, may my right hand forget its cunning . . . ," which was signed by 1,200,000 people. On 1 May dozens of senators, representatives, governors, mayors, clergymen and university presidents affixed their signatures to a cable addressed to Chamberlain. The cable stated that publication of the new British regulations would affect Anglo-American cooperation adversely and make it

> most difficult for European democracies to win sympathy of American masses for their cause if there should be grave violation of solemnly pledged covenant with Jewish people which pledge [is] rooted in the

finest religious traditions [of] humanity generally and England particularly.[38]

As 15 May, the expected date of publication of the White Paper approached, the Executive in London asked the American Zionists to perform an "act of desperation" and once more send an official delegation to the British ambassador in Washington to voice American Jewry's protest. The same request was made of the Zionist movements in Canada, Mexico and other Latin American countries vis-à-vis the British ambassador in each place. The organization of mass meetings was proposed as well, but time was running out.

In the few days that remained, it was decided to try to activate congressional bodies, in addition to individual congressmen. Fifteen members of the House Foreign Relations Committee and twenty-eight senators appealed publicly to the State Department to protest the restriction of Jewish immigration into Palestine. They particularly noted that they were concerned not only with the Jewish victims of Nazi persecution, but with the rights of the American people as provided for in the Anglo-American treaty. Influential congressmen declared on the floor of the House and Senate that the new British policy violated that treaty. These statements gave the Secretary of State an opportunity to reiterate publicly that American interests provided for in the treaty of 1924 had nothing to do with the Zionist enterprise in Palestine.[39]

Under steadily growing pressure, the State Department appealed to the President to make a public statement of policy which the Department could then use. In a confidential memorandum to Roosevelt, A. A. Berle, Assistant Secretary of State, explained the difficulties the State Department was facing. He complained that while the Zionists were agitating among congressmen and convincing them to protest Britain's policy, anti-Americanism was becoming ever stronger in the Arab countries because of what was considered American support for Jewish political hegemony in Palestine. Anything American policy-makers might say henceforth would be used against them.[40]

Roosevelt and the White Paper

The President of the United States seems to have been rather hard pressed between the Zionists and their friends on the one hand, and the State Department on the other. The outcome of these counterpressures is important, but for a better understanding of Roosevelt's moves it is helpful first to examine his connections with American Zionists. Those connections can now be quite reliably assessed, since many documents in Roosevelt's confidential files, as well as in State Department files, have been opened for public perusal.[41] A new picture emerges from these documents of the President's stand on the White Paper issue and of his relationship with American Zionists.

It may be said that until the end of 1938 Roosevelt had no more than a superficial interest in Zionism, to which he gave occasional lip service. His interest seems to have grown thereafter, primarily as a result of the appeals he received from various responsible public bodies that were concerned with the problem of refugees from Germany. The struggle over the White Paper brought him into direct contact with the Zionists, although on two different levels. Formal organizational contact with the President was maintained primarily through Rabbi Dr. Stephen S. Wise while more informally, a small group of men were in personal touch with him. Among them were the renowned Supreme Court judges Louis D. Brandeis and Felix Frankfurter, and Roosevelt's personal adviser, Ben Cohen.

During the 1930s and 1940s, Dr. Wise was more or less cast in the role of American Jewry's "foreign minister." His association with Roosevelt had begun when the latter was governor of the State of New York and Wise was a liberal rabbi pitting himself against a corrupt municipal apparatus.[42] The rabbi had remained an enthusiastic admirer of Roosevelt who, as President, always responded to Wise's requests for congratulatory messages to Zionist conferences, to the World Jewish Congress, to American Jews celebrating their New Year, etc. President Roosevelt, however, seemed anxious to avoid any suggestion that his intervention in the British government's plans for Palestine involved ethnic considerations.

The Hyde Park files evoke a picture of a rather strange relationship between Wise and Roosevelt. The Zionist leader is almost obsequious in his expressions of admiration, yet one feels that the things he asked of the President were relatively unimportant and could be complied with rather easily. Wise did not refer directly to the White Paper until just before its publication, and then only to assure Roosevelt of Jewry's gratitude for his endeavors, even though he had not succeeded in altering the British decision. The single overt concession the President seems to have made to Zionist leaders was in March 1939, when rising public pressure led him—at the meeting with Dr. Wise and Solomon Goldman—to issue the vague declaration of "sympathy for the Jews" quoted above.

More significant than Roosevelt's association with Dr. Wise was the contact he maintained on a personal level with several Zionists and other Jews who played outstanding roles in American intellectual, judicial and governmental life. True to his proclivity for surrounding himself with an intimate circle of advisers who had no official status but nevertheless influenced his decision-making, on matters pertaining to Zionism Roosevelt sought the advice of Brandeis, Frankfurter, Cohen and their associates.

Most of these men had been active in Zionist circles until 1921 when they resigned from all leading positions because of internal differences. Brandeis did not identify again with organized Zionism in America until the end of the 1920s and early 1930s when the movement's leadership again changed hands—and when the situation of German Jewry began to deteriorate. Rather than assume day-to-day leadership responsibilities, he now became the "grand old man" of American Zionism. A man of great personal prestige, Brandeis was consulted at critical times by the Zionist leaders as well as by the President, who called him Isaiah and had the highest respect for his advice.

When Brandeis learned that Great Britain was considering a change in its Palestine policy, he sent a note to Roosevelt asking what the world intended to do about Jews who were being forced into exile. Unless civilization had retrogressed to such a primitive state that it intended to annihilate homeless Jews, the note went on, it would have to encourage the one instrument that on the whole had proven capable of solving the problem of the lack of a Jewish homeland.[43] After receiving this note, Roosevelt had a number of discussions about Palestine with Frankfurter and Brandeis. They usually prepared for these sessions by exchanging documents, the President supplying Brandeis with material that enabled him to study the position of American and British representatives in the Near East, while Brandeis submitted cables and articles relevant to the Jewish situation and the Zionist stand.

Of the men included in this group, Ben Cohen, one of the advisers at the daily breakfast meetings held at Roosevelt's bedside, was closest to the President. With respect to discussions on Zionism and related problems, Cohen was mainly a connecting link between the President on the one hand, and Brandeis and Frankfurter on the other. This role befit both his position in the White House and his personality.

While discussing refugees, Zionism and British policy in Palestine, Roosevelt mooted the possibility of solving the problem of the refugees and also of Palestine by arranging to transfer the Arab population from Western Palestine to the neighboring Arab countries, in particular underpopulated and underdeveloped Iraq.[44] As this plan took shape in his mind, he began to conceive of it more and more as a financial matter. At the end of 1938, the British Foreign Secretary visited the United States and Roosevelt suggested such population transfer to him, requesting that the British government assess its feasibility. The response came in the form of a memo from the British ambassador in Washington. The idea was rejected not only because it was impracticable, but on the political–moral grounds that it contained an element of coercion. The most important reason given for its rejection, however, was that it was based on the erroneous assumption that settling Jews and Arabs separately on either side of the Jordan was only a matter of adequate financial resources.[45]

The memorandum made it eminently clear that His Majesty's Government did not believe, as others seemed to (a rather transparent reference to the President and his Zionist friends), that the problem of Palestine could be solved through economic means. H.M. Government was convinced that Palestine had become a matter of national sentiment throughout the Arab world, which ruled out even the most generous financial solution. This belligerent reaction to his suggestion deterred Roosevelt from making any further attempt at direct intervention. Moreover, just a few days later the American delegation in Cairo forwarded to the President a strong personal protest from Ibn Saud, ruler of

Saudi Arabia, against what the King described as America's support for Zionism.

When Brandeis received the first reliable information concerning the provisions of the White Paper, he wrote a long letter to Roosevelt, describing in detail the damage likely to accrue from the projected change in British policy. He concluded by saying that he wondered whether the President did not think that a timely word to London might still avert such an unjust, ill-considered turn of events.[46] Three days later Sumner Welles, Under-Secretary of State, sent a cable to the American ambassador in London to the effect that the President wanted him to mention in the proper places that it might be useful to temporarily postpone announcing the British plans for Palestine in view of the seemingly imminent international crisis.[47] The wording of the cable clearly indicates Roosevelt's ambivalence: he was indeed torn between the need to avoid implicating America in the Palestine problem, and his desire to satisfy his friends.

Roosevelt and the State Department

Throughout his presidency, Roosevelt referred most of the questions dealing with Palestine to his Secretary of State, Cordell Hull. Hull in turn referred them to Wallace Murray, an extreme anti-Zionist, who headed the Near East section of the State Department. As soon as the struggle was launched to deter the British from announcing their new policy for Palestine, Murray submitted memorandum after memorandum to Hull, hoping to minimize American intervention and diminish the effect of the public outcry.[48] He conscientiously handed on material sent by Americans stationed in the Arab and Moslem world (Turkey and Iran), who complained that America was acquiring a "false image" in those countries because of Zionist influence on the government of the United States. Murray even let it be understood that Middle Eastern countries were considering boycotting trade with America.[49]

State Department attitudes were also influenced by close association with British Foreign Office personnel. To their American counterparts, members of the British foreign service were the experts on the Middle East, and their views were dutifully reported back to Washington. The Jews seemed to have fewer and fewer friends, which made it quite reasonable to assume that newfound British realism would give increasing weight to the interests of the Arabs. Such an assumption had particular validity in view of the large numbers of Arabs and their importance for British Middle East strategy.

The State Department accumulated vast quantities of material relevant to Palestine, the British mandate etc., but there is reason to doubt that the bulk of it was ever submitted to the White House. On the one hand, Palestine was no more than a marginal problem as compared with America's direct interests in Europe on the eve of the war; on the other, the President had a rather low opinion of the State Department's ability to conduct the foreign relations of the

United States. One document that did reach the President, however, and enhanced the status of the Department in his eyes, was the aforementioned letter from Aziz Abdul Ibn Saud, King of Saudi Arabia. Dated the 17th of December, 1938, the letter contained a lengthy review of the history of Arab rights to Palestine. The all-powerful monarch based his claims entirely on Western democratic traditions, and maintained that Jewish-Zionist propaganda had falsified the Arab position for the purpose of misleading the people of democratic America.[50]

This was the first direct communication received from the head of an Arab country. Ibn Saud, presumably speaking in the name of all the Arabs, was their most important leader. In addition, his country bordered on Palestine, which seemed to give it a special position with respect to the solution of the Palestine problem. Hull felt, therefore, that the epistle merited a serious answer, not just acknowledgement of receipt. Eventually Roosevelt agreed to sign a rather noncommittal letter that defined American interests in Palestine as "spiritual," to the extent that they extended beyond those covered by the Anglo-American Treaty. In addition, he referred the King to the clarification of America's position on Palestine as formulated in a State Department declaration of 14 October, 1938, a copy of which was enclosed.[51]

When the failure of the St. James Conference became known and the American Zionists renewed their protest activities, Murray again tried, through Hull, to convince the President to allay Arab fears that America would assume a pro-Zionist stand. At this juncture, Murray formulated the position that was to become the official State Department stand throughout the war years and immediately thereafter. Maintaining that the British claimed to be hampered in their negotiations with the Arabs by American pro-Zionist pressure, he declared that all further efforts of such a nature must be opposed. The Zionists were trying to involve the United States in a problem that was essentially British, one for which America was obviously not prepared to accept any responsibility. It followed from this that American involvement would be detrimental to the United States, to the British, to the cause of democracy and in the long run to the Zionists themselves. Palestine, Murray wrote, does not solve the Jewish problem; the solution must be, and is being, sought elsewhere.[52]

The President's Personal Position

On 9 May, Brandeis brought the President a cable from London: it was actually a personal appeal from Weizmann to Roosevelt. In the name of the stateless Jewish people Weizmann asked the President to use his good offices to prevent repudiation of the Balfour Declaration, which would mean catastrophe in Palestine and would undermine all faith in promises to small nations. Roosevelt immediately sent a memorandum to the Secretary and Under-Secretary of State, declaring that he still believed it would be a mistake for the

British to issue a statement about Palestine at this point and that he felt the Americans should tell them so. He then asked what he could say to Judge Brandeis.[53]

This memorandum makes it quite obvious that Roosevelt did not fully endorse the State Department's position. When Sumner Welles sent him the news, transmitted to Kennedy in the name of Lord Halifax, that the British government had decided to postpone announcement of the White Paper, the President immediately passed the information on to Brandeis.[54] Only a week later, the British informed Roosevelt that the White Paper was being published. He then expressed his personal position in a highly interesting memorandum to the Secretary of State. The memorandum did not call for specific action, nor was it meant for publication. It was meant to be filed away. Five years later, pressed by the Zionists, Roosevelt agreed to make its contents public:[55]

MEMORANDUM FOR THE SECRETARY OF STATE

May 17, 1939

I have read with interest and a good deal of dismay the decisions of the British Government regarding its Palestine policy.

I wish you would let me have a copy of the original Palestine Mandate. Frankly, I do not believe that the British are wholly correct in saying that the framers of the Palestine Mandate "could not have intended that Palestine should be converted into a Jewish state against the will of the Arab population of the country."

My recollection is that this way of putting it is deceptive for the reasons that while the Palestine Mandate undoubtedly did not intend to take away the right of citizenship and of taking part in the government on the part of the Arab population, it nevertheless did intend to convert Palestine into a Jewish Home which might very possibly become preponderantly Jewish within a comparatively short time. Certainly that was the impression that was given to the whole world at the time of the Mandate.

The statement of your Page 6 paragraph 2, quoting the White Paper of 1933, bears out my contention.

This new White Paper admits that the British Mandate is "to secure the development of self-governing institutions." Frankly, I do not see how the British Government reads into the original Mandate or into the White Paper of 1922 any policy that would limit Jewish immigration.

My offhand thought is that while there are some good ideas in regard to actual administration of government in this new White Paper, it is something that we cannot give approval to by the United States.

My snap judgment is that the British plan for administration can well be the basis of an administration to be set up and to carry on during the next five years; that during the next five years the 75,000 additional Jews should be allowed to go into Palestine and settle; and at the end of five years the whole problem could be resurveyed and at that time either continued on a temporary basis for another five years or permanently settled if that is then possible. I believe that the Arabs could be brought to accept this because it seems clear that 75,000 additional immigrants can be successfully settled on the land and because also the Arab immigration into Palestine since 1921 has vastly exceeded the total Jewish immigration during this whole period.

Before we do anything formal about this please talk to me.

F.D.R.

If this was the President's view of the White Paper, why did he refrain from adamantly opposing it? Why did he not attempt at least to mitigate the drastic restrictions it imposed upon Palestine's Jewish community? One reason may have stemmed from the actual wording of the White Paper, in which certain qualifying provisions seem to have been introduced for the very purpose of blunting the edge of the American protest. Those provisions were intentionally deceptive and although Roosevelt took exception to some of them, they nonetheless helped justify his non-intervention.

On 15 May, two days before publication of the White Paper, the British embassy in Washington sent an aide-mémoire officially informing the President that the new policy was being declared and enlarging on its implications. The American government was asked to understand the special and difficult position in which the British government found itself with respect to this new policy—which would disappoint both Jews and Arabs. However, it would in no way prevent an ultimate solution on a federal basis, a solution consonant with the preference of the Jewish leaders. It further stated that the Colonial Minister would make it clear during the debate in Parliament that although the White Paper did not mention such a solution, it did not rule it out, and in due time it would be considered.[56]

The aide-mémoire then referred to the problem of immigration: such strong pressure had been exerted that Great Britain could not declare immediate and absolute cessation of Jewish immigration to Palestine. Here any objection Roosevelt might raise was forestalled as the Foreign Office took a leaf from his book and proposed the transfer of Arabs from Western Palestine to Transjordan, contingent on the good behavior of the Jews. With regard to land sales, the High Commissioner would do his utmost to abide by the recommendations of the last Commission of Inquiry. In view of the foregoing, the British were confident that the President had nothing to fear from the White Paper.

These explanations, all designed to deflect severe protest, obviously made an impression on Roosevelt. A further deterrent to direct action was the President's fear of jeopardizing Great Britain's safety, although the threat may have been exaggerated. Goldman's report to Ben-Gurion of the meeting he and Dr. Wise had with the President in 1939 contains some indication of this. Roosevelt cautioned them to bear in mind the British conviction that German and Italian propaganda had permeated the entire Arab and Moslem world. Therefore he could understand, although not necessarily condone, the readiness to sacrifice the Balfour Declaration and a Jewish Palestine on the altar of appeasement.[57]

A third reason for Roosevelt's failure to intervene firmly can be attributed to forces at work in America's hinterland. In his exhaustive study of American isolationism, Professor Zelig Adler concluded from the Hyde Park archives that Roosevelt was evasive because of the isolationists. They hated Great Britain and would have exploited to the utmost the slightest hint of discord between America and Great Britain.[58] Goldman mentions this in his report to Ben-Gurion, emphasizing the strength of American isolationism.[59] All these factors probably contributed to shaping Roosevelt's equivocal reaction to Britain's new policy.

Moment of Truth

During the anxious days just prior to the publication of the White Paper, many American Zionists began to wonder whether their president was sincere in his protestations of concern, and whether the American government was doing as much as it could. The President being almost sacrosanct, they sought a scapegoat; this would afford at least one satisfactory explanation of why American pressure on the British government had been so ineffective. There was no more appropriate candidate for such a role than Joseph Kennedy, America's ambassador to London. He was known to have isolationist leanings and even to be willing to compromise with the Axis Powers; he was also suspected—with some justification—of being a latent antisemite.[60]

By the end of 1938 there were persistent rumors of the ambassador's hostility to Zionism and of his friendship with pro-Arab circles in the British Foreign Office. This led Weizmann to suspect the reliability of Kennedy's reports to Washington. On the 10th of March, just before the original date set for the publication of the White Paper, Weizmann had made a last-minute attempt to circumvent Kennedy and communicate with the White House through other diplomatic channels. He made a quick trip to Paris where William Bullitt, a confidant of President Roosevelt who outspokenly opposed the Nazi regime, was serving as America's ambassador to France.[61] Weizmann asked Bullitt to inform the President that the Jews of Palestine were on the brink of despair, all his own efforts to influence London having failed. He had reached the conclusion that "nothing can save the Jews of Palestine and keep its gates open for Jewish refugees with the exception of a quiet word from you to the rulers of Great Britain."[62] Weizmann stressed that he was only asking that decision be postponed as any new decision taken just then would remain in force, no matter what changes might occur in the international situation.

The following day the Zionist Executive cabled Solomon Goldman information reported by reliable sources: MacDonald had told a Zionist sympathizer that Kennedy had indicated that there was no reason to fear America's reaction . . . the Jews would make some noise, but it would not be serious.[63] Goldman immediately transmitted the information to Brandeis and Frankfurter, to be brought to the President's attention.

These doubts concerning the trustworthiness of America's ambassador to Britain soon filtered down to the Jewish community. What had started as a whispering campaign quickly turned into an outright attack, particularly in the Yiddish-language press. Things came to such a pass that Kennedy cabled Goldman to deny that he had belittled the importance of American Jewish protests. He assured him that he supported the Zionist enterprise, declaring that he was doing all in his power to persuade the British to postpone publication of the White Paper.

It is in place to state here that Kennedy expressed his reservations—which bordered on hostility—only in personal comments. Where the issue involved governmental policy, he was entirely loyal to the instructions he received from Washington. In other words, policy-making remained the province of the President and the State Department.[64]

Once the ambassador's stand had been clarified, the question again arose as to whether the government of the United States had done everything it possibly could, or had failed to do so and therefore should be openly criticized. This was certainly a cardinal question and would exercise American Zionism for a long time to come. At that moment in history, however, it was left in abeyance as two perilous threats were becoming increasingly menacing: the external threat of Hitler and the internal threat of antisemitism.

Mobilizing American Jewry

Knowing that publication of the White Paper was imminent, American Zionists were overcome by a sense of helplessness and the Emergency Committee was pervaded by an almost tangible feeling of failure. Solomon Goldman nevertheless was determined to rouse a new wave of protest and induce a nationwide outcry against the White Paper. As the local Emergency Committees had been disbanded on the eve of the St. James Conference, other ways had to be found of reaching local communities. Goldman decided to try to mobilize the religious congregations—the basic unit of Jewish social organization in most parts of the country.

On the 15th May, after hearing from London that the White Paper would be published in two days, Goldman sent wires to thousands of congregations throughout the United States, urging them to let American Jewry's voice be heard immediately, before the House of Commons started debate on the White Paper. Each congregation was asked to conduct special prayers and report back to the National Emergency Committee.[65] The rabbis were also asked to report the number of participants in the services. Twenty-four hours later; Goldman was able to inform the press and the Va'ad Leumi in Palestine that more than 500 Jewish organizations, numbering 125,000 constituents, had already expressed protest over Britain's "betrayal" of the Jews.[66]

A final attempt to exert pressure was launched on the 22nd of May. Representatives of Jewish communities from 26 states met with Cordell Hull. They asked that Britain be requested to take no further steps until the government of the United States had had adequate opportunity to study the provisions of the White Paper. On the same day Dr. Wise sent the President a wire saying that it might still be possible to defer implementation of the White Paper "several times," thereby perhaps eliminating the likelihood that it would be implemented at all.[67]

The struggle continued even after the White Paper was officially published. Mass demonstrations held in hundreds of communities culminated in telegrams to the British ambassador in Washington demanding revocation of the new policy. The large number of local protests induced state and municipal authorities to forward protests to the President and Congress. These actions were supported by an overwhelmingly large section of the press, which published articles and editorials accusing Britain of violating its promise and ignoring the lessons of Munich.[68]

Soon, however, disturbing developments in Europe became of prime concern and all signs of protest vanished. The public struggle concerning American support for Great Britain overshadowed the problem of the White Paper policy.

* * *

Although the actions undertaken by the American Zionist movement during 1938–39 bore little practical fruit, the importance of what transpired should not be minimized. It was the first time since World War I that large segments of American Jewry engaged in public political action on behalf of Palestine, even though, in essence, the various manifestations of protest were little more than individual emotions channeled almost spontaneously into forms of mass pressure. The Zionist movement totally lacked organizational tools; it had no department of information and propaganda, no public relations section, no regular means of feeding news to the press or radio. When war broke out, American Zionism was still suffering the negative effects of the failure of its struggle against the White Paper, effects that to a great extent were responsible for the movement's impotency during the first year of the war.

Notes to Chapter 1

1. See *American Jewish Yearbook*, vol. XLI (1939–40), p. 220.
2. See Weizmann to Goldman, July 15, 1938, CZA, Z4/17055.
3. From letter in English from Weizmann to Goldman, October 3, 1938, Weizmann Archives.
4. Cable from Weizmann to Goldman, Lipsky, Wise, October 6, 1938, CZA, Z4/17055.
5. *New Palestine*, October 14, 1938, p. 6.
6. Reported on October 10, 1938, CZA, Z4/17055.
7. *Ibid.*
8. Wallace Murray, head of the Near East Section of the Department of State, in an internal memo to the Secretary of State dated March 4, 1938, estimated that over 100,000 wires and letters arrived during that period. See State Department files in Washington National Archives (hereafter, SDF), 867, N. 01/1506.
9. Original text appears in R. Fink (ed.), *America and Palestine: The Attitude of Official America and of the American People Toward the Rebuilding of Palestine as a Free and Democratic Jewish Commonwealth*, New York, 1944, pp. 24f.
10. Cable from Weizmann to Wise, Lipsky, Goldman, October 23, 1938, Weizmann Archives.
11. See Goldman's report to Weizmann, October 26, 1938, CZA, Z4/17055.
12. See editorial, *New Palestine*, November 11, 1938, p. 1.
13. See Ben-Gurion to Goldman, October 27, 1938, CZA, Z4/17055.
14. For a comprehensive picture of antisemitic activity in the United States on the eve of the Second World War, see J. R. Carlson, *Under Cover*, New York, 1968; J. L. Teller, *Strangers and Natives, op. cit.*, pp. 179–92.
15. See MacDonald's memorandum, January 19, 1939, Foreign Office (hereafter, FO), box 371/23221, file E700.
16. Wire from Lipsky to Goldman, February 16, 1939, CZA, Z4/17055.
17. See Ben-Gurion's memorandum to Goldman, January 20, 1939, Ben-Gurion Archives (hereafter, BGA), Sde Boker.
18. See Wise to Goldman, January 20, 1939, CZA, A243/125.
19. See Weizmann's cable to Ben-Gurion, January 20, 1939, BGA.
20. Ben-Gurion to Goldman, January 20, 1939, BGA.
21. From copy of memorandum sent to A. H. Silver in Cleveland (in Silver's Cleveland Archives, Zionist Activities files of 1939).
22. For example, the Bureau transferred a memo from the president of the ZOA to the Department of State, requesting that it be delivered to the American ambassador in London so that he could submit it to the British government.
23. See Emergency Committee minutes of December 18 and 30, 1940, and final decision to close Bureau in minutes of January 9, 1941. All minutes of the Emergency Committee meetings and Office Committee meetings referred to throughout the book can be found in the Minutes file of the New York Zionist Archives (hereafter, NYZA).
24. See Ben-Gurion's letter to New York of February 10 and 14, 1939, CZA, Z4/17055.
25. From draft of wire, February 27, 1939, *ibid.*
26. Ben-Gurion to Goldman, March 3, 1939, *ibid.*
27. Walter Elliot, Minster of Health, and Lord Cranborn, Under-Secretary for Foreign Affairs, were known to "leak" cabinet decisions to members of the Zionist Executive.
28. See letter from London Zionist Executive to the Washington Bureau, March 9, 1939, CZA, Z4/17055.
29. Cable from London Zionist Executive (Hebrew in Latin characters) to Washington Bureau, March 10, 1939, *ibid.*
30. Cable from Goldman and Wise to Zionist Executive in London, March 13, 1939, *ibid.*
31. Cable from Zionist Executive in London (Hebrew in Latin characters) to the Washington Bureau, March 15, 1939, *ibid.*

32. See letter from Zionist Executive in London to the Washington Bureau, March 16, 1939, *ibid.*

33. See main headline of *New Palestine*, p. 1. March 24, 1939.

34. FO, Box 371/23232, E2331. The Neutrality Laws were not changed, the government having been defeated in the Senate Foreign Affairs Committee by a vote of 11 to 12. For additional details, see S. Adler, *The Isolationist Impulse*, New York, 1957, pp. 248–9.

35. Britain's ambassador to Washington, Robert Lindsey, also noted Wise's unexpected moderation in a letter written on the 18th of March, 1939 (FO, Box 371/23232, E2480).

36. For discussion of the extent to which antisemitic elements infiltrated the isolationist movement, see D. Strong, *Organized Anti-Semitism in America, op. cit.*, and V. O. Key, *Politics, Parties and Pressure Groups*, New York, 1958, p. 129.

37. Wire in SDF, Near East Section, Block 10, no archival designation.

38. Copy of cable in Wise files, CZA, A243/34.

39. *New Palestine*, June 2, 1939, p. 8.

40. SDF (confidential file) 867 N. 01/1602 1/2.

41. There are two batches of confidential files in the Roosevelt Archives (RA); his personal files which will be designated PF, and those of his secretary, which will be designated SF.

42. See brief description of their relationship in Wise's autobiography, *Challenging Years, op. cit.*, pp. 216–32.

43. See F. E. Manuel, *The Realities of American–Palestine Relations, op. cit.*, p. 308.

44. See Sumner Welles' letter to Roosevelt, December 22, 1938, RA, SF.

45. From British ambassador's memorandum to Roosevelt, December 12, 1938, SF.

46. See Brandeis' letter to Roosevelt, March 16, 1939, RA, SF.

47. See coded wire of March 19, 1939, SDF, confidential file, 876 N. 01/1482 A.

48. See S. Adler in *Encyclopedia of Zionism and Israel*, II, New York, 1971, *sv* Roosevelt, Franklin Delano; see also J. A. DeNovo, *American Interests and Policies in the Middle East 1900–1939*, Minnesota, 1963, pp. 342–6.

49. See memo from Murray to Welles, December 11, 1938, SDF 867 N. 10/1353.

50. For English translation of letter, see *Foreign Relations of the United States* (hereafter FRUS), 1938, vol. II, Washington, 1955, pp. 994–5.

51. See letter from Welles to Roosevelt, January 9, 1939, FRUS, 1939, vol. IV, Washington, 1958, pp. 695–6.

52. See Murray's memorandum to Secretary and Under-Secretary of State, February 9, 1939, SDF 867 N. 01/1431 1/2.

53. Memo from Roosevelt to Secretary and Under-Secretary of State, May 10, 1939 RA, SF.

54. See Roosevelt's letter to Brandeis, May 12, 1939, RA, SF.

55. Memorandum to Secretary of State, May 17, 1939, RA, SF.

56. Aide-mémoire from British government to the government of the United States, May 15, 1939, RA, SF, FRUS, 1939, vol. IV, pp. 750–1.

57. See Goldman's letter to Ben-Gurion, April 6, 1938.

58. See Adler, in *Encyclopedia of Zionism, op. cit.* Professor Adler expressed similar ideas in his discussion with the author in September, 1971. In a letter to the author dated November 12, 1973, Ben Cohen also considers this factor—as well as the elections slated for 1940—primarily responsible for the fact that the President did not do more.

59. See n. 57 above.

60. See L. B. Namier, *Diplomatic Prelude, 1938–1939*, London, 1948, p. 96; see also W. L. Langer and S. E. Gleason, *The Challenge of Isolationism*, New York, 1962, pp. 76, 122; B. Rauch, *Roosevelt from Munich to Pearl Harbor*, New York, 1950, p. 85.

61. See S. Friedlander, *Prelude to Downfall—Hitler and the U.S., 1939–1941*, London, 1967, pp. 73f.

62. See report of ambassador dated March 10, 1939, "personal and highly confidential to the President," SDF, confidential file, 867 N. 01/1472.

63. Cable from Zionist Executive in London to Goldman, May 11, 1939, CZA Z4/17055.

64. For comprehensive analysis of Joseph Kennedy as a diplomat, see G. A. Craig and F. Gilbert (eds.), *The Diplomats 1919–1939*, Princeton, 1953.

65. Goldman wire as published in Jewish press on May 16, 1939, NYZA, ECZA file.

66. Announcement in press, May 19, 1939, *ibid.*

67. See wire from Wise to Roosevelt dated May 22, 1939 (microfilm).

68. See *New York Times* editorial, May 18; Dorothy Thompson in *New York Herald Tribune*, May 19; article by B. Noven in *Washington Post*, May 18; editorial in *The Nation* of week of May 20; and editorial in *The New Republic* of week of May 31.

2

1940—Year of Inaction

Never before has a single Jewish community been placed in such a position of responsibility. Our sacrifices must be commensurate with this responsibility and our coordination must make the assumption of this responsibility possible. It is the blindness of inertia, the paralysis of habit, that permits some American Jews to think that in the years ahead of us our organizations can go on moving in their separate orbits without regard to world events.

DR. S. GOLDMAN, 1940

The 21st Zionist Congress

ON THE 23rd of August, 1939, the world learned of the signing of the Molotov–Ribbentrop Pact. The foreign ministers of the Soviet Union and Nazi Germany had agreed that Russia would remain neutral in the event of war in Europe. The pact left Germany free to invade Poland with no fear of Soviet retaliation. War, therefore, seemed inevitable: Great Britain had abandoned her appeasement policy and was pledged to fight any further encroachments of the German army.

The 21st Zionist Congress, meeting in Geneva, decided to adjourn at once. The delegates hastily dispatched the most urgent items of business and dispersed, hoping to be able to get home before borders were sealed and civilian transport ceased. War-clouds had shadowed all the sessions until then. With the Nazis rapidly implementing Hitler's anti-Jewish policies in German-occupied Austria and Czechoslovakia, as well as in the Third Reich itself, Europe was filled with homeless refugees. They had no place to go—the only country prepared to accept them was Jewish Palestine, and the British were doing everything they could to keep them out. But Great Britain now spearheaded the anti-Nazi forces, forces that all Jews everywhere supported. Dr. Weizmann, in his opening address to the Congress, clearly expressed the ambivalence of the Jews—and the Zionists, in particular—toward the mandatory power: he could not hide the anger and frustration elicited by the White Paper, but neither could he withhold support for Britain's stand against further German aggression. Weizmann had no programmatic solution to offer; he could only hope that a united Jewry would find the strength to meet whatever trials the future held.[1]

Despite this overriding need for unity, inter-factional discord was rife at the Congress sessions. It is ironical that even as one delegate after another rose to emphasize the importance of unifying the people, dissension among the Zionist parties, factions and blocs reached new heights.[2] Two different approaches crystallized: some General Zionists, the Mizrachi and the Jewish State Party demanded a change in leadership and the adoption of a k ore radical anti-British stand. The majority of delegates, however, favored Dr. Weizmann's moderate position. The Congress adopted a political resolution that expressed gratitude for pro-Zionist sentiments voiced by distinguished members of the British parties, and welcomed the fact that the Permanent Mandates' Commission had rejected the White Paper. The same resolution declared that the White Paper had no legal or moral basis and that the mandatory government would have to accept responsibility for whatever might occur in the future.[3]

Weizmann put little hope in the American Zionist movement, in light of its performance during the struggle to avert publication of the White Paper. Others, however, believed that Zionism in the United States would eventually achieve enough unity and strength to turn it into an active force in the political arena and to make it an effective partner—even a stand-in, if necessary—for Jerusalem and London. The Americans, on the other hand, had expected the Congress to generate significant changes. The ZOA and Hadassah had gone to extraordinary lengths to sell shekels; they had been so successful that their delegation of 114 people was the second largest.[4] But despite their numerical strength and the fact that they functioned as a bloc, they made a poor showing at the Congress.

The majority of the American Zionists, led by Abba Hillel Silver and Solomon Goldman, advocated a moderate stand toward Great Britain and voted with the Labor Bloc and the Confederation of General Zionists. Silver and Goldman believed that it was too early to determine the final attitude toward the mandatory power, since not all avenues of approach had, as yet, been fully explored. Dr. Silver, in particular, was convinced that a great deal depended upon the Jews themselves. At that moment in history, he felt that there had to be a twofold response to the White Paper: the Yishuv—the Jewish community in Palestine—had to be strengthened, and the American Jewish community had to assume a new role. He proposed that a branch of the Jewish Agency be established in the United States: this would give American Zionism responsibility and influence commensurate with its size, and would ensure continuity if the war disrupted activities and severed contact with the European and Palestinian branches of the movement.

The delegates of the Palestinian Labor Movement—the largest delegation by virtue of its "double vote" (each Palestinian delegate had two votes) dominated the Congress and strongly opposed the creation of a new and rival power center in the United States. Weizmann remained sceptical: he saw little justification for

PLATE 2.   Rabbi Dr. Solomon Goldman, leader of the struggle against the White Paper, 1938–39.

PLATE 3. Rabbi Dr. Stephen S. Wise at the Zionist Congress, Geneva, 1939.

granting the American Zionists greater prominence and a more decisive voice in world Zionist affairs. (It should be noted that these views were never explicitly aired on the Congress floor, and only came to the fore in private discussions or at caucus meetings. Over forty years later, during interviews for this study, some of the delegates of the 21st Congress confided to the author that they had held such opinions.) When it was decided to adjourn the Congress early, the Zionist Actions Committee was granted emergency powers, and authorized to take whatever decisions the new situation called for.[5] Nevertheless, plans were discussed by the leaders of American Zionism and members of the Jewish Agency Executive to create a center of political Zionist activity in the United States. At the closing session, Dr. Goldman informed the tense, apprehensive delegates that in the event of war the American movement was prepared to shoulder the burden of whatever new responsibilities fell upon it.[6] On August 29, 1939, the official Zionist News Agency "Palcor" published the following item in its bulletin, datelined Geneva, 29 August:

AMERICAN COMMITTEE OF EXECUTIVE OF ZIONIST ORGANIZATION
At a meeting of the Executive of the Zionist Organization held in Geneva after the conclusion of the Zionist Congress, it was decided to establish a committee in America to represent the Executive of the Zionist Organization in that country. The Committee is to consist of Dr. Stephen Wise, Dr. Solomon Goldman and Mr. Louis Lipsky. A desire was expressed that the Committee should coopt representatives of the General Zionists, of Hadassah and of Labour in America.[7]

This vague statement, ending as it does with a pious wish, set the stage for the incessant defining and re-defining of the competence, functions and authority that subsequently consumed so large a part of the committee's time. Incidentally, the Palcor news item is the only recorded text of the Executive's decision to form such a committee.

"Committee of Ten" becomes "Inter-Party Committee"

The American delegation joined the multitudes converging on the roads, railways and ports of Europe. Most of the delegates who were heading directly for the United States managed to book passages on the "Queen Mary," and they used their time on board to discuss plans for the future. When news reached them on September 3rd that the Allied Powers had declared war on Germany, Solomon Goldman called the leading Zionists among his shipmates to a meeting. He informed them that he had been authorized to form an Emergency Committee in the United States to conduct Zionist affairs as long as the war lasted. Thus, in an overcrowded ship sailing under the British flag through submarine-infested seas, the foundation was laid for the political arm of

American Zionism—the Emergency Committee for Zionist Affairs.[8] Despite the many difficulties that would confront the committee in days to come, the many changes that would be made in its structure and personnel, it was destined to play a significant role in American Zionism.

Soon after the "Queen Mary" docked in New York on the 4th of September, Dr. Goldman reported to several Zionist leaders, including Wise and Lipsky, who had not attended the Congress. Their meeting culminated in a cable to Dr. Weizmann announcing that they were prepared to act as a committee for Zionist affairs for the duration of the "European war," as it was called then. The Political Department of the Executive in London cabled its approval on the 10th of September:

GOLDMAN, LIPSKY, WISE, ZIONISTS N.Y.

CORDIALLY WELCOME YOUR INITIATIVE STOP WAR SITUATION INCREASES POLITICAL ORGANIZATIONAL FINANCIAL RESPONSIBILITIES AMERICAN JEWRY STOP BELIEVE YOU SHOULD ESTABLISH NUCLEUS FOR NORTH SOUTH AMERICA STOP TAKE OVER SUCH WORK TOGETHER WITH REPRESENTATIVES MIZRACHI LABOR HADASSAH STOP PLEASE SEND MORE EXPLICIT INFORMATION REGARDING YOUR PLANS I HOPE COME OVER EARLY OCTOBER

CHAIM WEIZMANN[9]

Having acquired official recognition, Goldman, Lipsky and Wise decided to form a "Committee of Ten." The other members were to be one representative each from Mizrachi, Hadassah and Poale Zion, Dr. Abba Hillel Silver, in his capacity as chairman of the United Palestine Appeal, and Robert Szold, who was to serve as legal and financial adviser. Henry Monsky, president of B'nai B'rith, and Cyrus Adler, chairman of the non-Zionist American Jewish Committee, were asked to fill the remaining two places. When the problem of other Zionist groups was raised, it was proposed that they be represented in an advisory body.

The name "Committee of Ten" was soon found inappropriate as meetings were rarely attended by all ten members. The body was re-named "The Inter-Party Committee"—which immediately chose a small presidium consisting of Wise, Goldman and Lipsky. Wasting no time, the presidium arranged a meeting with Lord Lothian, newly-appointed British ambassador to Washington. Ever since he had served as secretary to Lloyd George, the ambassador had been known as sympathetic to Zionism. The "Inter-Party Committee" therefore felt that it was important to apprise him of the formation in the United States of a body representing the Jewish Agency, and to express a desire for mutual assistance and cooperation.

The meeting with the British ambassador was fixed for the 11th of September. The presidium had arranged to meet earlier that same day with Cordell Hull, the American Secretary of State. Still thinking in terms of the activities that had been undertaken during the First World War, the Zionist leadership wanted to clarify possibilities of recruiting American Jews for the British army, the status of Palestine now that Great Britain was at war, and the official American attitude to forming a Jewish legion. Hull was of the opinion that any form of recruitment on American soil for service in a foreign army would be tantamount to felonious, as it would be in violation of the United States Neutrality Law. Even establishing an information service on American territory to help young men find ways of enlisting, seemed to Hull "pretty close" to being a violation. As to the matter of sending supplies to Palestine, he was quite sure that since the country was under a mandate to Britain, ruled by a British High Commissioner and policed by British soldiers, it would be regarded as a country at war.

Lord Lothian received the members of the presidium most cordially. He made it clear that he personally could do nothing to facilitate the enlistment of American Jewish volunteers in the armed forces of the Allies, but he was aware that thousands of young Americans were leaving American territory in order to enlist. When asked whether those who volunteered for the British armed forces in particular would have to forfeit American citizenship, Lord Lothian pointed out that during the First World War special concessions had permitted citizens of the United States to pledge loyalty to the King for the duration of the war only, without renouncing their allegiance to the American government. He promised to investigate his government's current position and inform the presidium.

Wise, Lipsky and Goldman then met with the Polish ambassador, Count Pototski, to express American Jewish support of beleaguered Poland and to offer assistance. Specifically, they offered to contact influential individuals who had access to the communications media and could open various channels through which Poland's situation could be brought home to the American public.[10]

This initial spurt of activity seemed to bode well for the future and the following cable, datelined the 11th of September, was sent to Dr. Weizmann in London:

ASSUMING AUTHORIZATION IN USA FOR EXECUTIVE IN ALL MATTERS ARISING FROM WAR ... FORMING COMMITTEE INCLUDING PARTIES PLUS SILVER SZOLD ADLER MONSKY STOP ESTABLISHED CONTACT TODAY HULL LOTHIAN ...[11]

Weizmann wired approval on the 14th of September:

YOURS ELEVENTH AGREE YOUR COMMITTEE ACTING AS

SUGGESTED STOP PLEASE ESTABLISH CONTACTS IMMEDI-
ATELY ESPECIALLY POLAND POSSIBLY WITH ASSISTANCE
DIPLOMATIC PHILANTHROPIC CHANNELS STOP INFORM
JERUSALEM COMPOSITION YOUR COMMITTEE.[12]

Emergency Committee for Zionist Affairs

A full meeting of the Inter-Party Committee was held on 19 September. It was attended by Wise, Lipsky and Goldman of the ZOA, Leon Gellman of Mizrachi, Bertha Schoolman of Hadassah, and David Wertheim of Poale Zion. Abba Hillel Silver, Robert Szold and Hayim Greenberg, the ideological leader of the Labor Zionists, were also present. Samuel Caplan, editor of the *New Palestine*, was the Committee's acting secretary.

The first point on the agenda caused no friction—it was decided that the new body would be called the Emergency Committee for Zionist Affairs. The second point, however, elicited serious differences of opinion. The participation of non-Zionists was called in question, and there was controversy as to the number of representatives each Zionist organization would be entitled to. The issue of the non-Zionists was temporarily settled when all present accepted the explanation that Cyrus Adler of the American Jewish Committee and Henry Monsky, President of B'nai B'rith (who had been invited but did not actually attend the meeting) had been invited as individuals and not as representatives of their respective non-Zionist organizations. The problem of the Zionist constituency was solved by giving each Zionist party two representatives on the Committee. It was further decided that the committee represented the World Zionist Executive and that its decisions would have the same binding authority as those of the Zionist Executive. This last declaration was less significant—and certainly less definitive—than it sounded.

Having overcome these hurdles—at least for the time being—the members of the committee could now apply themselves to practical problems. A discussion ensued about the possibility of transmitting money to Palestine; a request for money to transport immigration certificate-holders from Germany, Austria and Czechoslovakia to Palestine was also considered. Other points on the agenda concerned ways and means of sending provisions to the Yishuv in Palestine and Dr. Weizmann's projected visit to launch a "national loan." Although the discussions on most of these issues were indecisive, for reasons that will be elucidated below, the members of the newly constituted Emergency Committee felt that it was now established as a factor on the American scene.

The committee's effectivity was diminished from the outset, undoubtedly due to the mental set of most of its members: they tended to think in terms of the activities that had been undertaken during the First World War. Although the international situation and the position of Jewry were now entirely different from what they had been in 1915, the concern was still how to send food to

Palestine's Jews and whether a "Jewish Legion" could be formed. No new initiatives were introduced, nor were there clear directives for political action. Another obstacle to effective functioning was implicit in the organizational setup: the committee bore within itself the seeds of future failure—inefficient management and bungling confusion were endemic. A certain amount of the mismanagement very likely reflected the chaotic condition of American Jewish organizational life as a whole, but this hardly justified the impossibly cumbersome apparatus that was established. The organizational hierarchy comprised a small presidium, several sub-committees to deal with specific areas, the full Emergency Committee and then a large, unwieldy advisory body representing every Zionist group in America, no matter how miniscule. The entire structure functioned on a voluntary basis; the administrative staff changed constantly—there was not even a permanent secretary.

Unprepared as the ground may have been, however, a number of processes were at work that made the emergence of the committee significant and almost inevitable. The first and most pressing of these was, of course, the outbreak of war. Members of the Jewish Agency was as recently as the month before, at the Congress, had objected to forming a permanent office of the Agency in America, now agreed that it was necessary. They were influenced by Britain's fear that Mussolini was strong enough on both land and sea in the Mediterranean and Red Sea areas to sever British supply and communications lines east and west of Suez. If Great Britain was afraid of being cut off, surely the danger to Jewry in Palestine—and in the rest of a wartorn world—was even greater. All correspondence concerning establishment of the Emergency Committee refers to the "war situation," "matters arising because of the war," "for the duration of the war."

A second process that spurred the formation of the Emergency Committee was the change slowly taking place in the relative positions of the Zionist movements. American Zionism had been gaining weight in the economic sphere since the 1920s, and since 1936 had been seeking expression in the political sphere. At the same time the centers of European Zionism were gradually declining, even though they remained influential with respect to policy. As the American movement grew, however, it began to aspire to a role as important as that played by Jerusalem and London.

Then an internal Jewish process was under way, perhaps the most important force leading to the formation of the Emergency Committee: recognition was growing among Zionists in America as well as among Jews in general that on matters concerning all of Jewry, cooperation and combined action had to supercede narrow organizational interests. They realized that it was desirable and necessary to work together on several fronts at one and the same time. Ways had to be found of combating antisemitism in America, of helping the Jews in Europe, and of augmenting Jewish achievements in Palestine.[13]

Another important element was the role visualized for America in the postwar world. It was becoming increasingly clear that no matter how America contributed to the actual conduct of the war, it would undoubtedly hold a central position after the cessation of hostilities. This had decisive implications for Zionism, as Arthur Lourie declared at the ZOA convention in 1940. Speaking for the Emergency Committee, he stated: "It was recognized that whether America entered the war or not, the attitude of this country was likely to be of decisive importance in determining the future of the Jewish National Home."[14]

Confusion Reigns

Before the Emergency Committee was even a month old, it was being bombarded by requests, appeals, demands from individuals and organizations in America and abroad—all in one way or another resulting from the war. Decisions had to be made, things had to be done, but the committee was woefully unprepared for the leadership role it was expected to play. In fact, during those final months of 1939 there were still many more questions than answers: was it only to be a united propaganda agency for the Zionist organizations? Should it send money to Palestine and, if so, for what purposes and from what sources? Was it responsible for financing the transportation of refugees and others to Palestine? And above all, what were its overall functions, goals, powers, and how was it to exercise those powers?

In the middle of November Louis Lipsky wrote to Joseph Linton, Secretary of the Zionist Executive in London, to inform him that "all matters that come under the direction of the Emergency Committee, dealing with emergency needs or foreign needs, should be sent to Mr. Caplan."[15] This loose description of the subjects to be brought to the attention of the committee's acting secretary is glaringly evasive. Caplan's first communication with Linton further confounded the confusion: he stated that although the committee's functions had not yet been defined, all Zionist bodies in the United States recognized its authority to act in the name of the Zionist Executive. He then gave assurance that the committee would perform whatever tasks it was given. In effect, he was saying that the Emergency Committee did not intend to initiate action, but would wait for instructions (presumably from Dr. Weizmann). Obviously, it was still not clear if the committee was to be the representative of the Zionist Executive in the United States or an independent authority to centralize political action initiated by the American Zionist parties.[16]

At this point it is in place to note the three different approaches that struggled for ascendancy through the first year of existence of the Emergency Committee:

1. With the exception of the Solomon Goldman, most of the ZOA leadership viewed the committee as an umbrella organization coordinating Zionist political work in the United States. The Executive in Jerusalem was the source of its authority, but the Emergency Committee would not be bound by any decision of the Executive that conflicted with or countermanded the sovereign decisions of the committee's constituent Zionist groups in America. An exclusively

Zionist body, the committee would not deal with general American Jewish issues; those were the province of the American and World Jewish Congress.

2. Chaim Weizmann, the leading members of Hadassah and Robert Szold believed that the committee should centralize and coordinate activities of all groups, individuals and organizations working to advance and develop the Jewish community in Palestine, whether they were oriented to Zionism, religion or philanthropy. The Emergency Committee, therefore, should be modelled on the expanded Jewish Agency and should be prepared to assume the functions of the Agency, should the war create such a contingency. This approach, emphasizing the general-Jewish aspect, tended to play down the Zionist role.

3. Solomon Goldman, Abba Hillel Silver and Emanuel Neumann of the General Zionists, David Wertheim, a leader of Poale Zion, and most of the Mizrachi leadership were aware of the need to strive for a transformation within the American Zionist movement which would equip it to take its place as the vanguard of American Jewry. They believed that were the Emergency Committee granted adequate power and authority, it would be able to mobilize American Jewry into a significant political and economic force to realize the Zionist goal after the war.

Abba Hillel Silver, in particular, had a clear perception of the varying implications of each of these approaches. He felt that on major policy issues it would be possible to reach a consensus that all the Zionist parties could subscribe to, regardless of which approach was eventually decided upon. Pursuant to Silver's proposal, the four largest parties agreed to form a sub-committee—a Council for Discussion of Zionist Policy to be chaired by Hayim Greenberg. Once again, however, each group involved had a different interpretation of why the council had been formed and what it should do. Some thought they should discuss worldwide peace aims, others felt they should concentrate on the postwar status of Palestine, and still others, convinced that Jewish–Arab relations were the crux of all future settlement, proposed that the council deal primarily with that problem . . . all of which amply demonstrated how very important such a forum for discussion of American Zionist policy would be. Yet the protagonists of the various viewpoints could not reach a consensus even about points for an agenda, and so the council was stillborn.

These divisive tendencies had repercussions with respect to Zionism's external policies as well. Very soon after the Emergency Committee was formed, Hadassah took independent action that caused embarrassment and confusion—if not outright damage: the Emergency Committee, in the name of the UPA, submitted a memorandum to the Intergovernmental Committee on Refugees that was meeting in Washington. Hadassah representatives helped prepare the memorandum, but, unknown to the other Emergency Committee members, the women simultaneously submitted a separate memorandum in Hadassah's name.[17] "Avuka," the Zionist Student Federation, had decided to work on the issue of Jewish–Arab relations and chose to use the platform of the UPA Conference to attack British policies in Palestine. Their target was Duff

Cooper, First Lord of the Admiralty, one of the speakers at the conference. The impassioned student representatives completely ignored the fact that Duff Cooper was one of the few friends of Zionism in the British government![18]

These are only two of the many examples that underscored the need for a disciplined political body invested with the authority to act in the name of all Zionist movements.

Internal difficulties notwithstanding, the Emergency Committee began to expand—which naturally helped to exacerbate the problems. One stimulus for expansion was the prestige accruing to membership in the committee as a result of the outstanding individuals who headed it. "Everyone wanted to be in on the show,"[19] and this included many wealthy fund-raisers for Jewish causes, as well as some of the smaller Zionist organizations, which felt that they deserved the privilege of serving on such an important body. Non-Zionist members of the Jewish Agency resident in the United States also claimed the right to belong to the Committee, which they considered an arm of the Agency Executive. Furthermore, interest in the Emergency Committee grew as the awful reality of the war in Europe was driven home; this led to widespread recognition of the need to pool efforts and share responsibility.

The basic question was still unanswered: did the Emergency Committee represent the World Zionist Organization or the Jewish Agency? Chaim Weizmann favored including non-Zionists in the Emergency Committee, possibly because he considered this a first step toward the reorganization of the Jewish Agency, something he had long had in mind to do. Hadassah favored Weizmann's position while Wise, Lipsky, Mizrachi, the Labor Zionists and Nachum Goldmann opposed it. Eventually it was decided that the Emergency Committee, having been "originally constituted as representing the World Zionist Executive . . . did not consider itself free to include non-Zionist members" without the authorization of the Executive.[20] Final and unequivocal though this declaration seemed, it was revoked soon after the arrival of Eliezer Kaplan, treasurer of the Jewish Agency Executive.

Kaplan came to the United States in 1940, hoping to ameliorate some of the financial problems of the Yishuv in Palestine and of the Zionist movement. It was only natural for him to establish close contact with the professional fund-raisers on the Jewish scene and to try to increase the extent of their involvement. He convinced the Emergency Committee to revamp its constituency and include non-Zionists. In May of 1940 the Emergency Committee passed a motion stating that it was the representative of the Agency Executive in the United States.

Pursuant to the decision, the committee was to be reorganized to include, in addition to delegates from the four major Zionist parties, representatives of non-Zionist groups active in public life, and "leading personalities in American Jewish life" as well.[21] The hope was that such an enlarged constituency would add political power through which pressure could be exerted on the American government, fund-raising activities would be coordinated and energies and talent would be freed to concentrate on Palestine's economic needs. Enlarging participation in the Emergency Committee also seemed to offer a broader base for conducting public relations and influencing public opinion.

Subcommittees were appointed to plan ways and means of achieving the above objectives, but when their reports were submitted to the plenum on 27 July, 1940, it was apparent that with the exception of the committee on economic activities, little progress had been made.[22] The lack of basic tools with which to work in the areas of political action and public relations seemed to present insurmountable obstacles.

Henry Montor, director of the UPA, who attended the Emergency Committee meeting of 27 July, 1940, analyzed the problem as hinging on the willingness of the Zionist movements to "sacrifice vested interests" and give the Emergency Committee "full power to act on all phases of the work concerning Palestine."[23] If such agreement were reached, each organization would retain its autonomy but would accept the Emergency Committee's guidelines with respect to educational, political and fund-raising policy.

A cable was sent to the Executive in Jerusalem requesting approval of the proposal to invest the Emergency Committee with the power and authority to act. Approval of the inclusion of non-Zionists was also requested. However, among the Americans an essential difference of approach still remained. Dr. Wise and Solomon Goldman wanted an explicit statement from Jerusalem and London endowing the Emergency Committee with authority. On the other hand, Henry Montor, Rose Jacobs of Hadassah and David Wertheim of Poale Zion felt that the American Zionist movement did not have to wait for its activities to be sanctioned by others. Eliezer Kaplan's tacit support of this latter group manifested itself in his suggestion—even before the Emergency Committee was reconstituted—that a small executive of six or seven people be empowered by the plenum to act on urgent matters.

Change of Heart in Jerusalem

Jerusalem had always refused to grant any representative American Zionist body the authority to act independently. Even at the height of the struggle against the White Paper in 1938–39, the Jewish Agency had hesitated to give an office in Washington the power to act effectively. By the spring of 1940, however, the attitude was changing: one of Eliezer Kaplan's tasks in the United States was to work out new forms that would govern the relationship between Jerusalem and American Jewry. The change of heart was taking place in response to two factors: the international situation, and the presence of certain new arrivals on the American Jewish and Zionist scene.

Mussolini declared war on the 10th of June, 1940, and it was obvious that before long the Middle East would be drawn into the conflict. The Agency Executive in Jerusalem realized the vital importance of a center of activity in America, which was still neutral and growing more powerful every day. From a base in the United States it might be possible to maintain international contacts and to some extent coordinate Zionist policy. This consideration began to override entrenched attitudes.

In the meantime, the active core of American Zionist personalities had been reinforced by two newcomers to the United States: Arthur Lourie and Dr. Nachum Goldmann. It was felt that the presence of these two experienced men would greatly enhance the movement's ability to act independently and authoritatively.

Arthur Lourie, who belonged to a prominent South African Zionist family, had been the political secretary of the Jewish Agency in London since 1933. His talent for preparing and editing political and diplomatic papers was almost unmatched, and he also had a great deal of experience in dealing with highly placed officials and diplomats. Lourie looked upon himself as a Zionist civil servant and therefore, true to the traditional British approach to civil service, was not a member of any Zionist party. Nevertheless, he had the respect and confidence of all the parties, and of the Zionist Executive and Jewish Agency as well.

Until war broke out, Dr. Nachum Goldmann was the World Zionist Organization's representative to the League of Nations. At the 21st Zionist Congress, he was coopted to the Zionist Executive as a member for political affairs. He was also chairman of the Steering Committee of the World Jewish Congress. Both Eliezer Kaplan and Dr. Wise felt that Goldmann could fill a void in the leadership of the American movement, particularly since the ZOA was then almost paralyzed. The old dispute between the Brandeis and the Lipsky–Weizmann factions continued to fester, with Solomon Goldman serving as the representative of the ailing Brandeis. Stephen Wise was unable to impose unity.[24] Edmund Kaufman, the ZOA's newly elected president, tried to move the organization's center to Washington D.C., where he lived. He had hoped to establish an effective power base in the nation's capital, but was too ineffectual to do so.[25] At the same time, the movement forfeited the massive Jewish support that was so readily available in New York. In many ways, the Emergency Committee was doing things the Zionist Organization should normally have done, and it was in this context that both Eliezer Kaplan and Dr. Wise looked toward Nachum Goldmann for assistance.

In July 1940 Dr. Goldmann was chosen to head the Executive of the Emergency Committee. Its other members were Stephen Wise, Solomon Goldman, Louis Lipsky and Eliezer Kaplan (for the duration of his stay in America). Some of the Zionist leaders were disturbed by Nachum Goldmann's prominent position—he had never been formally authorized to speak in the name of American Zionism, nor was he even officially a member of the Emergency Committee. He attended its meetings "by invitation" or as part of the administrative staff. To some extent, his detractors were afraid of the American dislike of the "alien"—particularly during wartime. Suspicion naturally centered on Communists, but "grass-roots" America tended to look askance at any foreigner active in political life. Another concern voiced by some people stemmed from Goldmann's dual role as repesentative of both the World Jewish Congress and the Zionist movement. They felt that the line of demarcation between the two bodies might thereby be blurred—to their mutual detriment.[26]

Goldmann's status was clarified in October of 1940 when a statement was issued that as a member of the Jewish Agency Executive, he was "cooperating with the (Emergency) Committee in all matters." This almost paralleled the status bestowed on Arthur Lourie who, in addition to "representing the London Executive," served as secretary of the Emergency Committee.[27]

Another Reorganization

In the autumn of 1940 it was decided to form a relatively small "Office Committee," since the Emergency Committee as a whole had been unable to reach decisions throughout its first year of existence.[28] Although this meant an even more cumbersome overall structure, for the next two years it was the Office Committee that conducted all business; its decisions were approved retroactively at monthly sessions of the plenum. The Emergency Committee as such apparently continued to exist only because it gave a rather large group of Zionists a sense of importance and enabled them to maintain the illusion that they were determining Zionist policy. More than thirty people attended those monthly meetings, which acquired the character of the "General Debate" that always appeared on the Zionist Congress agenda. Summing up the situation, Mrs. Shulamit Schwartz-Nardi, who was on the staff of the committee, remarked: "There were so many who wanted to be in the picture that they forgot to paint it!"[29]

The Office Committee had no formula for instant success, and when Ben-Gurion arrived in the United States early in November of 1940, he was profoundly disturbed by the situation he found. Deploring the amount of time and energy being wasted over organizational problems at the expense of political activity, he crystallized his own stand. It was his view that the Emergency Committee, having been organized to deal with Zionist affairs, could not bring in non-Zionists and function as an arm of the Jewish Agency without the approval of the Zionist Executive.[30]

Thus, at the end of 1940, we are left with a picture of the Emergency Committee buffeted by innumerable suggestions and counter-suggestions . . . little can be gained from a discussion of all the nuances proposed. There was one proposal, however, brought by Louis Lipsky in September of 1940, that became the framework for the committee's ongoing activities, although it was never formally adopted. Lipsky recommended the following seven points:[31]

1. The committee represents the WZO Executive in the United States and shall act in its name in every field in which the Executive will be unable to act, and in all urgent matters arising from the emergency situation.

2. The committee is to be the central Zionist body in the United States; the Executives in London and Jerusalem, as well as the Geneva office, will maintain direct contact with it.

3. The Emergency Committee is to carry out all political activities in Washington vis-à-vis the US government and foreign embassies in everything connected with Zionism and Palestine, implementation to be through a subcommittee for political activity headed by Dr. Wise.

4. The committee is to create favorable public opinion among Christians in the United States for the Zionist enterprise in Palestine through a "Committee for Palestine," such as had functioned in previous years.

5. The committee will deal with questions connected with economic problems of the Jewish community in Palestine through the Economic Committee headed by Robert Szold. The committee is to be expanded to include a Palestine Information Bureau to feed news of Zionist work to the Yiddish and Anglo-Jewish press, and to the general press when possible.

6. The Emergency Committee is to continue trying to get visas for European refugees.

7. The committee is to take responsibility for policies and activities of bodies established in the United States in the 1920s and 1930s for specific purposes and not under the discipline of the Zionist movement (such as the Security Committee for Hagana Affairs, the Shekel Committee, etc.). Such bodies are to report to the Emergency Committee and accept its guidance in everything involving policy and action.

Tragic Failures

The financial problems of the Emergency Committee were almost as severe as the organizational ones. Indeed, in large measure they were created by the lack of organizational clarity: neither the Jewish Agency nor the World Zionist Executive would agree to authorize the Emergency Committee to use any funds collected in their name. But almost the moment it was established in September of 1939, the committee began to receive appeals for funds to pay for the transport of European refugees to Palestine. There were also Zionist youth groups trapped in Europe; ways could be found of arranging transport for them—were money available.

The sudden need for funds for *aliya* confronted American Zionists with an issue they were not accustomed to handling. Until this time a one-man "Palestine Office" was all that was necessary to process the few Americans who wanted to take up permanent residence in Palestine. The "Office"—theoretically supported by all the Zionist parties, but actually by the ZOA—became somewhat more active when Nazi persecution intensified and American Zionists tried to help relatives leave Europe for Palestine. The numbers, however, were still very small.[32]

With the outbreak of war, the situation changed drastically. All contact was severed with countries from which large numbers of Jews had previously gone on *aliya*; contact with England, which issued the "certificates" attesting to legal permission to enter Palestine, was becoming more difficult every day—as was contact with Palestine. America became the focus of all those who hoped to extricate Jews from the European cauldron and finance their transport to safety.

On the 19th of September, 1939, at the Emergency Committee's second meeting, the agenda included discussion of an urgent letter from Eliezer Kaplan.[33] He requested money to pay for the transport to Palestine of 5,000 certificate-holders, 1,500 of them from "greater" Germany. Other, no less urgent requests arrived in quick succession from individuals and organizations. Among them was an appeal from the Palestine Office in Vienna for 36,000 dollars to arrange transportation for 600 certificate-holders; Recha Freier cabled from Berlin in the name of Youth Aliya, asking for 12,000 pounds sterling to finance a "shipment" of Jewish youth from Germany to Palestine; Josef Hyman of the Joint Distribution Committee asked for 100,000 dollars for 960 certificate-holders in Berlin, 1,200 in Prague, 600 in Vienna, 200 in Bratislava—money that would enable them to embark at Trieste for Palestine.[34]

The Emergency Committee decided to ask the Executive in Jerusalem for authorization to retain some of the funds collected in the United States for use in meeting these desperate appeals. The request was refused; the Committee was not authorized to use any money collected by the fund-raising drives in America. Other ways would have to be found of helping to rescue Europe's Jews. Solomon Goldman suggested that the Emergency Committee establish a fund of 100,000 dollars to be earmarked for financing transport to Palestine.[35] The ZOA decided to impose a voluntary tax on its members, and the other parties did likewise. A committee of four—one representative from each party—was appointed to plan ways and means of establishing the projected "Transportation Fund."

Secrecy was essential: under conditions then prevailing, "transport" implied clandestine organization of groups, stealing across borders, purchasing ships under assumed names and loading them with fictitious cargoes, bribing officials, and landing in Palestine at isolated beach-heads to avoid detection by the British. In other words, most of the necessary funds would be used for "Aliya B"—"illegal" immigration to Palestine. Little mention was made, therefore, of the projected fund, with the exception of an occasional brief report in minutes of the Emergency Committee. The minutes of the meeting held on 3 May, 1940, for example, record that the ZOA reported having collected 13,200 dollars, of which 10,000 had already been sent abroad; Hadassah had sent 25,000 dollars, and Poale Zion 10,000 dollars.

These contributions were welcomed by the people in Europe who were in direct contact with the refugees, but they were in need of more dependable financial sources. The Emergency Committee had been unable to set up a permanent fund, its remittances were sporadic and rescue work in Europe could not rely on it at this stage. The "Transportation Fund" never really materialized and, unfortunately, was only the first of many abortive attempts to raise money for the Emergency Committee to allocate as it saw fit.

Another attempt in this direction—also a failure—at least proved highly instructive with regard to the attitude of the State Department toward British policy in Palestine. The American Red Cross established a War Relief Fund for "war casualties." Abba Hillel Silver initiated an appeal to President Roosevelt to include the destitute, homeless Jews of Europe and the Jewish community of Palestine in the category of war casualties. Danger had become very real in Palestine: on the 24th of July, 1940, 20 Jews were killed by bombs dropped from Italian planes, and on the 9th of September, 1940, 112 people were killed, again by Italian bombers.

Silver wrote directly to President Roosevelt, who had been instrumental in founding the War Relief Fund. The President referred the letter to the State Department, which informed Silver that the appeal should be addressed to Norman Davis, president of the American Red Cross. After some further correspondence, it was arranged for Nachum Goldmann and Henry Montor to meet with Swift, deputy-chairman of the Red Cross. Swift explained that only one form of aid might be considered: an allocation of money to purchase food and equipment in the United States for shipment to the needy in Palestine.[36]

This was reported back to the Emergency Committee, whereupon the Hadassah representatives, supported by Edmund Kaufman of the ZOA, immediately attacked Silver, Montor and Nachum Goldmann for having encroached on territory generally recognized as belonging to the women's organization. The acrimonious debate that ensued was a sorry demonstration of the state of American Zionism. Personal and organizational rivalries were finally set aside long enough to approve further negotiations with the Red Cross.

After negotiations, Silver was sure that a considerable sum would be devoted to Palestine. As the discussions progressed, however, the State Department entered the picture. A report had been received from the American Consul in Jerusalem. He declared that the chief secretary of the mandatory government in Palestine did not consider the effects of war severe enough to require outside assistance, particularly in view of other complex issues that were involved. The State Department confirmed the other "complex issues," stressing that Alexandria, too, had been bombed—and Egypt was of crucial importance in the delicate situation existing in the Middle East. Furthermore, the views of the Arabs in Iraq, Yemen and Saudi Arabia had to be taken into account, as America did not want to upset the precarious balance of power in the area. The Red Cross, therefore, had to tread carefully.[37]

Finding themselves in an uncomfortable position, the Red Cross representatives were glad to help the Zionists arrange an appointment with Wallace Murray of the Middle East Section of the State Department. Murray made it quite clear that it was necessary to appease the Arabs in the hope of securing their loyalty to the British. In this respect Egypt and Saudi Arabia were particularly important. In addition, according to reports of Palestinian government officials, the situation of the Jews there was not as bad as the Zionists claimed. Confronted by these arguments, the representatives of the Emergency Committee could do nothing more than suggest that the Americans despatch a study mission to ascertain the true situation in the region—but, of course, nothing came of the idea.

Negotiations with the Red Cross fell through, but the Zionist leaders had learned an important lesson from them: henceforward, all attempts to work with members of the Middle East section of the State Department would take cognizance of the anti-Zionist influence exerted by mandatory officials on representatives of the United States in the Middle East, and particularly on the Consul-General in Jerusalem. As the latter was the highest American official on the spot, the British point of view reached Washington through a most authoritative channel. The Zionist leaders, particularly Silver and Neumann, had thus gained significant political insight as a by-product of their failure to get the support of the Red Cross; but the financial situation of the Emergency Committee remained untenable.

For the sake of perspective, it should be noted that the Emergency Committee was not the only Zionist body in the United States that suffered from lack of funds. Although the Zionist movements in America raised 70 to 75 percent of the money received by the Zionist Executive abroad, they had no say in the allocation of funds. With the exception of Hadassah, all the movements were heavily in debt. This, of course, did not make things any easier for the Emergency Committee. It had been established to respond to calls for help, but when the calls began to come, the Committee's hands were tied.

At the same time, there was need for constant vigilance: during 1940–41 many Palestinian Jewish organizations tried to engage in fund-raising in America, sometimes competing with the recognized UPA and UJA drives. The Federation of Industrialists, the citrus grove owners, the Doctors' Union, various educational institutions—all looked hopefully toward the large Jewish public in the United States. Orthodox groups and yeshivot in Palestine had been supported by the European Jewish communities. The war cut off their source of income, and now they, too, turned to America, particularly to the Jews belonging to Mizrachi. The Palestine Economic Corporation had a special angle. Being about to issue new shares, it wanted to advertise in the *New Palestine*, the ZOA journal, in the hope of encouraging Americans to buy shares.

This was viewed as a threat to the UJA and UPA, which considered the readers of the *New Palestine* as their donor public. The Revisionists, too, tried their hand at fund-raising, primarily through the "American Friends of a Jewish Palestine." This elicited a statement by the Emergency Committee wherein it declared unequivocally that settlement, education, immigration, health, etc. of the Jewish community in Palestine were the exclusive responsibility of the Jewish Agency. Jewish Palestine's needs could best be fulfilled, therefore, by increasing the financial resources of the Agency rather than by supporting separatist organizations.[38]

In most cases, the Emergency Committee tried to counter unauthorized fund-raising by encouraging its constituent organizations to insist that the official national funds be allocated in such a way that all sectors of Palestinian Jewry would benefit. Eventually one of those national funds—the United Palestine Appeal—agreed to allocate 100,000 dollars to the Emergency Committee itself, to be remitted in two installments.[39] But this was too little and too late to save the Committee's first year.

International Zionist Communication

The abysmal disappointment over the Emergency Committee's poor performance is best measured by the lofty expectations that accompanied its establishment. As soon as it became clear that war in Europe was inevitable, the World Zionist movement tried to make provisions for maintenance of inter-movement contact. Assuming that contact with the various European movements would be severed, London and Jerusalem looked toward the United States as a possible center for interchange of information and transmission of instructions, requests, etc. Even before the United States entered the war, however, this hope was frustrated; America's hostility to totalitarian regimes was well-known to the Rome–Berlin Axis; this almost entirely ruled out possibilities of direct contact with European Jewry. At the same time, during the early war years the expected severence of communication between Europe, Great Britain and Palestine did not occur. As it happened, it was the American Zionist movement that was almost completely isolated from the others.

It was originally planned that the Zionist offices in London, Palestine, Geneva and the United States would coordinate their activities, as long as conditions permitted. But with the international situation in a constant state of flux, rather than dividing their work geographically, each office tried to maintain contact with all branches of the Zionist movement everywhere. Efficiency and conservation of resources were knowingly sacrificed for the sake of "keeping in touch."[40] Largely due to objective conditions, the plans left a good deal to be desired. The Geneva center was little more than a contact office that occasionally managed to gather crumbs of information, but primarily worried about the ever-present threat of a German attempt to overrun Switzerland. The center in America, as we have seen, lacked the tools, the ideas, the desire, and, above all, the leadership to become in every sense a center of world Zionism.

From our historical vantage point over 40 years later, it is quite apparent that Jewry's traditional unity—a unity that comes to the fore at critical times—rather than any planned action, kept the world Zionist movement from disintegrating during the Second World War. This does not mean that the American movement made no attempt to play a role in inter-movement communications; it tried to function in areas where it had some natural advantage over the London and Jerusalem offices.

Latin America, geographically near the United States and to some extent under American political influence, had several Zionist organizations. Some were of long standing and others were relatively new, having been formed by refugees who arrived in Latin American countries during the 1930s. At the Emergency Committee meeting on the 4th of December, 1939, Solomon Goldman, urged by Dr. Landauer of the Jewish Agency's Organization Department in Jerusalem, recommended extending activities to include the countries of Latin America. Initially, the Emergency Committee tried to create some form of permanent contact there. Consultations were held in Washington with the political "oracles" of the Zionist movement—Frankfurter and Brandeis—and the Committee received their blessings. Cautious as always, Frankfurter suggested that the Zionist activity be camouflaged to appear in the guise of "cultural ties"—which the American government was interested in promoting.[41]

The suggestion was approved and as a first step it was decided to send someone there to study the situation in the Zionist movements.[42] The idea of sending a special envoy in the name of the Emergency Committee elicited immediate protest from Keren Hayesod in London and the director of the Department of Organization in Jerusalem. They considered the Keren Hayesod man—who also served as special representative of the Jewish Agency in Latin America—quite adequate, and refused to permit a representative of American Zionism to work there. Too weak to overcome such objections, the Emergency Committee did not press the issue. No one was sent and a void was created—particularly during the crucial early days of the war, a void that Dr. Nachum Goldmann tried to fill in the name of the World Jewish Congress. The Emergency Committee, therefore, at a very early stage forfeited any role it might have played in strengthening Latin America's Zionist movements.

Occupied Europe: From the very beginning, the Emergency Committee had considered contact with European countries to be its all-important function. Before it was even formally established, Dr. Weizmann had requested Dr. Solomon Goldman to try to establish contact with Polish Jewry and just two months later, Dr. Lauterbach asked Goldman to get whatever information possible about the large Jewish communities in Europe, communities in which important Zionist movements had flourished.[43]

The Emergency Committee decided to send Alexander Easterman, a reporter for the London *Daily Herald*, to the Balkan regions bordering on the German Reich. He was to investigate the situation and report back on the "conditions and prospects" of the Jews of Eastern Europe. The relatively large sum of 1,000 dollars was allocated for this purpose but, for a variety of reasons, nothing came of the idea.

The veteran Polish Zionist leader, Yitzhak Grinbaum, proposed that an American citizen be sent by the Emergency Committee to Lithuania to help the refugees and to establish contact with people in enemy-occupied areas of Poland. Richard Lichtheim, a member of the Executive who was posted to the Geneva office and may have felt that an American representative would encroach on his territory, declared that it would be "unnecessary and of no value." Two other offices in Geneva engaged in Zionist activity; both had been operating longer than the office Lichtheim headed. One was the office of the Agency's permanent delegation to the League of Nations, led, until the outbreak of war, by Nachum Goldmann and later by Dr. Cahani; the other was the Hechalutz office, headed by Natan Schwalb. Each office strove to be given "exclusive recognition" by the movement centers in Jerusalem, London and New York.

Lichtheim's office and the League of Nations delegation joined forces at the beginning of 1940 to prevent the Emergency Committee from sending its own representatives into occupied territories in Europe—which it could have done as an organization from a neutral country. To make sure that such an attempt would not be made by the American Zionists in the future either, Lichtheim wrote to the offices in London and Jerusalem, informing them that it was unlikely that the Emergency Committee could ever make contact with the Zionist organizations of occupied Europe.[44] Thus, the Emergency Committee was prevented from attempting to make an independent assessment of the situation in Europe. Thereafter it limited itself to as voluminous a correspondence with Lichtheim as conditions permitted, and depended upon him for information.

Canada and Australia: At that point, the Zionist organizations in the British Dominions remained the only possible sphere of activity open to the American Zionist Emergency Committee. South Africa's large active Zionist organization did not need an intermediary to maintain contact with other Zionist centers, as it was on a major junction of the British Empire's seaways. Therefore, Canada and Australia remained, both with less developed Zionist movements than that of the United States.

With the escalation of submarine warfare, the Canadian Zionists were isolated from their center in London, and they naturally turned to the United States. The Emergency Committee sent bulletins and educational material issued either by itself or by Palcor, and whenever the President of the Canadian Zionist Federation was in the States, he participated in Emergency Committee meetings.

One of the first joint undertakings of the two movements involved 270 European Zionist youth who had been members of *halutz* training groups in Europe or were Youth Aliya graduates and were caught in England on their way to Palestine. Under the British Emergency Regulations of May 1940, they were declared enemy aliens and expelled to Canada, where they were interned. After a simultaneous appeal to the British Embassy in Washington and to the Canadian government, many of those youth were freed from internment camps and placed in Zionist training farms, first in Canada and then in the United States.[45] The basis was thus laid for future cooperation between the American and Canadian Zionist movements.

The Zionist Federation of Australia and New Zealand was in a much more difficult position, as it was completely isolated. Remote from any other Zionist center, the two sections of the movement were also very far from one another, being at the extreme opposite ends of the continent. The entire Jewish community of Australia numbered no more than 25,000 and of New Zealand about 2,000.[46] Australian Jewry was in a particularly difficult position as the community had a very large proportion of young people, most of whom were called up for military service.

Nevertheless, the Zionists "down under" did their best to carry on, and turned to the Emergency Committee at their own initiative. To the extent that it could, the Committee tried to keep them informed of developments in Palestine and in Zionism in other parts of the world.

Isolation of the Emergency Committee

International communications were severely disrupted when war broke out, and this directly affected the Emergency Committee's contact with the Zionist Executive. In mid-1940, when Italy, too, declared war on the Allied powers, postal service to Palestine virtually ceased to exist. To the extent that letters arrived at all, they traversed unbelievably roundabout routes, spending months on the way. (The first letter sent from the Executive in Jerusalem to the secretary of the Emergency Committee arrived in July of 1940, some eight months after the Committee had been formed. Six earlier letters sent from Jerusalem either never reached their destination or were returned to sender two years later.

Initially, there was total cessation of overseas mail delivery. Then the Pacific Clipper, a special air service organized when the war started to secure America's connection with various parts of the world, began to carry mail through the Far East. By this route, it took between 23 and 32 days for a letter from the United States to reach Palestine. After Pearl Harbor and Japan's entry into the war, the Pacific route was blocked. Letters were then sent by the Transatlantic Clipper to England and from there to Palestine by sea, around the Cape of Good Hope, or by American planes crossing Africa in the width. Sacks of mail flying this route took several months to arrive. The difficulties of sending mail from Palestine to America were even greater, with the net result that answers to urgent questions, reaction to burning issues, were often sent so long after they had originally been raised that the issue had already become obsolete—or had been settled months before.

A different, but no less severe obstacle to communication was the draconic censorship exercised by the British in Palestine. Whatever was of major concern to the Zionist movement—immigration, settlement activities, the fate of European Jewry—was deleted or marred beyond recognition by the responsible governmental authorities. After completely mutilating minutes of a meeting or a letter, the clerk in question would append a cynical note to the effect that the British examiner is not responsible for the defacement of the communication . . . Minutes sent from the United States to Jerusalem were also decorated by great blots from the censor's pen or great gaps snipped out by his scissors (in one instance, only the letterhead and list of those in attendance remained of a whole set of minutes). The Executive was often completely in the dark as to the activities of the Emergency Committee.

The situation became so bad that in the middle of 1940, Eliahu Epstein (later Eilat) of the Jewish Agency Political Department was sent to Istanbul so that, among other things, he could be in a position to maintain contact with the American Zionists. Using the good offices of a friendly American journalist stationed in Istanbul, he was able to cable information to the United States, and even receive reasonably prompt answers.

The obstacles to communication that largely severed the Emergency Committee from the centers in Jerusalem and London further added to the complacent atmosphere prevalent among Zionists in the United States, fully a year and a half after the war had begun. Arthur Lourie, arriving in New York from the London office of the Jewish Agency, described the Committee as existing on a desert island, remote from the mainstream of Zionist life. As an example of this detachment, Lourie cited the casual reaction of the movement to a cable received from the Agency Executive in London on the 20th of February, 1940. The American Zionists were asked to initiate a public protest, parallel with efforts undertaken in London, to avert the implementation of land-purchase restrictions applying to Jews in Palestine. Differences of opinion concerning the form such protest should take were so great that on the 28th of February, when the restrictions became effective, no public protest at all had been made by the American Zionists.

The "Coffin Ships" and American Reaction

A crucial test of American Zionism's organized reaction to British policy in Palestine came in the wake of the sinking of the steamship _Patria_. Since 1934, Palestinian Jewry had been thwarting immigration restrictions by bringing "illegal" boatloads of refugees and landing them clandestinely on the shores of Palestine. After adopting the White Paper policy in 1939, the British patrolled the coastline more vigilantly; naval vessels would intercept the boats and turn the refugees away.

In November of 1940, 1,700 refugees, packed into two Haifa-bound "coffin ships"—as these overcrowded and often unseaworthy river-boats roaming the Mediterranean were called—were apprehended by the British Navy. They were escorted into Haifa and the passengers transferred to a French merchant vessel called the _Patria_, for deportation to the island of Mauritius. Before this plan could be carried out, an explosion occurred on the morning of 25 November in the hold of the _Patria_. It took less than half an hour for the ship to sink and over two hundred refugees lost their lives.[47]

During the two weeks that separated the interception of the "coffin ships" and the explosion, Palestine's Jewish leadership had desperately called upon American Jewry to protest the inhumane decision of the mandatory government to banish the unfortunate refugees, when they were at the very shores of a safe haven. (Incidentally, this was one of the occasions when Eliahu Epstein used his friend in Istanbul to make sure that news of the *Patria* would reach the United States.)

The Emergency Committee was convened on November 14 to discuss possible protest actions, but no decision was taken. Ben-Gurion, in the United States at the time, tried to initiate a large-scale public protest, but to no avail. The advisers in Washington—Brandeis, Franfurter, Ben Cohen—recommended "quiet diplomacy" to avoid embarrassing the British and rousing latent antisemitic sentiments in America. The majority of the Emergency Committee agreed with this stand although a minority, consisting of Louis Lipsky and Emanuel Neumann, advocated the militant position taken by Ben-Gurion. Discussion and clarification were still going on when the *Patria* blew up. (The British permitted the survivors to enter Palestine, reducing the number of certificates that would be available to Jewish immigrants by the number of survivors allowed in.) The only thing the American Zionist movement had done was meet with the British ambassador in Washington—and the meeting was not even covered by the press.

The *Patria* had additional, more far-reaching repercussions: Ben-Gurion castigated the Emergency Committee for not having moved heaven and earth to express their horror at the expulsion from Palestine of victims of Nazi terror. Weizmann cabled Ben-Gurion asking him to take a more moderate position as emotionally charged reactions would only complicate the situation. The cable added the reminder that the Germans had encouraged this shipment of refugees (the original boats, two of a convoy of three known as the "Sturfer" convoy, had been organized with the tacit agreement of the Gestapo in Vienna) to both get rid of the Jews and to embarrass the British.[48] Considering this a personal communication, Ben-Gurion did not show it to members of the Emergency Committee and continued to demand militant anti-British action.

When the contents of the cable were "leaked," the members of the Committee who had opposed public protest felt that their position had been considerably strengthened. Thus, when the third of the "Sturfer" boats—the *Atlantic*—arrived on the 24th of November and the British decided to banish its passengers despite the *Patria* story, two clearcut blocs were formed in America. (The Jewish Agency had again used its Istanbul channel and the news reached the United States quickly.) Stephen Wise, the Hadassah women and Robert Szold were among those who ruled out public protest; Solomon Goldman, Abba Hillel Silver, Louis Lipsky, Emanuel Neumann and the representatives of Poale Zion strongly advocated it. The deadlock resulted in the publication of a rather innocuous, carefully "balanced" statement expressing concern, in the name of American Zionism, over the expulsion of immigrants from the shores of Palestine. The peculiar document is almost apologetic in tone and concludes with a declaration of Zionism's support of the British war effort and the hope that the British government will not permit injustice to prevail.[49]

The constant tug of war within the Zionist parties, the incessant disagreement among outstanding personalities over methods and approach, added to the objective difficulties and the ambivalence resulting from support of Great Britain's war effort while condemning the mandatory government, left little time or energy to deal with the truly burning issues.

As its first year drew to a close, the Emergency Committee could claim credit only for having survived—and perhaps for having taken the first halting steps toward clarification of its organizational framework. In the sphere of practical activity it had accomplished nothing, and it had been quite helpless in the face of urgent demands. In other words, thus far the Committee had utterly failed to respond to the emergencies for which it had been created.

Notes to Chapter 2

1. 21st Zionist Congress—stenographic report, Jerusalem, 1938, p. 7.
2. *Ibid.*, Rabbi Berdin's address, p. 65.
3. *Ibid.*, pp. 52, 64, 99, 113.
4. *Hadassah Newsletter*, September–October 1939, p. 5.
5. *Ibid.*, text of decisions, pp. 249–51.
6. *Ibid.*, p. 242.
7. *Palcor Bulletin*, August 8, 1936, p. 6.
8. Described to the author by Mrs. Judith Epstein, then president of Hadassah and a delegate to the Congress, in an interview held on March 2, 1970.
9. Text of cables included in minutes of Executive Committee of Inter-Party Committee, September 10, 1939. (All minutes from this period are filed under Arthur Lourie, secretary of the Emergency Committee, NYZA.)
10. For descriptions of these meetings, see confidential appendix to minutes of Inter-Party Committee held on September 19, 1939.
11. See minutes of Emergency Committee meeting, September 18, 1939.
12. *Ibid.*
13. The most important example was the UJA. On the background and establishment of the UJA, see E. Ginzberg, *Report to American Jews*, New York, 1942.
14. *Report of the American Emergency Committee for Zionist Affairs to the Convention of the Z.O.A.*, n.d., Emergency Committee file, NYZA.
15. Lipsky to Linton, November 17, 1939, S5/409.
16. Caplan to Linton, November 11, 1939, S5/409.
17. See minutes of Emergency Committee meeting, October 24, 1939.
18. See minutes of Emergency Committee meeting, November 24, 1939.
19. See minutes of Emergency Committee meetings dated February 4, 1940; February 28, 1940; March 26, 1940; July 18, 1940.
20. See minutes of Emergency Committee meeting, March 16, 1940.
21. See minutes of Emergency Committee meeting, May 28, 1940.
22. See minutes of Emergency Committee meeting, July 27, 1940.
23. See minutes of Emergency Committee meeting, July 24, 1940.
24. Urofsky, *A Voice that Spoke for Justice, op. cit.*, p. 313.
25. See A. Gal, *David Ben Gurion—Preparing for a Jewish State. Political Alignment in Response to the White Paper and Outbreak of World War II 1938–1941*, Sde Boqer, 1985, pp. 69f (Hebrew).
26. The Brandeis group was especially critical of any "foreign" involvement in internal American Zionist affairs. Brandeis himself was vehemently opposed to it. See Brandeis to Szold, July 5, 1940, in M. I. Urofsky and D. W. Levy (eds.), *Letters of Louis D. Brandeis*, vol. V, Albany, 1976, p. 644.

27. See minutes of Emergency Committee meeting, October 29, 1940.
28. *Ibid.*
29. In an interview with the author, July 5, 1975.
30. See minutes of Emergency Committee meeting, September 20, 1943.
31. Proposal appears as appendix to the Emergency Committee minutes of September 9, 1940.
32. For report of activities of the Palestine Office, see report of its director to the ZOA Conference on May 18, 1938, CZA, Z5/136.
33. See minutes of Inter-Party Committee, September 19, 1939.
34. See minutes of Emergency Committee meeting, October 9, 1939.
35. *Ibid.*
36. Top secret report of meetings held by Breslau and Montor in Washington on October 8, 1940, Emergency Committee files (under Robert Szold).
37. *Ibid.*
38. See formulation in minutes of Emergency Committee meetings of December 27, 1939, of statement to be disseminated in the name of each Zionist organization. See also series of interviews with Hillel Kook, Dr. Raphaeli and S. Merlin carried out by the author for the Department for Oral Documentation of the Institute of Contemporary Jewry, Hebrew University, Jerusalem.
39. See report to Emergency Committee of November 23, 1939.
40. See outline of plan in letter from Lauterbach to Goldman, September 18, 1939, CZA, Z5/409; and to Nachum Goldmann, October 19, 1940, CZA, Z5/409.
41. See report by Goldman and Montor of their meeting in Washington on October 21, 1939, appended to minutes of Emergency Committee meeting on October 24, 1939.
42. See minutes of Emergency Committee meeting of December 4, 1939.
43. Lauterbach to Goldman, November 30, 1939, S5/409.
44. See Linton to Lichtheim, March 13, 1940; Linton to Lauterbach, March 26, 1940, and Lauterbach to Linton, March 26, 1940 (all S5/409). Folder L 11/165 in files of Jewish Agency representative in Geneva contains Lichtheim's reports of the situation (signed "Beit Or"), that were duplicated and distributed to Emergency Committee members.
45. See minutes of Emergency Committee meeting, November 29, 1940; also brief report on Emergency Committee's work submitted by A. Lourie to the ZOA Administrative Committee, 1941.
46. See report of Dr. Yona, president of the Australian Zionist Federation, to the Emergency Committee, November 29, 1940. For the story of Australian Zionism during the war, see memoirs of the head of the political department: J. M. Machover, *Toward Rescue—The Story of Australian Jewry's Stand for the Jewish Cause, 1940–48*, Jerusalem, 1972.
47. On the unintentional sinking of the *Patria* by the Haganah, see its official history: Y. Slutsky, *History of the Haganah*, vol. III, Part I, *From Resistance to War*, Tel Aviv, 1973, pp. 152–8 (Hebrew). For a detailed account, see the memoirs of the mission's commander, Meir Mardor: M. Mardor, *Shlihut Alumah* ("Secret Mission"), Tel Aviv, 1957, pp. 53–77 (Hebrew).
48. On Sturfer's activities, see D. Ofer, *Illegal Immigration During the Holocaust*, Jerusalem, 1988, pp. 160–204 (Hebrew).
49. See copy of press release in Emanuel Neumann Archives, file 51, original classification.

3

1941–42—The Search for Direction

It is my opinion that America could be converted not only into an arsenal for democracy but also into a tremendous reservoir of Zionist strength.

EMANUEL NEUMANN, 1941

AT THE beginning of 1941, when the Emergency Committee finally implemented an earlier decision to establish a Department for Public Relations and Political Action, the American Zionist movement seemed to be on the verge of adopting a more politically oriented stance. It also seemed to be waking up to the need to direct its information and propaganda to non-Jewish America, middle-level officials and the ordinary "man in the street"—not only to the Zionist and Jewish public or, in times of emergency, to high echelons in government. The formation of the special department appeared to be an indication that Zionism intended to emerge as an active political influence group on the American scene. And that was indeed the intention of some of the Emergency Committee's members. As we shall see, however, a cumbersome apparatus, personal and organizational rivalries, and ideological clashes thwarted those good intentions.

Department of Public Relations and Political Action

The subcommittee on reorganization set up by the Emergency Committee in 1940 recommended that a body be established to coordinate the public relations and political activities of the American Zionist movement.[1] Essentially, this was the major innovation proposed by the subcommittee, and it clearly demonstrated the importance attributed to the two areas in which the Department was to function. The proposal described the purposes of the

PLATE 4.   Emanuel Neumann, the dynamo behind the Emergency Council.

PLATE 5.   Dr. Walter C. Lowdermilk, initiator of the Jordan Valley Authority project.

Department as follows: a) to establish and maintain political contacts in Washington and other parts of the country; b) to meet with representatives of the press, radio, religious groups and other large nationwide organizations; c) to prepare appropriate material for use in education and propaganda. The Department was to be chaired by a member of the Emergency Committee, but a professional director, subordinate to the chairman, would conduct the activities.

The Department did not begin to function until 1941, when Emanuel Neumann undertook to direct it. Neumann had already filled many important positions in the American Zionist movement: until 1930 he headed the educational activities of the General Zionists; he was director-general of the United Palestine Appeal and chairman of its management committee from 1925 to 1927, and president of the Jewish National Fund in America from 1928 to 1930. In 1931 he was chosen to represent the American Zionist movement at the Jewish Agency Executive, in which capacity he formed the American–Palestine Committee to mobilize non-Jewish friends of Zionism. This organization was officially inaugurated at a gala dinner in January 1932. Soon thereafter, Neumann moved to Palestine with his family.

As a resident of Palestine, he was appointed to head the Department of Commerce and Industry of the Jewish Agency, where he gave first priority to encouraging the immigration of an entrepreneurial class capable of establishing private enterprises. At the same time, he sought ways of attracting capital investments from the United States. When the Labor movement took control of the Executive at the 18th Zionist Congress in 1933, Neumann left the Department of Commerce and Industry. Remaining in Palestine, he initiated and directed a number of economic projects and investment companies. He belonged to the faction known as General Zionists "B," and was active in the governing body of the parallel secret defense organization—the "National Hagana" (known also as Hagana Bet)—which in 1939 merged with the Hagana, the quasi-official Jewish underground. (A group opposing this merger split off at that time to form the Irgun Zvai Leumi—"Etzel."

For family reasons, Neumann returned to the United States in 1940, where he found himself rather estranged from the Zionist Organization of America. In his own words: from having been "at the top of the heap" when he left the States in 1931, he now saw himself as follows:

> an outsider . . . so completely involved in the immediate problems of Palestine and its future that I could not muster much interest for the Z.O.A. as such. What did attract me was the Emergency Committee for Zionist Affairs, which seemed destined for an important role.[2]

Convinced that it was of utmost importance to end the deadlock that had paralyzed Zionist political action in the United States since the publication of the White Paper and the outbreak of war, Neumann began to lend his weight to those forces that he believed could transform America into a second front for militant Zionist action. Certain that America would be of major importance on the international scene after the war and that Zionism's future would rest not with Great Britain but with the United States, he felt that American Zionist and Jewish public opinion had to be groomed to assume the role of a resolute, aggressive spearhead.

As has been indicated, not only American Zionist undertakings but Zionist propaganda as well suffered from a total lack of coordination. Neumann, with the sharpened perceptivity of one who was still uninvolved, was very much aware of this. He advocated a more extreme stand with respect to Great Britain's repressive measures in Palestine than did most of the members of the Emergency Committee—or the American Zionist movement in general. In this respect he and Dr. Wise opposed one another—which did not keep Dr. Wise from recognizing Neumann's talents and experience and approving his appointment to head the Department of Public Relations and Political Action.

On January 9, 1941, Emanuel Neumann became the executive director of the new Department, formally described as a subcommittee of the Office Committee. This description was designed to reassure the members of the Office Committee that they would maintain a controlling voice in the Department. Since public relations are necessarily conducted in accordance with a given political line, the immediate question which had to be tackled was who had the authority to determine policy. The rather unrealistic resolution of this problem was the decision that policy-making and political action would be supervised by the Office Committee—a decision that ignored the often tenuous line dividing public relations from political action.

Formulating a general political line to which all parties constituting the Emergency Committee could subscribe was another hurdle that had to be overcome before the Department could set to work. Neither in the United States nor in Palestine had the Zionist movement come out with a clearly defined statement of policy. The political stand of American Zionism, therefore, had to be derived from a number of different declarations that had been issued on a variety of occasions by a variety of bodies. The following points seemed to express a consensus: a) reconstitution of Palestine as a Jewish commonwealth; b) approval of the establishment of a Jewish fighting force; c) vigorous support of Great Britain's war effort, and equally vigorous condemnation of the British government's White Paper policy in Palestine. This was the clearest statement of policy that could be enunciated at the time without alienating one or another constituent body of the Emergency Committee.

Early in February of 1941, Neumann was already able to report on two meetings that had been held in Washington with Sumner Welles, Under-Secretary of State. The first, attended by Dr. Wise, Dr. Nachum Goldmann and himself, was to discuss the feasibility of forming a Jewish military force; Neumann accompanied Bernard Joseph, legal adviser to the Political Department of the Jewish Agency in Palestine, to the second meeting. There Joseph gave Welles a full report on the current scene in Palestine, Jewish participation in the war effort, the Arab situation, and the deportation of Jewish refugees from Palestine's shores.[3]

Perhaps more important than any single action or project undertaken by Emanuel Neumann as director of the Department for Public Relations and Political Action was his attempt to break through the parochialism that had limited the target of Zionist information and propaganda to Zionist-oriented— or at best Jewish—audiences. Neumann's targets included all influential political figures, men of letters, social and religious leaders, statesmen, and academics. Whether they were Jewish or not was immaterial, for these were the people who had to be convinced to support Zionism's aims, and they in turn would spread their conviction to ever-widening circles.

True to his precepts, Neumann constantly looked outward: he planned to revive the Christian pro-Palestine committee he had organized before his departure for Palestine, and began to enlist the support—on a nonpartisan basis—of senators and representatives. Plans to issue a monthly news publication entitled *Palestine Today and Tomorrow*, to be addressed to leaders of public opinion, had advanced to the point where Neumann approached Edgar Mowrer, Archibald Macleish, Pierre van Paassen and others of such calibre to serve on the editorial board (due to a lack of funds the publication could not be issued). Additional publication plans included a bulletin for circulation within the Zionist movement and a series of pamphlets to be prepared by authoritative scholars, which would present the fruits of research in a variety of academic fields, thereby attesting scientifically to the viability of the Zionist solution to the Jewish problem. Neumann also instituted bi-weekly conferences of editors of Zionist publications issued by the various movements, where attempts were made to coordinate the thinking and policies of these publications.

In his address to the Biltmore Conference in the spring of 1942,[4] Neumann summed up his conception of what the Emergency Committee's objectives in the field of public relations and political action should be:

> The Emergency Committee should develop into a combination of a Department of State and a Ministry of Information for the Zionist movement . . . if we can effectively mobilize our forces and talent throughout the country, if we go in now for an all-out effort for winning the battle of America, there is good prospect that we will win the battle of Palestine.[5]

The first step toward winning the "battle of America" required a total reorientation of the Zionist movement, a radical change in its posture. The "center of gravity" of world political action was shifting from London to Washington; America would henceforth have a much greater say in world affairs, which meant that it would bear greater weight in connection with the issue of Palestine and of the Middle East as a whole. The State Department had already established a special office to plan post-war reconstruction; universities, research institutions and committees throughout the country were debating postwar problems. Neumann believed that the Zionist movement must be revamped in a way that would prepare it to influence all those involved in postwar planning.

Following his own order of priorities, therefore, Neumann joined others in beginning to plan a dinner that would revive the nonpartisan "American Palestine Committee." Among the outstanding participants at the dinner, held on April 30, 1941, were William Green, president of the American Federation of Labor; Major Victor Cazalet, a member of the British Parliament on an official mission to the States; and Senate majority leader Barkley. Dr. Weizmann, the main speaker, reviewed the needs of Europe's Jewish refugees in light of the current situation, and spoke eloquently of Jewy's longing for its homeland. He declared, in part:

> . . . Fate, history, call it what you may, has linked the national destiny of the Jewish people with Palestine. And Palestine happens to lie at the juncture of three continents. It is close to the Suez Canal . . . the greatest artery of trade and commerce not only of the British Empire, but of the world. . . . It is therefore important for the peace of the world that the countries flanking this vital pass shall not be weak, under-populated and semi-desert, but strong, populous, progressive and passionately devoted to those basic principles which sustain the structure of the Western civilization. . . . The world has to choose today between two things: between the Bible and the Sermon on the Mount, or *Mein Kampf*, and there is no bridge between these two.[6]

The inaugural dinner aroused a great deal of interest; there was extensive advance publicity, and the main speeches (as well as the message sent by Senator Robert Wagner, who could not attend because of illness) were broadcast over 177 radio stations throughout the United States. Three cabinet members, two hundred congressmen, clergymen, well-known journalists and men of letters were among those present.

The Department of State was less than enthusiastic about the establishment of the American Palestine Committee; some of the Department's more prescient personnel may even have recognized that the Committee might presage an era of Zionist political offensive such as had been hitherto unknown. Wallace Murray, chief of the Near East and African Division of the State Department and an avowed enemy of Zionism, made several attempts to thwart the establishment of the Committee, and managed to persuade Vice-President Henry Wallace not to accept the honorary chairmanship.

The British embassy in Washington was even more concerned, fearing that the newly formed body would be anti-British and would buttress isolationism in certain segments of American public opinion. Neville Butler, adviser to the British embassy, convinced Wallace Murray that the Zionists in Palestine were undermining the British position in the Middle East, and causing the 70 million Arabs in that part of the world to rise in protest.[7] To this Murray added his own considered opinion that Arab unrest would be further exacerbated by this confirmation of Nazi claims that the United States and Great Britain supported a national home for the Jews in Palestine, thereby making Great Britain's position in the Middle East increasingly untenable.

Lord Halifax, the British ambassador, went so far as to pay a special visit to Secretary of State Hull, to impress him with the gravity of the situation. Hull's reaction was typical of men schooled in the traditional American way of thinking:[8] he said that he considered a group such as the American Palestine Committee an inseparable and inevitable part of America's political system.

When such high-level approaches brought minimal results, lower-grade diplomats on the British embassy staff expressed their "great concern" over the dinner. Assistant Secretary of State Adolph A. Berle finally agreed that in addition to "playing the matter down a little," the President would be dissuaded from sending greetings to the gala occasion (and this was one time when Roosevelt turned down a request from Stephen Wise to send official greetings to a Zionist or Jewish event). The embassies of Moslem and Arab states also made representations to the Americans.[9] The dinner was held, however, and, as noted above, was very favorably reported in the press and on the air.

Expanding rapidly, the American Palestine Committee soon took a small office in Washington D.C., in addition to the space it shared in the New York office of the Emergency Committee. The Emergency Committee supplied its regular budget, but as it became an increasingly important means of bringing Zionism to non-Jewish America, many activities organized by the communities were paid for by local Zionist organizations.

The importance of the committee lay primarily in its constituency, as it included policy-makers, people of "religion and morality," the elite of the academic world and outstanding leaders in many spheres of American life. Non-Jewish religious bodies, however, were not represented, and Emanuel Neumann decided to try to reach this vital sector of organized American life. The approach was made through leading clergymen, who were usually highly respected and who wielded powerful influence in the smaller cities and towns. Once such men were convinced to support Zionism, it was relatively easy to elicit the organizational support of their churches. Favorably slanted information about Palestine would thus filter down to the non-Jewish masses through the medium of their own spiritual leaders.

In mid-1942 Rabbi Milton Steinberg, supported by the Department for Public Relations and Political Action, organized a church-oriented group that could appeal to a non-Jewish religious public and in many ways supplement the American Palestine Committee. This group was the nucleus of what became the "Christian Council on Palestine," which initially numbered 400 members, and grew to a peak of 2,400. The Christian Council promulgated the view that the fate of Jewry was a matter of concern to the conscience of Christianity, that all believers in Christianity were responsible for improving the lot of the Jews and for combatting racial and religious discrimination.

The Council's members supported the concept of a homeland in Palestine for the Jews, and organized conferences and seminars on relevant subjects. Such gatherings took place all over the country under the leadership of renowned theologians and clergymen. An interesting side-effect of this surge of non-Jewish sympathy was its impact on certain Jews who had always feared that overt support for Zionism would evoke accusations of "dual loyalties" and "un-American activities." Their fears were allayed when they saw that well-known non-Jews in governmental, religious, and intellectual circles unhesitatingly expressed their support for Zionism in public. Lest this be construed as implying that all of Christian America supported Zionism, it must be stated that large segments of liberal Protestants remained either hostile or indifferent to the idea of a Jewish state.

Mass Media

The Department of Public Relations was determined to publicize the problem of Jewish refugees and the Zionist solution to Jewish homelessness. The mass media reached an audience that could be tapped in no other way.[10]

During the first year of war the general press gave Palestine minimal coverage; whatever did appear was incidental to news of other events taking place in the Middle East. In the context of Middle East news, the situation of European Jewry and of the homeless Jewish refugees was never mentioned. Neumann had contacts with many journalists whom he began to supply with background material for articles on Palestine, stressing its importance as the solution to the Jewish question. Columnists who were frequently under great pressure to submit daily articles to the major newspapers were eager recipients of this material, as it saved them the trouble of ferreting out the facts. Radio commentators, also pressed for new, authenticated material, gratefully accepted the informational bulletins the Department prepared for them. Hundreds of press releases were issued by the Public Relations Department, serving as source material for the local press in many remote parts of the United States.

It was not until the 1930s, when Roosevelt—aware of the potential power of the airwaves—inaugurated his "fireside chats," that the radio became a prime medium for mass communication. With the war, a new type of program was introduced that featured a commentator expressing his own views on political, military and social issues. Millions of listeners tuned in to these commentators, who began to personalize their styles and acquire nationwide reputations. The Department made every effort to win these people over to a sympathetic understanding of Jewish and Zionist issues. Raymond Gram Swing, for example, one of the most popular commentators, regularly used background material and information about special events prepared for him by the Department.

Attempts were made to "plant" articles in the reputable intellectual journals;

two articles by Reinhold Niebuhr of the Union Theological Seminary were outstandingly successful. Called "Jews after the War," they appeared in successive issues of *The Nation* in December, 1942.[11] These and other articles were reprinted in pamphlet form and distributed to influential individuals throughout the United States.

With respect to the situation in the Zionist movement itself, Neumann's bi-weekly meetings with the editors of Zionist publications began to show results: a certain degree of unanimity became apparent in the way they treated major themes. More space was also being devoted to discussion of political aspects of Zionism, at the expense of less demanding—if more picturesque—descriptions of tree-planting, swamp-drying, Youth Aliya, etc.

At that time a number of official bodies were being established in America to deal with wartime information and propaganda, and the Department of Public Relations and Political Action sought some form of association with them. Emanuel Neumann contacted "Wild" Bill Donovan's "Office of the Coordinator of Information," an intelligence-gathering service that Roosevelt set up as soon as war broke out. When this service was transferred to the Office of War Information headed by Elmer Davis, Neumann tried to keep in even closer touch, mainly in the hope that censorship of Zionist news would thus be prevented. (There were very few cases in which the American censor interfered with the publication of Zionist material, despite the objections of some British agencies.)

Activities in Washington

A major weakness of Zionist political work in the United States had always been the movement's physical distance from Washington. New York was the "Jewish capital," and all major Zionist organizations had their offices there. Attempts to transfer the center of action to Washington had always failed. It was therefore customary for Zionist leaders to make flying visits to Washington to meet with important personages about specific issues—an inefficient way of working which became altogether obsolete in the new wartime situation.

As America prepared for war and then became a belligerent, the governmental setup expanded tremendously. The Zionist movement had to maintain constant contact with many of the burgeoning official or semi-official agencies. Every time there was need to press for an entry visa for European refugees, whenever it seemed that American intervention could bring about the successful conclusion of a rescue operation, or when a discussion about Palestine was arranged with a senator or an ambassador, one or more of the leading members of the Emergency Committee would go to Washington for a day or two. When Neumann took over the Department for Public Relations, he found himself constantly rushing back and forth between New York and Washington.

From his personal experience, Neumann knew that the Zionist movement was not very popular in the capital. The Near East Division of the State Department, and other influential circles, were overtly hostile. To counteract this, Neumann began to consider mobilizing the many Jews who now held important positions in government. Few Jews had been in government service in Washington prior to the New Deal; that began to change when Roosevelt consolidated his extensive plan to pull America out of its deep economic depression through the establishment of public agencies designed to give both jobs and services. Washington began to fill up with academically trained personnel, particularly in fields related to economics and welfare. Many of those young college graduates were Jews from the cities of the East, for whom opportunities for advancement in commerce, banking and insurance had been limited. They were concentrated mainly in the Departments of Labor and Justice, and in economic and financial agencies such as the Securities Exchange Commission. Most of the professionals who came to Washington then were American-born children of immigrant parents, graduates of the free public universities—many of them from the highly respected College of the City of New York. Their entry into government service was not always graciously received; many members of Congress resented "that element," referring to them collectively as "the New Yorkers"—synonymous with "Jews."

Neumann looked for ways of involving these young professionals in pro-Zionist activity. One of the ways tried was to organize a "dinner club" of people who were either government employees or who worked closely with the government. Discussion at these dinners would be directed toward Jewish and Zionist themes. The utmost discretion had to be exercised, as the group included high-level civil servants such as the Commissioner of Labor Statistics, the economic adviser to the White House, a senior official from the Department of Budgets, a director of the "Lend–Lease" program, a member of the War Production Board, and even Benjamin V. Cohen, one of Roosevelt's close personal advisers. In the course of time, discussions were led by Dr. Bernard Joseph, Chaim Weizmann, Walter C. Lowdermilk and others of similar caliber. The "dinner club" subsequently became the nucleus of the American Palestine Institute, which took upon itself the promoting of the Lowdermilk Project, and which was founded by Israel Sieff, who was in America in connection with the British war effort.

Work in Washington was two-directional, the intention being not only to convince influential members of government bureaus that Zionism held the solution to the future of suffering European Jewry, but also to learn as much as possible about the Allied Powers' plans for the Middle East after the war. Since neither the World Zionist Organization nor the Jewish Agency had offices in Washington at the time, Emanuel Neumann, together with Nachum Goldmann, undertook to perform the function those bodies normally would have, while trying to amass as much information as possible.

The natural place to seek information about plans for Palestine was in the Near East Division of the State Department, which had largely been ignored by representatives of the Zionist movement. Until now, the movement had tried to influence the President through Dr. Wise and the people around Judge Brandeis. It had been very unusual for a memorandum to be sent to Hull or Sumner Welles in the hope that they would then approach Roosevelt.[12]

Neumann embarked on a cautious investigation of the situation at the Near East Division, and immediately became aware of the personnel's implacable hostility toward Zionism. In a rather curious fashion, he also glimpsed the State Department's general approach to the problems of the area. During Dr. Weizmann's visit to the United States in April 1941, A. A. Berle asked to see him for the purpose of discussing Britain's problems with the Axis-oriented Arab countries. Weizmann asked Neumann to go in his stead. Great Britain was then under severe pressure from all sides: Rommel was attacking in the Western desert, the British front had collapsed, its army had been evacuated from Greece, and Iraq was in the throes of a pro-Axis uprising. According to Berle, Arab opposition to Britain stemmed from fear that if the Allies won the war, they would permit the Zionists to assume control of the Arab world. Since Great Britain had to deploy forces to defend Egypt from the west, Singapore in the Far East and the Balkans to the north, her vital lines of communication from the Persian Gulf through the Tigris and Euphrates valleys to Turkey were inadequately protected and the Arabs could cut them quite easily.

Berle had a solution to offer: as he saw it, the situation of the Jews in Palestine was desperate, caught as they were between the German–Italian offensive advancing on Egypt, Vichy-controlled Syria, and the pro-German rebels rising to power in Iraq. If the British were too weak to defend Palestine, the Jews there would be helpless in the face of Arab attack, and the entire Zionist enterprise would be destroyed. It was imperative to arrive at an understanding with the Arabs. The Zionist movement, therefore, had to demonstrate "statesmanship" and relinquish its demand for a Jewish state in Palestine. Should the Germans nevertheless conquer the country, the Jews of Palestine would then be able to turn to Saudi Arabia for help and refuge. In compensation for renouncing their claims to Palestine, after the war the Jews might be permitted to establish a sort of "Vatican" in Jerusalem, while they would build their actual state in the highlands of Ethiopia (sic). When Neumann commented that Ethiopia was controlled by the Italian enemy, Berle answered that this would change after an Allied victory. To Neumann's rejoinder that the same held true for Palestine, Berle had no answer.[13]

In all fairness to Berle, he repeatedly declared that he was not speaking on behalf of the State Department but rather thinking aloud. Such naive thinking, naturally, was totally unacceptable to the Zionists, and it drove home once more the attitude prevalent—particularly in the Near East Division—where the "Zionist problem" and "Zionist dissension" were always the terms of reference when the problem of Palestine or the Jews was being discussed.

During the early 1940s, Sumner Welles was undoubtedly the Emergency Committee's best and most important contact at the State Department. Welles' attitude to Zionism differed from that of his colleagues, as borne out by his willingness to mediate between the Zionists and the British embassy in Washington after Halifax replaced Lord Lothian as ambassador. Relationships deteriorated to the point where an open argument broke out between Halifax and Emergency Committee members who came to him in March of 1941 to express their protest at British treatment of refugees trying to land in Palestine. Welles' readiness to intervene was an expression of goodwill such as was rare among State Department personnel.

Sumner Welles also demonstrated his sympathetic stand in the summer of 1941, when the American Zionists began to fear that Britain was preparing secret postwar political settlements in the Middle East, ignoring the interests of the Jews in Palestine. In May 1941, Alexander C. Kirk, the American minister to Cairo and Saudi Arabia, sent his superiors an evaluation of the situation in the Middle East. He attributed the constant deterioration of Great Britain's status and the growing Nazi influence in the area to England's support of Zionist aspirations. Kirk made two proposals: 1) that the United States issue a declaration about certain aspects of the Palestine problem for the purpose of mitigating Moslem hostility; 2) that an attempt be made to reformulate the idea of the Jewish national home based on other premises than the ones currently accepted. Vague as these suggestions were, they amounted to a clear anti-Zionist stand. On the 28th of July Kirk sent another message, this time to the effect that his "sources" assured him that the United States was in a most appropriate position to solve the "Arab problem" in the Mid-East—and in Palestine in particular—as America had no history of difficult entanglements and no political goals for the future in that area. It was, therefore, incumbent on the Zionists in the United States to reconsider their position with respect to Palestine, thereby relieving tension in the Middle East and reducing the influence of the Rome–Berlin Axis on the Arab world.

On 15 July, in Hull's absence, Welles sent a detailed answer to Kirk's first proposals.[14] He declared that under existing circumstances, the Department of State believed it undesirable to publish a declaration recommending appeasement of the Arabs and attempting to convince the Zionist leaders to change their minds about the Jewish national home. Welles, however, was virtually the only protagonist of such a view in the State Department, and he was far from representing the opinions of the Near East Division, where a bloc of extreme anti-Zionists was pressing for America to declare a pro-Arab policy. It was largely due to his efforts that some of this pressure was neutralized at that time, which meant that the United States maintained its "traditional" hands-off policy in the Middle East.

"Foreign Relations"

Discussion of Emanuel Neumann's efforts to expand the scope of his Department would be incomplete without brief mention of the "foreign relations" that he established. France, with its long colonial history in the

Middle East, still controlled large areas bordering on Northern Palestine. Through Henry Morgenthau, American Secretary of the Treasury, Neumann contacted René Pleven, head of the "Free French" representation to the United States. The two men met and had lengthy discussions about the implications for Palestine of the situation in Lebanon and Syria, particularly in view of the emerging British scheme for an Arab federation under British protection. The Free French were interested in eliciting the support of American Jewry in their struggle to be recognized by the American government as a French government-in-exile. Such status would entitle them to economic and military aid, which the United States hesitated to give. These contacts bore fruit after the war, when France came out in support of Zionist aspirations, assisted illegal immigration and cast its vote at the United Nations in favor of the establishment of the Jewish state.[15]

The Maronite Christians were another group which could be expected to oppose British–Arab plans for a postwar Arab federation. Initially, Neumann sought allies within the relatively large Maronite community in the States, contacts that were subsequently pursued both in America and in Lebanon by members of the Political Department of the Jewish Agency.

Another interesting relationship cemented during the early war years was with Dr. Taraknatt Das, an Indian Nationalist from Bengal who resided in the United States. Emanuel Neumann, Hayim Greenberg of Poale Zion and Dr. Das formed the "Asia League," intended to further the interests of peoples determined to rid themselves of the yoke of British imperialism. Membership of the League expanded to include Chinese, Koreans, and Burmese, some of whom had been living in exile for many years.[16] Neumann and Greenberg considered nascent Asia fertile soil for inculcating an awareness of Jewish hopes for Palestine. Little came of this effort, however, due to the recurrent problem of lack of funds.

The Lowdermilk Plan

In his constant search for new approaches to the problems of Zionism and for new people capable of disseminating Zionism's concepts, Neumann became associated with Professor Walter Clay Lowdermilk, chairman of the American Geophysical Union. A soil conservationist who viewed the problems he encountered in his profession not only from a scientific, but also from a humanist angle, Dr. Lowdermilk toured Southern Europe and North Africa in 1939, studying the effects of soil erosion in those lands.

He visited Palestine in the course of the same trip, and was so impressed by the soil reclamation and agricultural advances that had been brought about by the Jewish pioneers that he, a non-Jew, became a warm friend and admirer of Zionism. Accompanied by his wife, Inez, he traveled the length and breadth of the land with a view to analyzing its water and soil problems. The couple became emotionally involved, too, as they personally witnessed some of the "coffin ships" with "illegal" refugees packed under intolerable conditions into their holds. Lowdermilk's scientific observations resulted in a comprehensive program for exploitation of Palestine's soil and water resources; his human observations led him to believe that his plan might be vitally important in creating opportunities for the settlement of hundreds of thousands of Jews, while bringing prosperity to the Arabs of the entire region.

Great Britain tried constantly to magnify the claims of the 1930 Hope–Simpson report that Palestine's water, land and other natural resources severely limited the number of people the country could support. The conclusions of the Hope–Simpson report had never been refuted on scientific grounds. The mandatory power had countered the "humanitarian plea" to save Jewish refugees by permitting them to enter Palestine in unlimited numbers, with the equally humanitarian claim that "scientific" analysis had proven that Palestine was unable to absorb more Jews without harming the indigenous Arab population.

Both Ben-Gurion and Emanuel Neumann had been seeking ways to refute this conclusion with well-grounded expert opinion and incontrovertible facts, and such material now became available. Henry A. Wallace, Secretary of Agriculture, asked Lowdermilk upon his return to prepare a report on the agricultural development and exploitation of soil and water resources in Palestine. Wallace was profoundly impressed by the report and brought it to the attention of Judge Brandeis, noting that it was "the best pro-Zionist brief he had ever heard." Brandeis called together a group of people, including Supreme Court judges and some outstanding journalists, to discuss the material. He also saw to it that a copy found its way to Roosevelt's desk.

Neumann at once realized that Lowdermilk's report was indeed a powerful argument to be used in presentation of the case for Zionism, particularly the recommendation to establish a "Jordan Valley Authority" (a name inspired by the Tennessee Valley Authority). The essential points of the plan, as Lowdermilk outlined it first in his report and then in a book, are as follows:

> Palestine has two primary needs: water and power. Water is available in the flow of the Jordan and potential power is locked in the swift and turbulent descent of the river to the depth of the Dead Sea. The main aims of the Jordan Valley Authority are thus the diversion of the sweet waters of the Jordan and its tributaries for the purpose of irrigating the arid lands of the Jordan Valley and its slopes, and the utilization of the deep incline of the Jordan River channel for purposes of power development.
>
> In addition to the irrigation plan the J.V.A. calls for the development of power facilities. In order to understand this power program it is necessary to review the unique topographical features of the Jordan Valley. This rift valley has created the greatest inland deep on the face of the earth. Its total depth is up to 1300 feet. Owing to this low level the Dead Sea has a

dry, torrid climate. . . . The power programme calls for the introduction of sea water from the Mediterranean into the Jordan River Valley for the double purpose of compensating the Dead Sea for the loss of the diverted sweet waters of the Jordan and of utilizing the sea water for development of power.

The supply of water and water power could be further increased by the utilization of water resources which lie in areas adjacent to Palestine and which are now not being utilized. There is no doubt that a regional approach to the problem of water resources based on agreement of all potential interests involved would greatly enhance the economic significance of the project and redound to the benefit of all concerned.

Power and irrigation are only part of the J.V.A. project. Its general objective is the development of the land, water and mineral resources of the Jordan drainage in Palestine and Trans-Jordan, and the maritime slopes of Palestine . . . water conservation and flood control would be an important part of the J.V.A.'s activities. . . . The J.V.A. would also seek to promote conservation of land by controlling soil erosion and introducing measures to increase the soil's absorption of rainfall and to lead unabsorbed waters away from fields and terraces to natural drainage channels without cutting and carrying away the soil. . . . The important but long-neglected problem of scientific range management and grazing would also fall within the jurisdiction of the J.V.A., for a very large part of the total water-shed is best suited for grazing. . . . The reforestation of lands unsuited to farming and grazing would also be undertaken by the J.V.A.: reforestation will provide much needed fuel and timber and restore a more regular regimen of storm run-off water. . . . An important and lucrative phase of the J.V.A. would be the extraction of important minerals from the Dead Sea waters on a scale far larger than the present one.

. . . Also included within the scope of the J.V.A. would be the reclamation of the Negev, or South Country, which comprises an area almost equal to that of the rest of Palestine.[17]

After discussing the economic viability of the project, Lowdermilk goes on the consider: What of the 1.3 million Arabs in Palestine and Transjordan? They would benefit greatly from the J.V.A. The increased Jewish immigration it would make possible would enlarge the market for their produce and provide them with new opportunities for investment and labor. The most convinced Zionist could hardly have made a more cogent brief for Jewish immigration into Palestine and for the country's ability to absorb such immigration.

The Department of Public Relations of the Emergency Committee made every effort to give the report wide publicity. Neumann, however, felt that publishing the report as part of a book in which the author could include subjective evaluations of the situation in Palestine and descriptions of personal experiences, would best serve the purposes he had in mind. When the subject of a book was broached to Mrs. Lowdermilk she was doubtful, declaring that "Walter was living on borrowed time,"[18] as he had suffered a severe heart attack. Fortunately he lived for another 30-odd years, and with his customary vigor, set about preparing a book.

In September of 1942 Dr. Lowdermilk was sent to China by the State Department, and the final editing as well as publishing of the book remained in the hands of Mrs. Lowdermilk and Emanuel Neumann. An editor, Shulamit Schwartz-Nardi, and a publisher, Harpers & Brothers, were found, but the mountain of red tape that had to be surmounted because of wartime regulations (all of which were applied in the fear that this might be construed as an anti-British document) presented the most difficult obstacle. This, too, was eventually overcome, and in 1944 the book was published in America by Harpers, and in England by Victor Gollancz.

The plan itself was not implemented in those chaotic years, but after the State of Israel was established, the entire idea was turned over to Israel's Water Planning Authority, and certain important aspects of it were executed. Other parts of it are again timely today, fifty years later, when the project of bringing water from the Mediterranean to the Dead Sea to be used for both consumption and electricity production is under consideration.

Dr. Lowdermilk's interest in Israel did not end with his proposal for a T.V.A. on the Jordan. In 1951 he volunteered to help set up a soil conservation service in the new country. A year later, the United Nations' Food and Agricultural Organization appointed him as its representative in Israel, in which capacity he continued his work for another year and a half. In 1954 he was back in Israel again, this time to head the new agricultural engineering department of the Technion in Haifa.

Lowdermilk "discovered" Zionism and the Jewish pioneers in Palestine by himself. But Dr. Neumann, recognizing the influence wielded by the American scientist, threw whatever strength the Department for Public Relations and he personally had into ensuring the publication of the book, *Palestine, Land of Promise*. This was just the type of activity Neumann felt his Department should be doing but could not because of the Emergency Committee's internal situation. After his resignation in 1943, he continued to work with the Lowdermilk proposal.

Organizational Hurdles

We have noted above that Emanuel Neumann was working as director of the Department for Public Relations and Political Action—and both determining and implementing policy—for some time before his appointment was officially recognized. He had undertaken a number of independent actions, so it was not long before he was instructed to submit all material—even press releases—to the Emergency Committee for approval. The Emergency Committee was anxious to control the new Department, first of all because of its own internal situation—which was so bad that only the direct intervention of Bernard Joseph kept the ZOA from dealing it a death-blow,[19] and secondly because after Neuman's initial successes, everything began to revolve around the Department.

To ensure control, the Office Committee invented an arrangement that was as much fiction as fact: all members of the Office Committee would be ex-officio members of the Department, but each would delegate authority to a specialist in public relations, who would function as proxy. All matters of policy, naturally, would be decided by the Office Committee.

One of the specialists brought in under this arrangement deserves special mention. He was Meyer Weisgal, who had been involved in editing and writing for Zionist publications since World War I. By the time Weisgal became Dr. Weizmann's personal representative in the United States, he had had a successful career in theater as well as journalism. (He had produced two large pageants—"Romance of a People" in 1933 and the "Eternal Road" in 1937, both dramatizations of the story of Jewry and Zionism. He was also the creator of the highly successful Palestine Pavilion at the New York World's Fair in 1939.) He brought to the Department, along with his very varied experience, a long roster of influential people all over the United States to whom he had easy access.

Weisgal was in full sympathy with Neumann's conception of the Department of Public Relations, essentially believing that it should become the central propaganda instrument of the American Zionist movement. He, too, recognized the importance of convincing non-Jewish Americans of the validity of Zionism, but he was particularly concerned about the need to crystallize thinking within the movement itself. Convinced that the lack of coordination—in thinking as well as action—thwarted all efforts to improve the movement's public relations, he proposed the regular publication of a journal that would express the Zionist precepts in carefully considered terms and in contexts to which all the movements could subscribe. Naturally this proposal was turned down at once, the respective movements fearing, as usual, that a coordinated, combined enterprise of such a nature might infringe their sovereignty. Frustrated by similar obstacles each time he came up with a new idea, it was not long before Weisgal left to direct the office that the Jewish Agency opened in New York after the Biltmore Conference.

The Department's development was also severely hampered by the chronic lack of funds. Neumann had originally proposed a budget of 100,000 dollars to cover the first year's activity (which represented only two percent of all money raised in America for Palestine). The entire Emergency Committee had been promised a total of 25,000 dollars from the national funds for the year 1941—and even that ridiculously small sum was never remitted. Dr. Weizmann, who had hoped to raise a "political fund" of 500,000 dollars, was also thwarted by the refusal of the Zionist parties to sanction or contribute to an independent fund for political purposes, but he did instruct the Jewish Agency to allocate 27,000 dollars for Public Relations, which enabled some action. Neumann continued to work alone until the middle of 1941, when he hired Dr. David Petegorsky—an energetic, capable, young man.

During the second half of 1941, Neumann and Petegorsky worked together, and as Neumann told the author (in a personal interview on 2 June, 1974), this was probably the one and only high point of the Department's activity. Petegorsky was eminently qualified to assist Neumann in the field of political action. A Canadian with Orthodox rabbinical training, he had been an outstanding student at the London School of Economics and Political Science, and had extensive training in political research. When he resigned in frustration in March of 1942, he submitted a memorandum to the American Emergency Committee in which he offered full explanation of his feeling that "the Committee at present is failing utterly to cope with its tasks or adequately to discharge its responsibilities." He attributed this failure to at least three factors:

1) A defective organizational and administrative structure;
2) The failure of many members of the Emergency and Office Committees to exercise the responsibility that both their positions and the gravity of the moment demand;
3) A conception of the Committee's functions that is utterly inadequate for the complexity and urgency of the problems we confront.

In discussing the organization and structure, the memorandum stated that:

> The present organization of the Emergency Committee and its operation suffer from: a) a lack of centralized authority and coordination both in policy-making and administration; b) a lack of any clear and consistent political orientation and purpose; c) an unhappy method of selection of the personnel of the Office Committee; d) a misconception of the functions of the permanent staff. . . . There has been an extremely loose diffusion of authority which had amounted in most instances to the absence of any effective authority whatever. . . . Even more serious has been the failure of the Emergency Committee to appoint a director or chief executive officer charged with the general administration of the Committee's functions. . . . There has been, as a result, no integration or coordination of the Committee's various activities. There has been no adequate or effective allocation of duties and responsibilities.

The memorandum goes on to state:

> It is a most distressing—and almost unbelievable—fact that absolutely no provision has been made for the systematic organization of political work, for a planned program of political activity or for an effective

implementation of whatever programs existed. . . . There has been no clarity of purpose, of method, of goal. Thus, for example, there has been in the Emergency Committee a distinction between public relations and political work which my brief experience has convinced me is wholly untenable. . . . Lack of planned political activity and of a clear political orientation has served further to throw the Committee's work into confusion.

With respect to the Office Committee, Petegorsky declares that:

> It is overwhelmingly clear to me that the Office Committee, which is empowered to make decisions which involve the most complex and vital social and political issues of our time, is a body which can scarcely be considered competent for that purpose. . . . Virtually every one of its members is carrying a staggering burden of professional, business, personal and Zionist duties . . . but it is abundantly clear that the decisions the Committee is called upon to make . . . require nothing less than continuous and full time consideration of the problems they involve. . . . The Office Committee has regarded as one of its functions the closest scrutiny of every item of work done by the staff. . . . Meetings of the Office Committee are given over excessively to problems of procedure rather than of principle; and trifling details are given precedence over fundamental and vital issues.

The most important part of the memorandum, however, is the section headed, "Inadequacy of the Assumptions on Which the Work of the Emergency Committee Rests." Petegorsky claims:

> . . . most of the present work of the Emergency Committee seems to be based on the assumption that the world which will emerge after the war is over will be organized in very much the same way as it was before the outbreak of hostilities; that its problems will be similar in nature. That, of course, dictates that Zionist political activity follow the line it has traditionally taken. . . . I am overwhelmingly convinced, however, that there is another and vastly more realistic assumption to be made about the years that lie ahead. And that is that the postwar world will be a radically different one from the world we knew in prewar years. . . . Momentous developments are under way in China, in India, in Russia—in all of Asia. . . . These vast and revolutionary political, social and economic changes mean that we shall have to adjust ourselves to a wholly new world; that we must embark on an extensive revaluation and reapplication of our concepts; that we must begin to develop new contacts and relationships; that we must begin immediately to plan our program for the postwar world; that we must think 'in the grand

manner'. . . . At the present time we are probably the most poorly equipped of all groups in the world to cope with the vast problems by which we are encompassed. There are tremendous problems of federation, of regionalism, of world organization, of economic development, of political forms and institutions, of racial and national conflicts, etc. We have in our possession scarcely an ounce of material, hardly a single piece of adequate research, no cooperative or organized effort on which any political thinking or planning can be based.[20]

The memorandum then includes carefully thought-out structural suggestions for remedying the organizational and administrative anarchy—none of which were implemented during the period reviewed in this chapter.

Losing Momentum—The Struma Disaster

Aggravating all the problems raised by Dr. Petegorsky in his revealing memorandum were the ever-present problems of lack of funds, and the Emergency Committee's recurrent attempts to restrict Neumann's activities by insisting that his mandate extended only to the conduct of public relations. The activities Neumann had initiated so vigorously at the beginning of 1941 began to flag, and by the beginning of 1942, most had come to a standstill.

One of the first manifestations of the damage caused by the Emergency Committee's hesitancy to support Neumann's initiatives was in connection with the National Conference of Christians and Jews. This interfaith committee, organized primarily to combat antisemitism in the United States, had expanded after the outbreak of war to include many social and religious groups that were concerned over the preservation of American democracy. No Zionists had ever participated in this organization, a situation Neumann tried to change as he felt that a Zionist presence was essential there. In July 1941, he asked the Emergency Committee to send a representative to the Conference of Christians and Jews, but there was no response, which left the field free for the non-Zionists. The following autumn Rabbi M. Lazaron, the most extreme anti-Zionist rabbi in the States, left for England as part of a delegation of the Conference of Christians and Jews.[21] Had the Emergency Committee placed its own man there, the harm done by Rabbi Lazaron's anti-Zionist statements might have been averted. Indeed, a few months later Dr. Abba Hillel Silver was sent to England, among other things to repair some of the damage.[22]

Further damage to the cause of Zionism resulted from the Emergency Committee's failure to react to an article advocating the establishment of a binational state in Palestine within the framework of an Arab federation. The author, Dr. Judah L. Magnes, was president of the Hebrew University in Jerusalem, and his article in the *New York Times* of July 20, 1941, caused quite a stir. Some members of Hadassah supported the views expressed by Magnes, but more important, Wallace Murray of the Near East Division of the State

Department called the article to the attention of his superiors, noting that the views expressed were "worthy of close attention since they are based on a reasonable estimate of practical possibilities."[23] At the insistence of Hadassah, the Emergency Committee as such refrained from publishing a negative reaction to the article. Magnes and his supporters pressed their point of view during the following year and thereby postponed the crystallization of a uniform American Zionist stand with respect to the postwar aims of the Zionist movement.

One of the most unfortunate failures of the Emergency Committee was its inability to mobilize Zionist reaction to the tragedy that befell a boatload of refugees. On December 16, 1941, over 750 refugees boarded a small boat at the Romanian port of Constanza. The *Struma*, as the boat was called, set out frightfully overloaded for Haifa, but developed leaks and engine trouble and tried to dock at Istanbul for repairs. The Turks would not let any of the passengers land who did not have an entry certificate to Palestine. No one aboard the *Struma* had a valid immigration certificate, and the British refused to issue any, claiming that the annual quota for Jewish immigrants was exhausted. Altogether unseaworthy, the boat remained at anchor for ten weeks, after which the Turks became impatient and towed her out to sea. Knowing that they could never make the trip to Palestine, the captain tried to return to Romania. Just a few miles out the boat exploded and sank. Two of her passengers survived.

Turkey was neutral, which meant that there was no censorship to prevent information from reaching America about the plight of the refugees during those long weeks on the crowded ship. Both Jerusalem and London had sent urgent calls for action. Emanuel Neumann had met with the Turkish ambassador to Washington in the hope of getting permission for the passengers to disembark temporarily in Istanbul. When the boat sank on February 24, 1942, the news reached the United States quickly, appearing in the newspapers on the following morning. From Washington, Neumann called the members of the Emergency Committee in New York and Ben-Gurion in Chicago to make sure that a statement would be issued by the Emergency Committee for immediate publication in the press. The *New York Times* even extended the deadline for the make-up of its front page the following day, in expectation of the statement from the Zionists.

Some of the members of the Emergency Committee had second thoughts, hesitating to print a harsh protest to the British about the mistreatment of refugees and referring to an "understanding" that had been reached with Ambassador Halifax (in reference to an entirely different situation). The statement was therefore postponed until the Office Committee could meet the next day. The full picture of the process to which an urgent declaration was subjected—a process that completely nullified its value—is clearly described in a memorandum from Arthur Lourie to the members of the Emergency Committee:[24]

The process of consulting the parties, individual members of the committee and Mr. Ben-Gurion then began. A number of changes were suggested and were incorporated in a completely revised text which was ready next morning (Tuesday). Again there was the process of individual consultation with all concerned and the difficulty of reconciling different points of view where there has been no community of discussion. The statement was held up for the meeting of the Office Committee on Tuesday afternoon and with certain very minor changes the text as proposed was accepted. The Secretary was later informed that Dr. Wise would be arriving in New York that night, and since the cables were to be signed by him they should be submitted to him before dispatch. The telegrams were at Dr. Wise's office on Wednesday morning, but it was not until after five o'clock in the afternoon that Dr. Wise was able to let the Secretary know that he was unable to sign the cables in their then form. The cables were therefore again held up and came before the meeting of the full committee on Wednesday night. At this meeting the text which had previously received general approval was subjected to severe criticism by a number of those present. In the result, the cables were once again held up for radical revision and changes and the advantages to be derived from an immediate reaction have been dissipated.

"Muddling Through"—A Formula for Failure

The cumulative sense of frustration deepened, while the impression received by the outside world was that the Zionist movement was helpless, perhaps even indifferent. Neumann was close to despair and on 3 March, 1942, submitted his resignation. A subcommittee consisting of Dr. Israel Goldstein and Rose Halperin met to discuss proposals Neumann had made several months before about activities for the Department; he was asked to withdraw his resignation. He did so, stayed on until after the Biltmore Conference, and finally resigned early in 1943.

David Petegorsky's memorandum to the Emergency Committee constitutes a condemnation of uninspiring leadership with an underlying note of sorrow over missed opportunities. Trying to work with an impossibly inefficient apparatus which permitted each constituent of the Emergency Committee— whether individual or party—to pull in a different direction, the Committee at best could only succeed in "muddling through." The concluding sentence of Petegorsky's memorandum is both a warning for the future and admonition over the past:

Unless the members of the Emergency Committee can rise to the heights of leadership and statesmanship that the gravity of the hour demands, unless they can demonstrate those changes through which alone effective and significant results can be achieved, they will have failed the Jewish people in the saddest hour of their history.

The time for "muddling through" had long since passed, but there was still no serious attempt to think "in the grand manner," to plan for the future and to act decisively in the present. The leadership of the American Zionist movement indeed seemed about to fail the Jewish people in the saddest hour of their history.

Notes to Chapter 3

1. See minutes of Emergency Committee meeting, September 14, 1940.
2. E. Neumann, *In the Arena—An Autobiographical Memoir*, New York, 1976, p. 150.
3. Minutes of Office Committee of Emergency Committee (henceforth, OCEC), February 6, 1941.
4. Report of conference held from May 9 to 11 at the Biltmore Hotel, New York City.
5. See Neumann, *op. cit.*, p. 170.
6. *Ibid.*, p. 153.
7. See memorandum sent by Murray to Hull, Wallace and Berle, reporting on his talk with Butler on April 10, 1941; FRUS, 1941, vol. III, pp. 583f.
8. Cordell Hull was a judge whose political career began when the Tennessee Democratic Party sent him first to the House of Representatives and then to the Senate. Roosevelt appointed him Secretary of State in 1933, an office he held until 1944.
9. See Turkish ambassador's declaration to P. Alling, Murray's assistant as of April 24, 1941, to the effect that "every such activity as that of the APC only further inflamed Arab opinion"; FRUS, 1941, vol. III, p. 601.
10. From preliminary report by Emanuel Neumann on Department of Public Relations and Political Action, March 12, 1941; in portfolio on Department of Public Relations, Neumann Files.
11. *The Nation*, December 21, 1942, pp. 215f; December 28, 1942, pp. 253–5.
12. In the long run, most issues had reached the State Department's Near East Division, but the only direct contact had been in connection with securing visas for certain individuals, arranging flight priority for Zionist leaders coming to America from Palestine, among them Ben-Gurion—SDF 810; M. Shertok (Sharett)—SDF 867 01/1827; and others.
13. See Neumann's report to the OCEC of April 24, 1941. In a memorandum about the same meeting, Berle claimed that he had made no proposals whatsoever.
14. See Welles' message to Kirk, July 15, 1941; FRUS, 1941, vol. III, p. 615; also S. Welles, *We Need Not Fail*, Cambridge Massachusetts, 1948.
15. See Neumann's report to Weizmann of May 11, 1941, about political activities undertaken in Washington, CZA, Z5/1392.
16. Neumann, *op. cit.*, p. 166. Dr. Singman Rey, future President of South Korea, also participated.
17. W. C. Lowdermilk, *Palestine, Land of Promise*, London, 1944, pp. 122–7.
18. Neumann, *op. cit.*, p. 176.
19. See Bernard Joseph's report to the Jewish Agency Executive on his mission to the United States (Jewish Agency, April 13, 1941); see also Lourie to Lauterbach, letter of August 29, 1941, CZA, Z5/1392. In December 1941, the antagonistic leaders of the Lipsky–Szold factions resigned from the Emergency Committee, but their resignations were not accepted; OCEC minutes, December 4, 1941.
20. Memorandum presented by D. Petegorsky to Emergency Committee, March 30, 1942 (Petegorsky File in Neumann Files).

21. Minutes of OCEC, July 31, 1941. Three weeks before the Conference was to take place, Neumann again asked the Office Committee to send a representative, without success.
22. Minutes of OCEC, March 3, 1942.
23. See memorandum by Wallace Murray to Secretary, Under-Secretary and Assistant Secretary of State, February 6, 1942, SDF, 867 B. 01/1797.
24. Appended to minutes of OCEC, March 3, 1942.

4

The Biltmore Conference

The most important event in the internal development of the Zionist movement in the war years was the adoption of the "Biltmore platform."

JEWISH AGENCY EXECUTIVE REPORT, 1940–1946

THE BILTMORE resolution marked a watershed in the history of the Zionist movement in that it set forth, for the first time, a clear political goal for the movement. During the first 45 years of its existence, Zionism was forced, for a host of political reasons, to refrain from inscribing such a goal on its flag. And so, when in mid-1942 an American Zionist conference adopted the resolution, urging that

> the gates of Palestine be opened; that the Jewish Agency be vested with control of immigration into Palestine and with the necessary authority for upbuilding the country, including the development of unoccupied and uncultivated lands; and that Palestine be established as a Jewish Commonwealth integrated in the structure of the new democratic world . . .,

friends and foes alike were taken completely by surprise. What caused such an about-face in Zionist policy at the most hopeless moment in the Second World War?

Political Background

"Palestinianism" in Crisis

Side by side with the "classical" Zionism imported into the United States by East European immigrants at the end of the nineteenth century, another, a native American brand of Zionism had evolved over the years. The trend may be called "Palestinianism";[1] its greatest protagonist was Louis D. Brandeis. As the social structure of American Jewry gradually became transformed, this type of Zionism became increasingly dominant, serving as an ideological base for the existence of a certain section of the American Jewish community. Palestinianism was based on the proposition that it was the responsibility of all Jews to participate in building up a Jewish national home in Palestine. American Zionism was thus supplied with an ethnic status and self-respect denied the nationalist Jew by the surrounding majority.

On the other hand, Palestinianism was devoid of any characteristic which might provoke conflict between Zionist beliefs and American obligations. In consequence, the majority of American Zionist activity in the 1920s and 1930s consisted of "practical Zionism on behalf of others"; this deprived Zionism of both its cultural-national and its political dimension, so that it was converted into a quasi-philanthropic movement.

The emphasis on "practical work" gave the American Zionists and their many supporters in the American Jewish leadership a concrete task; this was the only way they could make Zionist philosophy relevant to American conditions. The outstanding example of this line of thought was the women's organization, Hadassah, which during the 1920s became the largest, most powerful and best-organized branch of the Zionist movement in the United States. From its inception, the organization stressed its practical mission—responsibility for the health services of the Palestinian Jewish community. Many more women could identify with this goal than with vague philosophical abstractions, which had never attracted a community that fought shy of any involvement in political-ideological controversy.[2]

The drastic changes in British policy in the late 1930s, which reached their apex in the MacDonald White Paper and the outbreak of World War II, led to a crisis among the supporters of this approach. The American Zionist leadership and the Jewish community as a whole were faced with a feeling of total failure. Palestinianism had not succeeded in solving the Jewish problem, any more than the large-scale philanthropic activities among European Jewry initiated by the AJJDC. It became apparent that a much more comprehensive political solution than that achieved at the end of World War I was necessary. The atrocities of the war and a feeling of complete impotence strengthened the awareness among Zionist leaders that it was necessary to return to political Zionism. These feelings slowly overcame the counter-arguments which had prevented the majority of American Zionist and other Jewish leaders from supporting the demand for a Jewish state.

Euphoric Postwar Visions

The entry of the United States into the war in December 1941 gave wings to an ideological current which had first come to the fore during the period of the First World War and which came to be called "postwar messianism" or "postwar millenarianism." America's involvement in the "European war" was

PLATE 6. Opening session of the Biltmore Conference, May 9, 1942. Weizmann at the podium.

seen not merely as a military–political act, but as something of an apocalyptic struggle, a battle of the "sons of light against the sons of darkness," that would cleanse the world of all evil.[3]

From the Marxist left to the extreme nationalist right, all shades of American society were represented among adherents to this view. This explains the resounding cheers that greeted Mrs. Roosevelt's naive declaration that the war was being fought so that every child in the world would have a glass of milk every morning, and President Roosevelt's statement that the United States was fighting for a "new world free from fear and want." This "ideology" became America's declared policy and was adopted as Section 6 of the Atlantic Charter,[4] meaning that it was the basis of the war aims of both Great Britain and the United States.

This was also the ideological basis of hundreds of organizations that arose in the United States and began to plan various aspects of the postwar world. They had one common goal: the solution of all the problems of humankind, starting with hunger in India and ending with Poland's borders. A directory published by the Council for Foreign Affairs in 1942 listed over 300 such bodies and organizations. A few of their names will suffice to illustrate their supreme sense of self-importance: World Community Movement, World Federalists, World Citizenship Movement, World Peace Association.[5] Most of them had an internationalist approach to world affairs and believed that now was the time to rectify the world's ills through international cooperation. Their common denominator—involvement in postwar planning—seemed to have had a magical effect, and whether the organization or movement was religious, social, economic, scientific or political in its nature, the words "postwar planning" were incorporated in its statement of aims. Many of the organizations were not particularly important, but as a collective phenomenon they were significant harbingers of a trend. In addition, some very influential research institutes as well as retired statesmen and ambitious politicians also jumped on the "postwar" bandwagon.

The body that had overall governmental sanction was the Advisory Committee on Postwar Foreign Policy, chaired by the Secretary of State and established by presidential decree. Its members came from universities, Congress, the business world, the State Department, and other governmental agencies. The committee was directed to prepare a detailed political plan of America's position in the postwar international scene. Substantive guidelines were contained in three brief questions: "What does the United States want? What do other states want? How do we obtain what we want?" In 1942 the committee's scope was broadened to include several independent research institutions.[6]

In the Jewish world, the American Jewish Congress was the first public Jewish organization to sponsor an institute for peace research. As early as February 1940, the Congress approached the American Jewish Committee, the Alliance Israélite Universelle in France, and the Board of Deputies of British

Jews in Great Britain with the proposal to establish a body that would prepare a "Jewish plan" to be presented to the future peace conference. The American Jewish Committee refused to participate and set up its own institute to study Jewish problems in the postwar years—which meant that by mid-1941 two parallel institutes had been created for the same purpose.[7]

Naturally, the Zionists in America were aware of the growing interest in postwar planning, and the names of Zionist organizations can be found in the directory published by the Council for Foreign Affairs. But, reeling from the successive blows of the White Paper, outbreak of war, Land Transfer Regulations, heartless treatment of "illegal" immigrants and the threat to the survival of the Jewish community in Palestine, the movement had little strength left for consideration of problems that seemed less immediate.

Emanuel Neumann, who, as head of the Emergency Committee's Department of Public Relations and Political Action was closer than most of his colleagues to the Washington nerve center, was quite aware of the importance of injecting the Zionist viewpoint in the plans for postwar political settlements. As we have seen, however, most initiatives of the Department were thwarted either by shortsightedness, bungling or narrow partisan interests, and the problem of planning for the world after the war was no exception.

David Ben-Gurion, in the United States in September 1940, was deeply impressed by the scope of planning that was being undertaken. In London, before coming to the States, he had already interested himself in the papers on war aims that were being prepared by the Royal Institute for International Relations, the renowned "Chatham House." This intense activity in both America and England convinced Ben-Gurion that the Zionist movement could not wait until the end of the war to plan the position it would present at the future peace conference. A clear, comprehensive Zionist policy had to be formulated at once, so that it could be brought before the Great Powers at the earliest possible moment. Immediately upon returning to Palestine, Ben-Gurion set to work on a proposal to create committees to consider different aspects of the Zionist solution. He visualized such planning as based on professional research by trained economists, who would prove "by facts and figures" that Palestine could absorb masses of Jews after the war. In 1940 and 1941, however, little was done to crystallize such plans.

The Zionist Movement's Peace Aims

Zionism was now paying dearly for the many years during which it had permitted definition of its major objective—the establishment of a Jewish state in Palestine—to be replaced by the obscure term "national home," that could be variously interpreted to fit different times, places and purposes. The White Paper of 1939 pointed up the danger of this vague formulation. Maintaining that the "national home" had already been created in Palestine, and that Great Britain had therefore fulfilled its promise to Zionism, the mandatory government was now imposing whatever restrictive measures it saw fit on Jewish immigration and land-purchase. It was becoming clear that Zionism's political aim would have to be restated in unambiguous terms; parallel discussions—independent of one another—were instituted in Zionist circles in Jerusalem, London and New York.

Ben-Gurion's Position

If Ben-Gurion had secretly hoped that Great Britain would delay implementation of the provisions of the White Paper because of the war, he was soon disappointed. Final proof of Britain's perfidy came in February 1940 with publication of the draconian "Land Transfer Regulations," pursuant to the directives of the White Paper. As the German air force "blitzed" the Low Countries and France and the British government fell, Ben-Gurion set out for London, hoping to convince the new government to give Palestine's Jews a role in the war effort.

After his discussion, he wrote: "the difficulties in obtaining renunciation of the policies of the White Paper are almost insurmountable," even though the new prime minister and several of his colleagues—as well as the leader of the opposition—opposed it. The British government "from now on [will] be absorbed in the urgent and tremendous task of waging war." Ben-Gurion concluded that it should be made perfectly clear to the British government that there could be no other solution to the problem of Palestine than the creation of a Jewish state either as a "sovereign state or an autonomous commonwealth within the British Empire or a state that would be part of a Mid-East Federation." World Jewry, particularly that of Palestine and America, would have to be mobilized to achieve that goal.[8]

In the United States, at the end of 1940, Ben-Gurion found the American Zionists not only fragmented, but terrified to act lest they be accused of "dragging America into the war." This reinforced his conviction of the need to draft a clear and well-defined formulation of Zionist aims. During this visit Ben-Gurion convened a private meeting of the American Zionist leadership, after a dispute with Brandeis and Wise on the question of protesting the deportation of "illegal" immigrants from Palestine. At the meeting, which took place at the Winthrop Hotel in New York on December 5, 1940, Ben-Gurion urged the participants to support his formulation of the plans for a Jewish army and a Jewish state. The latter, in his view, could absorb 4–5 million European Jews who would be in dire need after the war, and would ensure free Jewish immigration and settlement. To further this aim, he proposed the establishment of a permanent link between American Jewry and the Yishuv—which, he claimed, were the only remaining Jewish communities of any significance in the world.[9] He requested that the American Zionist leaders work to activate the Jewish masses, and the youth movements in particular, in pursuit of this goal.[10]

Only two of those present—Nachum Goldmann and Abba Hillel Silver—

accepted Ben-Gurion's "maximum Zionist program," which constituted an open attack on the White Paper. The others were more cautious, with Wise opposing any action which could hamper the British war effort. He came under immediate attack by Silver, who declared that Wise was "talking himself into a position disastrous to Zionism." This stand, he added, was that of some members of the State Department, who had adopted the British view on Palestine. Ben-Gurion recommended that an all-American conference be convened to present the activist Zionist plan. Although the proposal was accepted, the conference did not, in fact, take place.

The day he was leaving the States, Ben-Gurion wrote to Goldmann elucidating his program for Zionist activity, which he divided into a "war platform" and a "peace platform." The focal point of the peace platform consisted of a plan to establish a Jewish commonwealth in Palestine that would undertake a large-scale program of government-fostered *aliya* and would resettle millions of Jews from Europe and other countries through absorbing them into agriculture, industry, and all other branches of the economy.

Ben-Gurion undoubtedly chose the term "commonwealth" (which he transliterated in Hebrew characters) for reasons of political expediency. It was a sufficiently broad concept to serve as the external framework within which Palestine's Jewish body politic could accommodate itself, but at the same time it would not limit Jewish sovereignty in the conduct of internal affairs such as immigration and settlement. Concerning the country's international associations, he suggested a number of possibilities, among them ties with the British Empire or with an Arab–Jewish federation. This letter, written to Goldmann on the 17th of January, 1941, is of particular interest as it offers insight into Ben-Gurion's entire political program.[11]

Upon his return to Palestine, Ben-Gurion drafted the carefully considered political document which spelled out in detail his views on Zionism's postwar aims: "Guidelines for a Zionist Policy." His objective was to achieve a maximal Zionist solution to the question of postwar political control of Palestine and the problem of the destruction of the Jewish world in Europe (and other countries). He had a single solution for both issues: to establish a government in Palestine that would facilitate settlement throughout the country and would enable a representative body of the Jewish people (the Jewish Agency or a Jewish government) to effect the rapid transfer to Palestine and resettlement there of millions of Jews who would constitute a nation that could stand on its own feet. Ben-Gurion brought these "Guidelines" to the Executive of the Jewish Agency and to the smaller Zionist Actions Committee, hoping to have them adopted as the Zionist movement's official policy. Both bodies rejected the proposals.[12]

At the end of June 1941, Ben-Gurion again set out for the United States, stopping in London on the way. He learned that Lord Moyne, the new Minister of Colonies, would make no change in Britain's Palestine policy. In Ben-Gurion's presence, the Minister declared that "it was necessary to find a territory other than Palestine."[13] Lord Moyne also rejected the idea of establishing a Jewish division in the British Army on the feeble grounds that not enough equipment was available. This strengthened Ben-Gurion's conviction that nothing could be expected from Great Britain and that Zionism had to seek allies among the "forces of tomorrow"—Russia and the United States—who would shape the postwar world. He tried to interest Maisky, the Soviet ambassador to London, and Winant, the American ambassador, in his political plans.[14] Winant encouraged him to present his views to the American government and American Jewry (even securing the "priority" needed to enable him to board a ship sailing for the United States, as Ben-Gurion recorded on the 11th of November, 1941, in his diary).

Ben-Gurion was not continuing on to America empty-handed: in his baggage was the English version of his "Guidelines for a Zionist Policy," the message he intended to deliver to American Jewry. That message had more far-reaching repercussions than anticipated: upon his departure, Ben-Gurion's luggage was searched by the British authorities, "Guidelines" was found and photographed and his plans were thus divulged. Thereafter, he was considered a "dangerous individual" by the Foreign Office.[15]

A Meeting of Minds

Abba Hillel Silver's stand at the December 1940 meeting with Ben-Gurion indicated that his Zionist outlook had undergone a radical transformation. As mentioned above, Silver's first encounter with the State Department had taken place a month earlier, when he had petitioned for Red Cross funds on behalf of Jewish war victims in Palestine. The request met strong opposition from the State Department, which stated cynically that America did not wish to upset the precarious balance in the Middle East, and skilfully avoided addressing the question of the Jews and their future. Any timidity which Silver may still have possessed from his Geneva Congress days (when he was identified with the Weizmann line) vanished in the wake of this rebuff. Although it is difficult to ascertain whether Silver's volte-face on the American political scene resulted solely from this incident, it is clear that the Zionist cause benefited from losing its one-party affinity, and the inter-party competition to gain Jewish support that developed in consequence.

In August 1940, Silver came out publicly in favor of Wendel L. Willkie, the Republican candidate for the presidency. He placed several advertisements in the press, quoting at length from Willkie's commitments to utilize America's might in the cause of democracy and on behalf of the Jewish people. These were indications of a new Zionist approach more dynamic and more independent than that of the majority of the Zionist leaders who, from Wise downwards, supported Roosevelt. This new Zionist activism may have been strengthened by Silver's constant contact with the Yishuv in Palestine through his position as chairman of the United Palestine Appeal.[16] The Arab "rebellion" of 1936–39 had toughened the Yishuv, which was now more or less ripe for political independence. Silver may have been influenced by this fact more than his peers. Neumann, who had arrived from Palestine only a year earlier, could also vouch for the Yishuv's new maturity. Silver's respect for the political potential of the Yishuv and its leader, Ben-Gurion, increased accordingly.

During Ben-Gurion's next visit to America, he met Silver on the evening of October 8, 1941. Earlier that day, Silver had been badly shaken by the State Department's brutally effective intervention against American Red Cross aid for Jewish refugees, and he was in the mood to take radical action on behalf of the Zionist cause. The meeting was to prove of crucial significance. To Ben-Gurion's inquiries on the state of American Zionism, Silver replied that contrary to the image of weakness generated by the internal squabbles within the ZOA, pro-Zionist forces among American Jewry were on the increase. These elements did not subscribe to any political ideologies, or flock to join the ZOA. Nevertheless, interest in a Jewish state and the desire to work toward it were gaining momentum. The United Palestine Appeal spearheaded this movement, which was making inroads in circles that for years had been alien to Zionism. The younger generation was also becoming attracted to Zionism: the chief UPA activists were mainly college graduates. To Ben-Gurion's question: "Will American Jewry react favorably to the Zionist political demand when its time will come?" Silver answered in the affirmative.[17] It was against this background of growing activism that Silver formulated a statement on an independent United Palestine Appeal in reaction to the refusal by the Joint (JDC) to raise the percentage of the funds collected by the United Jewish Appeal to accommodate the growing needs of the Yishuv.[18]

To launch the independent United Palestine Appeal, Silver decided to convene a "National Conference on Palestine." It was at this conference that Ben-Gurion and Silver raised the public banner of the proposed Jewish commonwealth.

Weizmann's Position

Dr. Weizmann, in London, had also come to a realization of the need to formulate a new Zionist political policy despite his generally "gradualist" approach. Since the autumn of 1939, he had demanded a Jewish state in the western part of Palestine, permitting the substantive implications to vary with changing circumstances, but giving the impression that he envisioned Palestine as an autonomous unit within either a Middle-East federation or the British Commonwealth.

Finally, however, shaken by the destruction of European Jewry and the tragic certainty that the end of the war would find countless masses of homeless, desperate Jews who would want to put Europe behind them and go to Palestine, Weizmann felt compelled to formulate Zionism's aims more explicitly. He believed that the refugees—those Jews who would somehow survive the Nazi hell—would constitute the Jewish majority needed for the establishment of a Jewish state. In formulating the policy calling for the creation of such a Jewish political entity in Palestine, Weizmann relied on two sources: the first was the demographic theory developed by his associate and friend, Louis Namier, who analyzed the numbers and condition of the Jews who would remain in Eastern Europe after the Allied victory. The other source was Weizmann's own first-hand contact with leaders of the various governments-in-exile in London, with whom he discussed the possibility that Jewish survivors of the Holocaust would be accepted into their countries when peace finally came.

Louis B. Namier, a renowned historian and one of Weizmann's closest advisers, developed a theory about the fate of European Jewry. One of his hypotheses was that the Soviet Union, emerging victorious with the Allied forces, would "adjust" its borders westward, more or less in accordance with the demarcation lines of the Ribbentrop–Molotov Pact. This would, in effect, "remove" some two million Jews from the context of the "Jewish problem" in Europe.

Outside of the Soviet Union, three-and-a-half to four million Jews would remain in Poland, Romania, Hungary and Slovakia; they would constitute the most acute aspect of the postwar "Jewish problem," and Professor Namier believed that an immediate solution would have to be found for them. In his opinion, the lot of these three to four million Jews would not really improve with the victory over the Axis powers. German conquests had effectively entrenched a process in Central and Eastern Europe that had begun even before the First World War and gained ascendancy in the period between the wars: the "de-judaization" of the economy, public services, culture and society in general. For many generations antisemitism had been rabid in those countries; furthermore, they would be staggering under the weight of destruction wrought by the war. They would hardly be a haven of refuge for postwar Jewry. Namier concluded that over a period of some twenty years after the war ended, the emigration of several million Jews would have to be organized. Such an enterprise could be undertaken only by a Jewish state or Jewish commonwealth in Palestine.[19]

Weizmann's main reservation about this theory was the horrifying assumption that a million Jews would almost surely be annihilated by Nazi brutality. (As the war went on and the terrible news kept coming to him, he constantly revised the expected number of Jewish casualties in Europe upward.) No matter what the number, however, the only solution for the survivors would be emigration and resettlement in Palestine. To implement such a plan, it would be necessary to grant "fiscal autonomy, freedom of immigration and land purchase" to the Jews living in Palestine and "that means a state."[20]

Weizmann found confirmation of this viewpoint in his discussions with leaders of the European governments-in-exile who were making London their temporary seat of government. Wanting to clarify the status envisioned for the Jews of Eastern Europe in those countries—where they had been so populous before the war—Weizmann met, among others, with Benesc of Czechoslovakia and Sikorsky of Poland.

Edouard Benesc (Czechoslovakia's prewar Prime Minister who was considered a friend of the Jews and faithful to the precepts of his predecessor, Masaryk) made it absolutely clear that his country would not be able to reabsorb more than about two-thirds of the Jews who had lived there. Any attempt to revert to the status quo ante would, in his opinion, merely aggravate the situation of the remaining Jews. On the other hand, he promised that they would be given adequate compensation for property, which would cover the cost of emigration and resettlement in Palestine.

Weizmann's meeting with Sikorsky, head of the Polish government-in-exile, had similar results. Sikorsky started with a declaration of his personal friendship for the Jewish people and then made it clear that at least a third of the Jews who had lived in prewar Poland—where there had been the largest concentration of Jews in Europe—would be unable to find their place in a renewed Poland and would have to emigrate. Weizmann's general conclusion was that a third of the Jews of Central and Eastern Europe—some two million in number—would be forced to emigrate.[21]

* * *

While the proposals brought by Weizmann and Ben-Gurion were being discussed in inner circles in London and Jerusalem, Zionists in America were awakening to the need for an all-encompassing Zionist solution to the Jewish problem. A number of elements were responsible for this development: the growing demand of the Jewish public that something be done for the Jews of Europe, the increasing awareness of the many official and semi-official plans being devised in the United States for the postwar world, and the growing influence of the Yishuv leadership on some sectors of the American Zionist leadership.

The National Conference on Palestine was the first public body to declare Zionist postwar aims. At its conference on the 26th of January, 1941, it resolved that

> in the conditions which will prevail in post-war Europe, Jewry will be faced with the task of finding a home for large masses of Jews from Central and Eastern Europe . . . and only by large-scale colonization of these Jews in Palestine, with the aim of its reconstitution as a Jewish Commonwealth, can the Jewish problem be permanently solved.[22]

In Silver's impassioned address to the Conference, he quoted Danton's call to the people during the French revolution: "Boldness! More boldness and always boldness!" He called upon the Jews of America to let themselves be heard, to cast off all fear of rousing antisemitism at home, of being accused of "double loyalty" and, above all, of "embarrassing" the President. This was the first call to arms addressed to the American Zionists, and it came from the man who would eventually lead them on the political battlefield. In January of 1941 it was still a lone "cry in the wilderness," but it began to reverberate through the Jewish communities. Under Silver's leadership the fund-raising campaigns for the United Palestine Appeal, the Keren Kayemet and Keren Hayesod became arenas for political indoctrination; public pressure for the formulation of a clear Zionist policy began to build up.

Peace Program of the Emergency Committee

In April of 1941, the Office Committee of the Emergency Committee decided unanimously that "it was essential to formulate some kind of tentative program of Zionist postwar plans," and set up a subcommittee for that purpose. Dr. Solomon Goldman, erstwhile president of the ZOA and leader of the struggle against the White Paper in 1938–39, was named chairman. The other members of the subcommittee were Mrs. de Sola Pool, president of Hadassah; L. Gellman, president of Mizrachi; Hayim Greenberg, ideologue of the Labor Zionists; Robert Szold; Emanuel Neumann; and Stephen Wise.

On the 19th of June the subcommittee presented its proposals to the full Emergency Committee and invited guests—members of the Zionist Executive who were in the United States at the time. Solomon Goldman prefaced his presentation of the Zionist "peace aims" with a statement that the subcommittee had considered its purpose to be the formulation of a position solely for internal clarification. The proposals were as follows:

1. *Aliya*—In light of the fact that by the end of the war millions of European Jews would be homeless, a practical plan for their resettlement in Palestine had become an urgent necessity, the more so since Palestine's limited economic absorptive capacity was becoming the battle cry of anti-Zionists and non-Zionists.

2. *Borders and Political Status*—Sensitive and complex as the problem of borders might be, the subcommittee believed the time had come to outline a "maximalist position"; since millions of Jews would have to be resettled, Transjordan should not be severed from Palestine; it was not deemed advisable, however, to stake out exact geographic boundaries at the moment.

The subcommittee had concluded that "for obvious reasons," the Zionist movement should not be interested in perpetuating the mandate which had become, in practice, a British colonial administration under the League of Nations. The program therefore called for the "early reconstitution of Palestine within its historic boundaries" as an autonomous Jewish commonwealth where "full equality before the law" would be granted all residents and the various ethnic and religious groups would have "autonomous rights."

3. *International Associations*—Intentionally formulated in vague terms because of the war and the unclear political situation in the Middle East, this

section included a call for close cooperation between the Jewish commonwealth and the other countries of the region, as well as with the British Commonwealth or any other umbrella organization encompassing the democracies that might be created in the future.

4. *Finances*—As most of Europe's Jews would be totally destitute after the war, it was suggested that the Zionist movement ask for governmental assistance in financing the mammoth projects of emigration and resettlement.

A stormy debate followed presentation of the plan; the participants split into two opposing camps, one claiming that the proposals were vague and not sufficiently maximalist, the other claiming that they were too extreme. The first camp included Meir Grossman, leader of the Hebrew State Party, who rejected the program outright, and Israel Mereminsky (Merom), Histadrut delegate to the United States who feared the various interpretations that might be given to terms such as commonwealth, federation and autonomy; he felt that in view of the unstable international situation, all efforts should be concentrated on opening the gates of Palestine at once to masses of Jews. Isaac Neiditch, a veteran French Zionist in exile in the United States, objected that the program contained no demand for a completely autonomous Jewish Palestine.

Rabbi Perlzweig of Great Britain was one of the spokesmen of the second camp; he warned against "terms that might do damage to the relations that had been built up between Zionism and Britain." Rose Halperin of Hadassah was the only one to object to the term "commonwealth," claiming that it would rouse the antagonism of liberal Arab public opinion; she recommended demanding unrestricted massive immigration to both sides of the Jordan.

Meyer Weisgal, attending the meeting as an observer, was among the few who fully accepted the program, although he felt that the question of the status of Jews living outside of Palestine and their relationship with the proposed Jewish commonwealth should have been addressed.

Responding to critics in both camps, Solomon Goldman emphasized the fact that the demand for a Jewish commonwealth was something entirely new; at the same time, however, it took into consideration the constantly changing situation of the world at war.

Levy Bakstansky, liaison between the Jewish Agency Executive in London and the Emergency Committee, stated that this proposal was quite similar to the program suggested in London, in that both recognized the need for international assistance to implement the large-scale immigration and resettlement programs involved. The differences were primarily the inference that London's proposed Jewish commonwealth would be included in a Middle-East federation or in the British Commonwealth, while the American plan, vaguer in its description of international associations, could be interpreted as a clear demand for an autonomous Jewish state in Palestine. In addition, the British Zionist proposal referred to a "transfer" of Palestine's Arab population to neighboring Arab countries—in consonance with the position of progressive circles in Britain that viewed "population transfers" as an important element in all postwar settlements.[23]

All three proposals for a postwar Zionist program—that of David Ben-Gurion in Palestine, of Weizmann in London and of the Emergency Committee's subcommittee in America—met the same fate. They were neither accepted nor rejected, and therefore had no immediate effect on Zionist policy. This does not mean, however, that the attendant discussions in all three Zionist centers had been futile. First of all, the movement's leadership was shaken out of complaisant acceptance of the political status quo and began to think of redefining Zionism's aims. Secondly, Isaac Neiditch's suggestion that a world Jewish conference be convened in the United States to discuss and adopt a Zionist peace program, eventually bore fruit.

This was not the first time that it was suggested that a worldwide Zionist Conference be convened in America. Stephen Wise had been trying unsuccessfully to convince the Zionist Executive to hold an international conference in the United States since the latter part of the 1930s. In 1938, when there was already reason to believe that Britain might not carry out the policy outlined in the Balfour Declaration, Weizmann and Ben-Gurion suggested calling a worldwide conference in the United States to deal with the problem of Palestine in the light of Jewry's situation. After publication of the White Paper, David Ben-Gurion strongly advocated calling a meeting of the Zionist Actions Committee in America. He believed that Britain was trying to drive a wedge between the Jews of Palestine and the world Zionist movement, which posed a serious danger to the movement's very existence. He also felt that the concentration of all decision-making in Palestine, without involving Jews of America and other places, was unhealthy for the movement. Discussion of Neiditch's proposal elicited several other suggestions, although no practical steps were taken at the time, largely because of the blockade of the Mediterranean and the submarine war in the Atlantic—which made it extremely dangerous to travel to the States.

Throughout the spring and summer of 1941, however, there was growing public pressure to adopt a clear political stand more pertinent to the needs of the hour. The call for a Jewish commonwealth that had been included in the resolutions of the National Conference on Palestine in January of 1941, was echoed in the decisions adopted by a conference of Mizrachi held in May, and of the League for Labor Palestine (a public, nonpolitical body close to the Labor Zionists).[24] By the beginning of September, the continuing bad news from the North African front, the *Struma* tragedy and its aftermath, the growing volume of hair-raising information about the fate of European Jewry— juxtaposed with an increasing tendency on the part of the British to appease the Arabs at the expense of Jewish rights in Palestine—made it clear that merely opposing British policy was no longer enough: a positive Zionist solution had to be offered. On 2 September, the Emergency Committee decided to oppose the incorporation of Palestine in a Middle East federation; it also decided that henceforth the demand for an autonomous Jewish commonwealth in Palestine was to be included in any public declaration of the Zionist movement.

At its annual conference a few days later, the ZOA issued the following statement:

> We solemnly declare that the rapid resettlement and rehabilitation of the homeless Jewish masses can be effected only by the reconstitution of Palestine, in its historic boundaries, as a Jewish Commonwealth. The solution of this otherwise insoluble problem can and should be achieved after the war under intergovernmental auspices and with intergovernmental assistance. There can be no substitute for Palestine as a permanent National Homeland.[25]

At the same conference, the Zionist Organization of America elected Judge Louis Levinthal of Philadelphia as its president; in this capacity he became chairman of the Office Committee of the Emergency Committee. A dynamic, forceful personality, Judge Levinthal quickly put through a decision to convene a nationwide Zionist conference. After consulting with Dr. Weizmann, he asked Meyer Weisgal to organize the conference, which was to set itself the following goals: 1) to define the aims of Zionism; and 2) to mobilize American Zionism for large-scale political and financial action. It was decided that the conference, to include a festive dinner in honor of Dr. Weizmann, would last three days.

Thus, as 1941 drew to a close, American Zionism was on its way to giving unified expression to an unequivocal formulation of the movement's political aim.

Goals, Constituency and Agenda of the Conference

In drawing up the agenda for the conference, Meyer Weisgal had two goals in mind: 1) the adoption of resolutions that would have an effect on the Jewish and non-Jewish "outside" world; and 2) resolutions that would alter the internal organization of the American Zionist movement and enhance it in the eyes of the public. To achieve these two objectives, the conference would have to address the following issues: dissemination of information and propaganda geared to making the strongest possible impact on the public; cohesion and galvanization of all Zionist forces in the United States; coordination of all Zionist diplomatic activity in the United States by the Emergency Committee for Zionist Affairs; establishing a base for the possible organizational unification of all Zionist bodies in America; formulation of a clear Zionist political position. Weisgal attached importance to the last point, as there was "an urgent necessity for an authorized declaration both for ourselves and for the world, of what the Zionist program is."

Since there was no way of convening the Zionist Congress, the projected conference would be vested with the maximum possible authority and would be comprised, as far as wartime conditions permitted, of the responsible leadership from London, Jerusalem and the United States. As stated in the conference program, it was incumbent upon it to accept the challenge of "authoritatively determining Zionist policy which will guide the Zionist movement, as well as the Jewish and non-Jewish worlds regarding the political future of Palestine."

Weisgal therefore proposed that the following issues be discussed: 1) Jewry's situation throughout the world; 2) the exact status of Palestine in Jewish life, with a detailed breakdown of the components, problems and possibilities in economic, political and military spheres; 3) the influence of the war on Zionist thought and action; 4) the postwar goals of the movement and the groundwork necessary to achieve them; and 5) formulation of Zionist policy.

Weisgal stipulated that speeches, discussions and even background briefings were to be prepared in advance in meticulous detail. The documents and reports would be prepared by the most appropriate personages, regardless of their organization affiliation or personal standing. "Only a discussion on a high political and intellectual level can contribute to the strengthening of the Zionist movement at this hour of severe crisis."[26]

From the structural standpoint, Weisgal planned to have the conference resemble the World Zionist Congress as closely as possible. With this in mind, it was necessary to select delegates representing every branch of the movement in the United States. Weisgal's proposal to base representation of the Zionist parties on their proportional representation in the Emergency Committee was rejected by the smaller parties, Poale Zion and Mizrachi. Arguments over representation continued through March and April, until Stephen Wise proposed a compromise calling for equal representation for all four major parties to "advance the spirit of unity in the American Zionist camp." Robert Szold proposed an addendum to Wise's suggestion, stipulating that no vote would be taken in the plenary sessions on "central Zionist issues" unless the subject had been unanimously agreed upon in advance.

It was thereupon agreed that the conference would be a "consultative deliberative gathering," and that its resolution would be subject to the approval of the highest bodies of the various organizations. The conference would deal with substantive matters, while the means of implementing resolutions would be discussed in subcommittees, not in plenary sessions. Some of the authority that its organizers had hoped would be vested in the conference was thereby vitiated, and it seemed doubtful that such a consultative assembly could alter and reinvigorate the face of political Zionism, particularly in the United States.[27]

Conference Deliberations

The Conference met from 9 May to 11 May, 1942, in New York's Biltmore Hotel:[28] 586 delegates took part, 519 of whom represented American Zionist groups and organizations, and 67 represented Zionist organizations from abroad. Among the latter delegates were the leaders of the Canadian Zionist Federation, members of the Provisional Executive Committee for General Zionist Affairs, refugee Zionist leaders from Europe, and representatives of Palestine's Jewish community. The American participants represented a broad spectrum of bodies, parties and organizations, including the smallest and most marginal. The Zionist youth movements were represented by 28 delegates, and a special session was devoted to their problems.

Stephen Wise, speaking in the name of the Emergency Committee for Zionist Affairs, opened the first session. He stressed that the primary aim of the conference was to achieve unity within the Zionist camp, which would be expressed through cooperation in the struggle to realize the aims of Zionism. Such cooperation, overriding organizational and party rifts, could attract a sizeable portion of American Jewry to Zionism. Rabbi Wise then declared that the conference would *not* deal with the two central issues that were then dividing American Jews and Zionists—formation of a Jewish army, and protest against the implementation of the British White Paper in Palestine. Wise cited Dr. Weizmann's negotiations with the British government and his handling of the question of the Jewish army as sufficient reasons for the conference to avoid the issue; he also argued that with America and England fighting as allies, it was desirable to act with discretion toward England—which precluded pursuing the immigration issue. In a single sweeping gesture, therefore, Wise attempted to strike two major issues from the conference agenda.

For Dr. Wise, the special importance of the conference was to convert the United States into "the heart of the arena of Zionist activity." As a Zionist congress could not be called because of the war, American Zionism would assume the right to safeguard Zionist interests: it would return this authority to the first Zionist congress to be held after the war.

Dr. Wise was followed by Judge Louis Levinthal, who emphasized the importance of the conference from the standpoint of American Zionists. He saw it as inaugurating a new chapter in the history of the Zionist movement, one in which American Zionists would play a central role. The cooperation of the Zionist movements within the framework of the Emergency Committee indicated that "the things upon which we Zionists all agree are far more important than the things about which we differ." In Levinthal's view, the conference had to "achieve that unity of purpose, that solidarity of action, which would bring to the Zionist movement its maximum strength." It was imperative to enlist American Zionists, Jews, and as many non-Jews as possible in the struggle to achieve three goals: 1) the establishment of a Jewish army in Palestine; 2) support for large-scale Jewish immigration to Palestine under Jewish supervision; 3) the reestablishment in Palestine of a Jewish common-wealth with self-rule.[29]

Although the conference was being held during one of the darkest periods of World War II, it was permeated by an atmosphere of optimism stemming from the certainty that a better future was in store. One of the signs of these bright hopes for the postwar world was the striking fact that no major current political issue was discussed. All the issues raised were focused on political developments anticipated after the war. Discussion centered on the attempt to crystallize policy in three crucial areas: the future of Palestine, the Arab question, and the problem of internal unity in the American Zionist camp.

Political Future of Palestine

As expected, Weizmann and Ben-Gurion set the tone on this theme. Weizmann, the key figure at the conference, delivered a speech typical of the opening addresses to the Zionist Congress, dealing with "the state of the Zionist movement." He expanded on the situation of European Jewry after the war, contrasting the fate of Jewry with that of other conquered nations. Weizmann calculated that a quarter of the Jews of Eastern and South-Eastern Europe would probably be liquidated by the end of the war,[30] and those remaining would be writhing under a yoke of brutal oppression such as had never before been known. After the war other peoples would begin to rehabilitate their countries, but the Jews would find themselves ". . . a floating population between heaven and hell, not knowing where to turn." He predicted that the number of survivors would range from two to four million. The responsibility for finding a solution to their predicament rested with those whose task it would be to shape a better world. Thus, Palestine would become part of the overall postwar settlement, and would be the only solution for the Jews.

With this in mind, Weizmann proposed a two-pronged line of political action for the duration of the war: first, it was essential to change the image of Palestine as a land too small to absorb masses of refugees; and second, in considering relations with the Arabs, Jewry's historical right to the land, combined with strategic-imperial considerations, must constantly be stressed. As a strategic international crossroad, Palestine was of great importance during wartime. The well-developed Jewish community of Palestine would serve the interests of the Allies, and the Arab residents of the country, benefiting from the economic development, would surely cooperate.

The overall goal had to be based on the beginning of the creation of the Jewish commonwealth which could only be established through the efforts of the Jewish people, under the "corporate responsibility" of the entire nation. Weizmann did not hide his disappointment with British policy, particularly as manifested in connection with the Jewish army and the *Struma*. Nor did he try to engender hope for a change in the near future—except for greater goodwill within the bounds of the White Paper. On the whole, his words reflected a willingness to adhere to a structural relationship with England. He called for total Jewish unity on Palestine, as he believed that the solution to the Jewish problem depended on Jewish and Zionist solidarity, and concluded on the hopeful note that ". . . those who survive will carry the torch proudly."

Ben-Gurion's address, another major focal point of the conference, opened the second day's sessions. He spoke of the role of Palestine as the solution to the Jewish problem. From several standpoints, this may have been the most important speech of the conference. Ben-Gurion expressed his faith in an Allied victory, but maintained that the victory would confront the Zionist movement with its supreme test—the test of realization. From a political viewpoint, he saw two essential differences between the post-World War I period and the present: the first difference was in the critical situation of European Jewry which Dr. Weizmann had already described; the second was the political situation in the Middle East. No well-defined political units had existed in the Middle East at the time of World War I, but now, with several independent Arab states and others that had been promised independence, an Arab Palestine was being demanded as part of an "Arab Empire." Any postwar settlement, therefore, would have to include a decision about Palestine.

The fulfilment of Zionism depended on the ability to solve two central problems, one economic and the other political. Like Weizmann, Ben-Gurion considered Palestine's economic ability to absorb immigrants as a central problem. By way of solution, Ben-Gurion detailed the agricultural potential of different parts of Palestine, emphasizing development in the Negev and absorptive possibilities in fishing and other industries. Combined, these potentialities produced an economic absorptive capacity which would increase as the number of Jewish settlers increased. Unlike Weizmann, Ben-Gurion did not consider the Arab problem as the second most important one to be tackled. After a balanced, detailed analysis of the Arab question, he reached the conclusion that an even more central question was that of the nature of the government in Palestine. He concurred with the Peel Commission's conclusion that the mandate was unworkable, because of the direct clash between the objectives of the Balfour Declaration and the mechanism that had been set up to realize those objectives. The mechanism was suited to a colonial regime in a backward colony but not to a dynamic, developing community like Palestine's. Large-scale postwar immigration to Palestine would have to find a new instrument fitting the needs and special conditions that would prevail. "Only a Jewish administration could carry out this goal."

After 25 years of experience with mandatory rule, it was clear to Ben-Gurion that the governmental authority and responsibility necessary for building the land would have to be put into the hands of the Jewish people. This process would unfold in several phases, the first being the transfer of all authority in matters concerning immigration and settlement to the Jewish Agency. A new government would have to be created in Palestine that from all standpoints— legal, fiscal, commercial and administrative—would lend itself to maximal development of the land's resources, with the aim of absorbing mass immigration. It was not in place yet to determine the exact political structures and patterns for postwar Palestine, but it was imperative to establish guiding principles for immediate political action by the Zionist movement. Such action would have to be directed toward convincing the Jewish and general public in the United States, Great Britain, the Soviet Union and other countries of concepts derived from a unified Zionist solution to the problems of Jewry and Palestine.

The guiding principles would be:

1. Reiteration in no uncertain terms of the original intent of the Balfour Declaration and the mandate, namely as President Wilson had declared on 3 March, 1919, the reestablishment of a Jewish commonwealth in Palestine.

2. The transfer to the Jewish Agency, as representative of the future immigrants, of full supervision over Jewish immigration and of the authority necessary to develop and build the land and maintain internal security.

3. Full equality for residents of Palestine in civil, political and religious spheres; assurance of self-rule on the level of municipalities and granting of autonomy to various communities—Jewish and Arab—in the administration of internal affairs such as education, religion and other fields.

The final decision as to whether Palestine should be an independent entity or annexed to a broader unit such as a Mid-East federation, the British Commonwealth, or some Anglo-American union would have to be postponed until the war was over.

The critical hour had come for the Zionist movement: either it would provide an expedient and total solution to the burning problem of masses of homeless Jews and through mass immigration lay secure foundations for a Jewish Palestine with self-rule, or it would lose all meaning. Execution of this political goal depended upon the independent efforts of the Zionist movement: "We must do the job ourselves. Palestine will be as Jewish as the Jews will make it."

These ideas were not new, having been raised in discussions and considered in articles in Jewish and Zionist journals, especially the important article published by Weizmann in the journal *Foreign Affairs* in February 1942.[31] What was new was the crystallization at the conference of these ideological and programmatic tenets into a "Jewish commonwealth" formula based on mass immigration, and positing this formula as the postwar political future for Palestine. Ben-Gurion's forceful, substantive address, in tune with the emotional current that had begun to flow through American Zionism, made a stronger impression than Weizmann's cautious speech. The conference delegates, regardless of the differences they might have had on other issues, were in almost total accord with respect to the Jewish commonwealth formulation which became, in fact, the common denominator linking all factions.

Detailed reports on Palestine's tremendous economic development during the first years of the war were presented by A. K. Epstein and Abraham Dickenstein. Social developments and groupings in the Palestinian Jewish community were analyzed by Israel Mereminsky and Yehudit Simchonit, representatives of the Histadrut and Pioneer Women respectively. These presentations emphasized and substantiated the economic and social potential for mass immigration and absorption of European refugees at the end of the war.

The optimistic spirit was somewhat jolted by Nachum Goldmann's discussion of "World Jewry after the War." Goldmann warned against pinning too much hope on the immigration of war refugees to Palestine and their role in establishing a Jewish commonwealth. He had three main reasons for this: first, it was almost certain that far fewer Jews would remain alive in Europe than Weizmann and Ben-Gurion had estimated. The situation was far graver than the free world knew; there was also a possibility that before its final defeat, Germany would exterminate as many Jews as it could. Secondly, Europe's surviving Jews would be not only economically impoverished, but crushed and broken physically and spiritually. Goldmann cast doubt on the readiness and ability of many of the survivors to continue being Jews. Many of them would try to assimilate, in the desire to forget what had happened to them. Thirdly, he took issue with Ben-Gurion about the number of Jews Palestine would be able to absorb. He felt that the figure of two to two-and-a-half million Jewish immigrants in a short period of time was unrealistic and impractical, and should not be mentioned to the world's statesmen. On the other hand, Goldmann stressed the need for strong, well-organized Jewish support for the commonwealth of the future, which would require the renewed integration of Russian Jews into world Jewry, and the overall strengthening of the Jewish diaspora; this Goldmann considered inseparable from the struggle to establish a commonwealth.

The main opposition to the commonwealth formula came from Mizrachi, its members considering both the slogan and the arguments vague and erroneous. Rabbi Gold voiced his suspicion that the new formula as expressed by Ben-Gurion was a cover-up for something less than political statehood. More serious than that—it sanctioned, to some extent, the idea of a territorial division of Palestine. He warned against the self-deception that it was possible to "accept what was offered right now, and fight for the rest later on." Like his fellow party-member, Gedalya Bublick, he objected to basing the claim for a Jewish state on the need to absorb refugees; the basis for Jewry's claim to Palestine had always been and still was the nation's ancestral right rooted in the Torah.

Meir Grossman, representing the Revisionists, castigated Zionist diplomacy of recent years, calling it appeasement of Great Britain, appeasement of non-Zionists, and appeasement of the Arabs in Palestine. Zionism had abandoned its political base and political goals and therefore had lost its momentum. Now, on the brink of failure, the movement was adopting not only the policy of those it had denounced as political extremists and fanatics, but their goals and even their slogans. Because of its dearth of vision and unwillingness to fight, the movement lagged far behind the needs of the hour. In his view, a Jewish government in Palestine such as Ben-Gurion suggested would be worthless unless Jews from all parts of the diaspora gathered in Palestine and formed a Jewish army capable of defending the country.

At the request of Dr. Wise, Nachum Goldmann rose to answer Grossman's scathing remarks. Refuting the claim that "official Zionism" was only now calling for what the Revisionists had called for years ago (a Jewish state, Jewish army, mass immigration, etc.), Goldmann maintained that a political slogan should be put forward only when there was a chance—even if a very small one—that it be realized. Apt timing is the essence of political wisdom. Ideas that were foolish yesterday may well be sophisticated tomorrow; it was simply a matter of timing. In a way Goldmann was thus expressing the optimistic spirit of most of the delegates and their conviction that the time had come to achieve a decisive solution to the problems of Jewry and Zionism.

The Arab Problem

It was clear that prior to setting forth its political goal, the Zionist movement had to face one of its oldest dilemmas—the formulation of its policy regarding what it called the "Arab Question," a question hotly debated ever since the early days of modern Jewish settlement in Palestine. In all those years of confrontation between Arabs and Jews, the Zionist movement had not adopted a clear-cut policy on the political relationship between Zionist goals and Arab reality in Palestine. Yet, as long as the goal was not defined, the character of the relationship remained ambiguous.

The general outlook was that the rapid economic development, time, and the growing number of Jews in the country would neutralize the conflict and bring about co-existence between the peoples. This, in the eyes of many, was to be based upon the belief that Arabs sharing the economic progress spurred by the Jewish in-gathering would gradually mollify the Arabs whose animosity, jealousy and hatred stemmed, they believed, from poverty and under-development, much of which was seen, by some, a result of the class system in the Arab society. Different groups, parties and individuals in the Yishuv and in the world Zionist movement had their own blueprints for co-existence of the two peoples in the land.

Much time was devoted at the conference to the Arab question, primarily because of the divergent views of some leading Hadassah women and Ben-Gurion. Ben-Gurion had made his position entirely clear on many occasions since his arrival in the United States in December 1941, and it clashed with those held by women such as Tamar de Sola Pool, Rose Jacobs, Mrs. Schoolman, and others who had became prominent in Hadassah during the 1930s.

Tamar de Sola Pool was president of the organization from 1939 to 1943, and at her initiative Hadassah set up a committee in 1941 headed by distinguished scholars to study Arab–Jewish relations in Palestine. The objective was to arrive at a proposal for a "compromise solution" in Palestine that would allow for development of the Jewish national home with the consent of the Arab population. The committee aspired to convert itself into a body that would shape Zionist policy on the issue of a binational solution for Palestine, encouraged by the Committee for Investigating the Legislative Development of Palestine that had been established by a resolution of the 21st Zionist Congress on the eve of the war. Mordechai Bentov's report summarizing the majority position of the latter committee, which recommended a binational solution (no agreed-upon proposal was reached), was published in English for the express purpose of influencing American Zionist leaders.

Rose Jacobs, speaking for Hadassah, said that the conference was not equipped to decide on any of the complex issues involved in the solution to the Arab problem, and that preparatory research must be done by a small team of experts. The trend in the world was toward forming large geographical units, such as were being fostered by certain Arab leaders and British statesmen. One could not dismiss the possibility that unification of several Arab countries would be effected in the framework of a postwar settlement, since the Arab claim to Palestine had not been rejected by the Allied powers and the British were propelling the Arabs in that direction.

The Zionist movement had to realize that central groups in the American public (liberals, academicians, church circles) had not yet fully grasped the meaning of Jewish aspirations for Palestine. It was already clear that America would have a pivotal say in determining postwar settlements, including the issue of Palestine. Jews and Zionists therefore had to convince the above groups of the justness of their position, and to this end would have to crystallize new concepts in connection with Jewish–Arab relations. Without extensive background material, Zionist leaders would be unable to present Zionist objectives convincingly to American public opinion. Whatever the proposed solution, emphasis had to be placed on educating the public, and Hadassah had decided to take the initiative by establishing a commission to study the organization of peace, had raised a large fund for comprehensive research on the Palestine problem, with emphasis on Jewish–Arab relations, and had appointed a special "informant" in Palestine to provide the committee with daily reports of events there (a broad hint that Hadassah did not rely on Jewish Agency reports). Hoping that this extensive research project would become the joint enterprise of all American Zionists, Mrs. Jacobs urged the conference to refrain from making decisions about the political future of Palestine until such time as the study would be completed.

The address of the Hadassah representative constituted a direct attack on the position of the majority of those present, and, as one of the participants put it, was "an indirect rejection" of the call for establishment of a Jewish commonwealth in Palestine. In his rebuttal, Weizmann clung to the traditional Zionist position on the Arabs, whom he did not consider a major obstacle to the fulfilment of Zionist goals. He felt that only a minority of Arabs in Palestine opposed Zionism, while most of them enjoyed the prosperity that Zionist development had brought. The Arab position had been distorted by politicians, but he felt that a solution satisfactory to both sides could be found, given goodwill and hard work on the part of the Jewish people and of the world's statesmen.

Ben-Gurion, on the other hand, after more than a decade during which attempts had been made to negotiate a solution in a series of meetings with Arab leaders, had given much time and thought to the problem.[32] After analyzing the political situation and reporting on his own contacts with the Arabs, he made his position clear:

> There is an Arab question—and the problem must be overcome by a decision of the Great Powers, as in the last war. Any attempt on our part to achieve a Jewish–Arab accord is doomed to failure unless we give up on immigration—and there is no point trying to achieve such an accord, as Hashomer Hatzair and Hadassah are trying to do, without giving up immigration. The Arab opposition is firm. . . . We must explain the true situation, with all its difficulties, to public opinion, and if justice is with us, justice can triumph.

Ben-Gurion explained his position at length. He believed that the entire matter called "the Arab problem" was erroneously conceived by most Zionists, and should be viewed in the light of three fundamental issues: 1) There is no "Arab problem" in the sense in which there is a Jewish one. The Arabs live in homogeneous concentrations in their own countries, vast territories either sparsely populated or almost entirely unpopulated. 2) The Jews do *not* settle in Palestine "at the expense" of the Arabs. The contrary is true: the fact that the Arab population had doubled in exactly those areas where Jews had settled, testified to this. 3) The mass Jewish immigration expected at the end of the war would not in any manner or form be detrimental to the Arab community.

In this context he ruled out the idea of transfer of Palestine's Arabs, which American Zionists had frequently discussed in the past and which Weizmann had advocated. All future plans for the rebuilding of Palestine must be based on the assumption that one would have to reckon with the presence of something like a million Arabs. In his opinion, there was no economic conflict between Palestine's Arabs and Jewish settlement. What was called the "Arab problem" meant in reality the political opposition of the Arabs to Jewish immigration into Palestine. Many people, ignoring this simple, although disagreeable truth, attempted to solve the Arab problem where it did not exist. Ben-Gurion also referred to the proposed political solutions, expressing his opposition to a binational state on the grounds that the Arabs would reject any form of compromise. On the same basis, he rejected "parity" which, in his view, could be realized only under the mandate as no independent government could function under a system which, by its very nature, froze all attempts to govern.

The crux of the question was the will of the Jews to immigrate to Palestine; if the extent of Jewish immigration depended upon Arab consent, there would be no immigration at all. Therefore, the solution was to create a fait accompli; the

Arabs would agree to Jewish immigration and would reconcile themselves to the new reality, once it became a fact. He saw the immigration of millions of Jews, enforced by the Allied powers, as the only solution to the Jewish problem.

This line was followed by several of Ben-Gurion's party colleagues, as well as by Meir Grossman, who protested that the conference was devoting too much time to one of the less important problems of the moment. Judge B. Rosenblatt, then a resident of Palestine, broached the "Palestinian Federation" plan which had been devised by leading Zionists from different parties who met in Haifa at the end of the 1930s. He proposed a federation on both sides of the Jordan, comprising a Jewish unit and an Arab unit. After a territorial exchange which would annex Samaria to Abdulla's state and the Huran to the Jewish unit, there would be a "Jewish commonwealth within a federated Palestine." In the course of time it was assumed that the federation as such would become a dominion belonging to the British Commonwealth. Judge Rosenblatt felt that America could be persuaded to support such a plan as it was based on democratic principles, the federal principle and the commonwealth idea, with America itself as a model.

Opposition to Ben-Gurion's position was also expressed by the Zionist Left. Bezalel Sherman, secretary of the Left Poale Zion in the United States, saw the solution of the Arab problem as the crux of everything. Following traditional socialist thought patterns, he maintained the "Arab laborers whose interests are identical with those of many Jews in Palestine" were the most likely and most natural candidates for Arab–Jewish negotiations.

Moshe Furmansky, Palestinian representative to Hashomer Hatzair in the United States, openly opposed the new political line because of his position on the Arab question. He stated that Zionism had to face the following facts: 1) there were a million Arabs in Palestine; 2) in principle, one nation should not rule over another; and 3) the necessity after the war for millions of Jews to enter Palestine immediately. Only the establishment of a binational state could combine these facts into an appropriate legislative framework. This solution was consonant with the ingrained progressive spirit of the Jewish people and the Zionist movement, and it would attract the cooperation of the progressive forces in the world.

Summarizing the discussion, Weizmann supported Ben-Gurion's position. He attacked Hadassah's independent action, stating that he did not negate research as such and that study committees could be of assistance to policy-makers, but conducting negotiations and making decisions should be left to the central authority, *primarily in Palestine*. Practically speaking, Weizmann considered that all those who sought compromise and "understanding" with the Arabs were deluding themselves. Jews active in the field of Arab–Jewish relations had often promised him that the Arabs would agree to the immigration of millions of Jews—but he had not yet seen any such declaration signed by an Arab leader. As for the Arabs, they would not want to negotiate with the Zionists as long as they could "get everything they wanted from

MacDonald." The only way to break the deadlock was for the democratic powers, recognizing the justice of the Zionist claims, to make it clear to the Arab world that the Jewish claim, based on historical grounds and strengthened by Jewish enterprise in Palestine, had not harmed the Arabs, and that Jewish settlement would continue.

Ben-Gurion's position was approved by most of the participants. Even in Hadassah, a tendency emerged to accept the tenet that the realization of Zionism is *not* contingent on Arab consent to a compromise. The turnabout was neither drastic nor immediate, but it did signal the inception of a process that would soon begin to change the spirit of American Zionism.

Officially, the conference merely reiterated the accepted formula of Zionist Congress resolutions expressing Jewry's readiness for full cooperation with its Arab neighbors. But Ben-Gurion's thesis that there was no solution to the problem, that mass Jewish immigration had to be "forced through," that the Jewish commonwealth had to be presented as a fait accompli and thereby evoke de facto recognition on the part of the Arabs, was accepted.

Internal Unity of American Zionists

A central motif of all speeches at the conference was the heavy responsibility resting on American Zionists, but until the third day not a single concrete proposal as to how American Zionism could fulfil that responsibility had been put forward. The agenda had allotted only two hours to a discussion of "internal Zionist unity," but the subject of unity did not appear in any advance draft resolution—it having become almost taboo on the Zionist scene in the United States. To everyone's surprise, the issue eventually became a central topic of discussion. Professor Haim Fineman (a leader of Poale Zion), in the name of his party, called for the establishment of an American Zionist federation—a proposal that created a sensation on the conference floor.

This proposal would not have come as such a shock had it been made in any other country, as the 19th Zionist Congress had passed a resolution to establish "united national federations." The Zionist movement in the United States was an extreme example of the class of centrifugal and centripetal forces that resolution had hoped to mitigate. The various Zionist parties in America, despite periodic attempts at coordinated activity, were on the whole separatist, even hostile, and concern for the grave situation of European Jewry had not fundamentally changed the picture.

Fineman's proposal was essentially simple: such a federation would not negate the legitimate right of the various parties to give their own interpretations to Zionism, but would facilitate action on certain basic issues on which the parties could not act separately. The most vital of these issues was the education of the American public toward a genuine understanding of Jewish needs and ways of meeting them. This could best be done by a single Zionist organization combining the resources and energies of all the organizations.

This, in Fineman's opinion, was only the first stage in a "struggle for unity," the central goal of which had to be Jewish unity throughout the United States as a means for realizing the objectives of Zionism.

Membership in the projected federation would be direct, through payment of individual annual dues. The federation's purpose would be to bring about the political involvement of its members of instilling in them a sense of deep responsibility for the Zionist enterprise. Dr. Fineman brought the idea as an official motion of Poale Zion to be placed before the conference presidium, and he proposed forming a committee of representatives of all the Zionist organizations to draft a constitution for the federation—in accordance with the organizational lines of the Zionist Congress.

This proposal turned into the key issue at the conference. It created something of an uproar, disrupted the planned agenda based on speeches prepared in advance, and it gave the delegates an opportunity to speak their minds. It was the only time the sessions became an arena for real discussion. The Mizrachi delegates came out in vociferous opposition to the proposal. The president of Mizrachi summed up his party's position by warning the delegates against a proposal "that could bring Karl Marx into your Zionism." On the other hand, widespread support for the proposal came from hundreds of delegates from outside of New York who had not been heard from until then. So many people asked for the floor that the agenda had to be set aside.

The large parties were unwilling to consent to a proposal that had not been included in the agreed-upon agenda, although Judge Levinthal expressed the opinion that to attain their goals the Zionist parties must "cut themselves loose from the straitjacket of party lines and factional thinking. . ." But breaking the bonds did not mean creating a homogeneous Zionism; rather, it entailed consultations and joint activity. The Emergency Committee served as an example of the kind of unity to be desired—unity of action. Therefore, any question of a federation had to be brought to the committee for a ruling. The aim of such a federation would be to attract millions of Jewish sympathizers to take part. It would have to harness American Jewry's best political talents in anticipation of the United Nations peace conference, since any internal conflict once the war ended was liable to jeopardize the future of the Zionist undertaking in Palestine.

Hadassah preferred to reject the proposal outright. Mrs. de Sola Pool cited the amount of bickering and dissension that went on in the Emergency Committee as proof of the great risk involved in going "with one fell swoop into anything that might weaken the individual organizations." She seconded the idea of referring the issue to the Emergency Committee for decision.

By now, little more survived of Weisgal's comprehensive agenda than cursory references to such important topics as Zionist youth group activities, pioneering, the national funds and above all, to consideration of the *present* situation, whether of American Jewry, or Jewry in general. The possibility of helping Europe's Jews was not discussed, nor was Zionist political activity in the United States mentioned; the entire thrust of the conference seemed to be toward the postwar world.

Emanuel Neumann, speaking on the basis of his experiences during the past two years, made an effort to direct discussion to possibilities for political action on the American scene. He criticized the conference for devoting most of its time to an attempt to pinpoint the political goals of Zionism, but avoiding discussion about practical ways of accomplishing those goals. He considered the main problem to be a radical revamping of the role of American Zionism. Emphasis had to be placed on creating a "sympathetic climate in the American public." In general, the Zionist solution involving concentration of European Jewry in Palestine and the reconstitution of Palestine as a Jewish state was not acceptable to American statesmen, although there was an awareness that this problem was of great concern to American Jews.

Neumann had learned from experience that there were reserves of pro-Zionist sentiment in "Christian America," but there was vast ignorance regarding Zionist goals and the actual situation of Palestine and the Middle East. All political levels in Washington, as well as the general public, needed factual information which could serve as the basis for American policy in support of a Palestinian solution to the problem of European Jewry. Neumann expanded on his theory of integrated and parallel activity on political, religious-traditional and intellectual levels, cautioning that Zionism must renounce its isolationism and reintegrate itself into the mainstream of thought and society in the United States. This isolationism was responsible for the fact that each and every one of the bodies dealing with the postwar world ignored Zionism's goals, and not one of the American experts on the Mid-East supported Zionism.

With respect to the Emergency Committee, Neumann said that in order to become an effective political organization it had to stop wasting energy on problems of internal organization, and become a crystallized group represent-ing overall Zionist interests in the United States; its budget would have to be increased and its activities expanded, while it had to become a policy-making body with clearly defined functions and authority. However, unless the Committee encompassed the majority of American Jewry by reaching out to the local communities all over the country, none of these recommended internal changes would alter the essence of its activity.

The political Zionist spirit in America had to be renewed and a unified line of policy would have to be determined on all Zionist issues. Since American Zionism had minimalized the importance of ideas and ideologies, he proposed the establishment of a center for Zionist thought. With such support, the Emergency Committee could become a combination of "a State Department and Information Ministry of the Zionist movement."

Few delegates dealt with this issue during this session of the Biltmore Conference. As might be expected, criticism issued from both extremes of the Zionist political spectrum. Grossman of the Jewish State Party spoke of the lack of self-confidence of American Zionists, of obscure goals, uncertainty and

Jewish and American isolationism, as well as an ideological vacuum. He attributed all these unhappy phenomena to "Zionist appeasement" during the past twenty years. Moshe Furmansky of Hashomer Hatzair attacked the movement for the same shortcomings, but from a socialistic outlook. Zionism to him was the vanguard of the Jewish people, and its duty was to galvanize the masses into a "national collective." American Zionism had maneuvered itself into a position of alienation from the Jewish "masses" by forgoing any attempt to educate and lead them. American Zionists now had to unite and take an active part in the struggle to shape the national future with an inevitable "new form of social life" destined to materialize in the future. The vanguard of Jewry was not the Jewish army, but rather the pioneering movement. Activity now had to concentrate on two things: educating the masses and molding them into a public Zionist front; activating this front for the realization of Zionist goals.

These last three speakers were the only ones who attempted to define the sort of action that might achieve the goals visualized for the conference. On the whole, stark reality seems to have been shunted aside by the tendency toward messianic optimism. When the conference was over, therefore, American Zionism found itself with general basic lines of political strategy, but no tactical directives as to how to realize them.

The Resolutions

As was often the case at Jewish conferences and conventions in America, there was little direct connection between the sessions and the resolutions passed.[33] This was conspicuously so with the Biltmore Conference, where the parties had agreed that no resolution would be presented unless approved by them in advance. During the conference sessions, Robert Szold and a subcommittee of representatives of the parties engaged in the formulation of resolutions. The subcommittee received groups and individuals who wanted to propose resolutions or to alter the drafts of those that had been prepared in advance. On the final night of the conference, 11 May, the subcommittee submitted its proposed declaration (see below), after having thrashed out several of the more controversial points.

An issue that was conspicuously underplayed was the plight of European Jewry. The American Zionists had no operative suggestions to make and could only offer their brothers in the "ghettos and concentration camps" "a message of hope and encouragement" and "a prayer that their hour of liberation was not far distant." The "Arab question," as we have seen, was passionately debated in the plenary session, but to make the resolution palatable to all the parties, it was rather obliquely worded to reflect Ben-Gurion's thesis that the solution lay in mass Jewish immigration forced on the Palestinian Arabs by the Great Powers.

The most serious discussion in the subcommittee[34] turned on the formulation of the resolution calling for the establishment of a Jewish commonwealth. Here there was a direct collision between the approaches advocated by Weizmann and Ben-Gurion respectively. Weizmann's position (as presented by Meyer Weisgal) placed the emphasis on opening Palestine to unlimited Jewish immigration and on nullifying other articles of the White Paper by giving the Jewish Agency broad jurisdictional powers and by facilitating settlement. The commonwealth was presented as a political demand, a "maximalist goal" to be submitted to the "forum of nations" at the end of the war. Ben-Gurion's position (presented by Robert Szold) was that the commonwealth should be the Zionist movement's declared goal in order to make the immigration and absorption of millions of refugees in Palestine possible. This was the reverse of the position implied by Weizmann's contention—namely, that the commonwealth would come about as a result of the immigration and absorption of millions.

A compromise formulation was devised here too: the "final goal" of Zionism was divided into three sub-categories. The first demanded that "the gates of Palestine be opened"; the second "that the Jewish Agency be vested with control of immigration into Palestine and with the necessary authority for upbuilding the country"; and the third "that Palestine be established as a Jewish commonwealth integrated in the structure of the new democratic world." These sub-categories could be interpreted either as phases of development leading to a Jewish commonwealth (as per Weizmann) or simultaneous components of this development (as per Ben-Gurion). The divergent attitudes of the two leaders toward the Great Powers also becomes apparent here. Weizmann still put his faith in Great Britain which, he indicated, would mend its ways after the war and continue to serve as "patron" of Jewish immigration. In Ben-Gurion's view, America would play the most active role in transporting masses of Jews and in the political solution.

The declaration that was brought to the floor on the last session of the conference was first approved by representatives of the major Zionist parties and then by Weizmann and Ben-Gurion. Arthur Lourie, political secretary of the Emergency Committee, put the finishing touches on the final version and was largely responsible for the verbal gymnastics that made the resolutions generally acceptable. The vote itself was little more than a formality. The declaration was accepted by a show of hands, the only opposition coming from Moshe Furmansky. The text read as follows:

DECLARATION ADOPTED BY THE EXTRAORDINARY ZIONIST CONFERENCE ("Biltmore Conference") MAY 11, 1942

1. American Zionists assembled in this Extraordinary Conference reaffirm their unequivocal devotion to the cause of democratic freedom and international justice to which the people of the United States, allied with the other United Nations, have dedicated themselves, and give expression to their faith in the ultimate victory of humanity and justice over lawlessness and brute force.

2. This Conference offers a message of hope and encouragement to their fellow Jews in the Ghettos and concentration camps of Hitler-dominated Europe and prays that their hour of liberation may not be far distant.

3. The Conference sends its warmest greetings to the Jewish Agency Executive in Jerusalem, to the Va'ad Leumi, and to the whole Yishuv in Palestine, and expresses its profound admiration for their steadfastness and achievements in the face of peril and great difficulties. The Jewish men and women in field and factory and the thousands of Jewish soldiers of Palestine in the Near East who have acquitted themselves with honor and distinction in Greece, Ethiopia, Syria, Libya and on other battlefields, have shown themselves worthy of their people and ready to assume the rights and responsibilities of nationhood.

4. In our generation, and in particular in the course of the past twenty years, the Jewish people have awakened and transformed their ancient homeland; from 60,000 at the end of the last war their numbers have increased to more than 500,000. They have made the waste places to bear fruit and the desert to blossom. Their pioneering achievements in agriculture and industry, embodying new patterns of cooperative endeavor, have written a notable page in the history of colonization.

5. In the new values thus created, their Arab neighbors in Palestine have shared. The Jewish people in its own work of national redemption welcomes the economic, agricultural and national development of the Arab peoples and states. The Conference reaffirms the stand previously adopted at Congresses of the World Zionist Organization, expressing the readiness and the desire of the Jewish people for full cooperation with their Arab neighbors.

6. The Conference calls for the fulfillment of the original purpose of the Balfour Declaration and the Mandate which, "recognizing the historical connection of the Jewish people with Palestine," was to afford them the opportunity, as stated by President Wilson, to found there a Jewish Commonwealth.

The Conference affirms its unalterable rejection of the White Paper of May 1939 and denies its moral or legal validity. The White Paper seeks to limit, and in fact to nullify Jewish rights to immigration and settlement in Palestine, and, as stated by Mr. Winston Churchill in the House of Commons in May 1939, constitutes "a breach and repudiation of the Balfour Declaration." The policy of the White Paper is cruel and indefensible in its denial of sanctuary to Jews fleeing from Nazi persecution; and at a time when Palestine has become a focal point in the war front of the United Nations, and Palestine Jewry must provide all available manpower for farm and factory and camp, it is in direct conflict with the interests of the allied war effort.

7. In the struggle against the forces of aggression and tyranny, of

which Jews were the earliest victims, and which now menace the Jewish National Home, recognition must be given to the right of the Jews of Palestine to play their full part of the war effort and in the defense of their country, through a Jewish military force fighting under its own flag and under the high command of the United Nations.

8. The Conference declares that the new world order that will follow victory cannot be established on foundations of peace, justice and equality unless the problem of Jewish homelessness is finally solved.

The Conference urges that the gates of Palestine be opened; that the Jewish Agency be vested with control of immigration into Palestine and with the necessary authority for upbuilding the country, including the development of its unoccupied and uncultivated lands; and that Palestine be established as a Jewish Commonwealth integrated in the structure of the new democratic world.

Then and only then will the age-old wrong to the Jewish people be righted.

* * *

On the closing evening of the conference, a representative of the Jewish Telegraphic Agency approached the leading delegates with a cable that had just arrived from Polish sources in London. It was headlined "Mass Murders of Jews in Lithuania," and cited the names of towns in which the entire Jewish population had been systematically exterminated. Reactions were mixed. Levy Bakstansky, general secretary of the Zionist Federation of Great Britain, heard a prominent American Jewish leader say, "Just another Belgian atrocity story."[35] Abba Hillel Silver, however, received the news with the words: "We cannot truly rescue the Jews of Europe without the right to build the Jewish commonwealth in Palestine—they are interlinked and inseparable."[36]

Notes to Chapter 4

1. J. Shapiro, *Leadership of the American Zionist Organization 1897–1930*, Urbana, Illinois, 1971, pp. 251–6. It is interesting to note that this position is parallel to that of the German Zionists of the Oppenheimer–Bodenheimer school.
2. Hadassah consciously disassociated itself from political Zionism. The organization never requested any of its members to accept a Zionist program or even to sign the Basle Declaration, and at the time of the Brandeis–Weizmann controversy was even ready to resign from the World Zionist Organization. For a general analysis of the positions adopted by Hadassah from the organization's inception, see D. H. Miller, *A History of Hadassah, op. cit.*
3. For detailed discussion see R. W. Slosson, *The Great Crusade and After—1914/1918*, New York, 1930.
4. Pt. 6 of the Atlantic Charter, as published in *The New York Times* of August 14, 1941, reads: "After the final destruction of the Nazi tyranny, they hope to see established a peace which will afford to all nations the means of dwelling in safety within their own boundaries and

which will afford assurance that men in all the lands may live out their lives in freedom from fear and want."

5. See R. Savord, *American Agencies Interested in International Affairs*, New York, 1942.

6. H. A. Nutter, *Postwar Foreign Preparation 1939–1945*, Washington D. C., 1959, p. 151.

7. In actual fact, by 1940 the American Jewish Committee had already established a committee for peace research. See N. Cohen, *Not Free to Desist, op. cit.*, pp. 265f; N. Schachner, *The Price of Liberty*, New York, 1948, pp. 132–5. For American Jewish Congress activities, see *Congress Weekly*, February 7, 1941, p. 4; February 21, 1941, pp. 5–6; March 28, 1941, p. 4; October 24, 1941, p. 5; January 2, 1942, p. 4; January 9, 1942, pp. 5–7; February 20, 1942, pp. 5–6.

8. From "Comments on the Current Situation," May 14, 1940. It is interesting to note that this is one of the few places where Ben-Gurion makes a clear distinction between the Jewish state and the Jewish commonwealth.

9. See minutes of the meeting, December 5, 1940, BGA. Seven leading Zionists were present: Nachum Goldmann, Israel Goldstein, Tamar de Sola Pool, Louis Lipsky, A. H. Silver, Robert Szold and Stephen S. Wise.

10. *Ibid.*; also M. N. Penkower, "Ben Gurion, Silver and the 1941 U.P.A. National Conference for Palestine. A Turning-Point in American Zionist History," *AJH*, 1973–1980, vol. LXIX, pp. 72f. See also A. Gal, *David Ben-Gurion—Preparing for a Jewish State, op. cit.*, pp. 74–7.

11. The original letter can be found in the Emergency Committee Box, NYZA.

12. See D. H. Shpiro, "The Political Background of the 1942 Biltmore Resolution," in M. I. Urofsky (ed.), *Essays in American Zionism 1917–1948, Herzl Year Book*, vol. 8, New York, 1978, p. 170.

13. As stated in Ben-Gurion's report of the discussion: "On the Way to an Army and to the State of Israel": Article 28 of a series of articles that appeared in *Davar* in 1966.

14. Ben-Gurion's memo to Maisky is in the Ben-Gurion Archives. These undertakings are all decribed in Article 28, *ibid.*

15. See FO 371/31380, E6946.

16. For one of these advertisements, see *Opinion*, vol. X, no. 12 (October 1940), p. 25. In it there are numerous quotations from Willkie's speeches against the oppression of Jews in Nazi Europe and against Father Coughlin's antisemitic campaign. On Silver's activity in the UPA, see N. Orian (Herzog), *The Leadership of Abba Hillel Silver in the American Jewish Arena, 1938–1949*, unpublished Ph.D. dissertation, Tel Aviv University, 1982, pp. 44f (Hebrew).

17. Ben-Gurion's diary, October 8, 1940, unpublished manuscript, BGA.

18. On the struggle concerning funds collected in the United States for "overseas Jewry," see M. Kaufman, *The Non-Zionists in America*, Jerusalem, 1984, pp. 44–50.

19. This theory was published later as an essay entitled "Numbers and Exodus" in *New Judea*, February–March 1942, and republished in L. Namier, *Conflicts: Studies in Contemporary History*, London, 1942, pp. 132–7.

20. From Weizmann's address to a joint meeting of the staff of the Jewish Agency Office in London with the Board of Deputies of British Jews, October 1941, FO 371/27129 E8556.

21. For report of meeting, see Weizmann's statement at meeting of Office Committee, April 16, 1942.

22. For the full text of the resolution, see *New Palestine*, January 31, 1941, p. 22.

23. Minutes of Emergency Committee meeting, June 19, 1941.

24. For wording of decisions, see *New Palestine*, vol. 32, September 19, 1941.

25. *Ibid.*

26. Weisgal's memorandum to Emergency Committee about organization of the Extraordinary Conference of American Zionists, March 20, 1942, Biltmore Conference file, Emergency Committee Box, NYZA.

27. Minutes of OCEC of March 23, 1942, and April 22, 1942.

28. Although the official name was "Extraordinary Zionist Conference," it became generally known as the "Biltmore Conference."
29. The address of Dr. Wise and Judge Levinthal and all subsequent reports of the conference proceedings are taken from the stenographic minutes of the conference in the New York Zionist Archives.
30. For the first time Weizmann quotes the term "liquidated," used by the Nazis with respect to the Jews.
31. N. Rose, *Chaim Weizmann: A Biography*, London, 1986, p. 377.
32. For Ben-Gurion's descriptions of such meetings see his book *Meetings with Arab Leaders*, Tel Aviv, 1957.
33. Some of the issues included in the final decisions, such as the question of Jewish participation in the war, were not discussed on the conference floor at all.
34. It is difficult to reconstruct the exact proceedings, as no minutes were recorded. The information included here is based on interviews with, and recollections of, various individuals who participated in the formulation of the decisions. These include an interview Professor Yehuda Bauer had with Judge Louis Levinthal on June 11, 1964; interviews the author had with Judge Levinthal on June 11, 1973 and on August 17, 1974; the author's interviews with Arthur Lourie on June 14, 1974, and on January 11, 1976; and an interview with Lourie that appeared in *Ma'ariv* on January 4, 1963.
35. Quoted to the author by the late Professor Jacob L. Talmon.
36. From an interview with Joseph Cohen, January 17, 1972.

5

Leadership Crisis

American support for a Jewish State in Palestine is the key to our
success.

DAVID BEN-GURION, 1942

The center of gravity for Zionists, no less than for world affairs today, is
in the United States.

CHAIM WEIZMANN, 1942

Discordant Voices

IT WAS not until the Biltmore Conference ended that its importance was
actually put to the test. The highest body of each Zionist party had to approve
the resolutions before they could become the official policy of American
Zionism. Thus, the real battle for the Biltmore program was about to be waged
in the parties and in certain peripheral groups. Each party had its own
interpretation of the commonwealth resolution defining Zionism's ultimate
objective. To some it said too little; to others it said far too much. The major
opposition, however, emanated not from the parties, but from extraneous
elements. The Biltmore Resolution engendered the unified opposition of all
those who favored a binational solution for Palestine and precipitated an all-out
struggle to have the binational state, rather than the Jewish commonwealth,
declared as the goal of Zionism.[1] Some supported this solution out of genuine
belief in binationalism; others out of fear that agitation for a Jewish state would
result in accusations of dual loyalty.

On August 11, 1942, a new political body that advocated binationalism—
the Ichud (Union)—was formed in Palestine. Dr. J. L. Magnes, rector of the
Hebrew University, and Henrietta Szold, head of Youth Aliyah, officially joined
the movement that comprised elements previously active in Hashomer Hatzair
and Brit Shalom.[2] We have noted above that some of the American Hadassah
leaders favored binationalism, and through them the newly formed Ichud tried
to influence American Zionist policy. At the time of the Biltmore Conference,
they were still too weak to do more than demand that no decision at all be taken
with respect to Palestine's ultimate status. By early September, however, the

PLATE 7.   Orator in action—David Ben-Gurion, leader of the Yishuv.

PLATE 8.   Weizmann taking leave of the Zionist Congress on August 31, 1939: "I do not know if, and under what circumstances, we shall meet again."

proponents of a binational state within Hadassah, strengthened by the formation of the Ichud in Palestine, raised the issue of the political goal of Zionism at a meeting of the Emergency Committee.[3] The majority of the Emergency Committee opposed the Ichud's political position and expressed support of the Biltmore program, while confirming Zionism's willingness to work in cooperation with the Arabs. Hadassah's representatives, following the directives of their Executive, withheld support of the Emergency Committee decision.

Ben-Gurion felt that a major purpose motivating those who formed the Ichud was to destroy organized Zionism and attempt, through the use of insidious propaganda, to convince the American government that "there was a cheaper solution to the Palestine problem than the Jewish Commonwealth."[4] It was essential, in Ben-Gurion's opinion, for American Zionists to react. They had to make it clear to the American government and the public that Zionism did not support Magnes, despite the impresssion created by his friends, including the Sulzbergers and their paper, *The New York Times*.

Support for the Ichud was the central issue at Hadassah's national board meeting where Mrs. de Sola Pool spearheaded the pro-Magnes forces and Judith Epstein led the fight for confirmation of the Biltmore formulation. A two-third majority of the board members finally approved the resolution calling for a Jewish commonwealth, a decision that marked more than one turning-point: internally, it denoted the inception of a "change of guard" in Hadassah's leadership; externally, it in effect decided the fate of the Biltmore program in America.

By the time the joint national convention of the ZOA and Hadassah was convened in November of 1942, Hadassah's position was clear. Robert Szold led the fight for approval of the Biltmore program, declaring himself firmly in favor of the commonwealth plan and against all minimalistic alternatives.[5] He even took issue with those Zionist leaders who stressed only the need to open the gates of Palestine to mass immigration, as this implied the "whittling down of Jewish rights to Palestine." This was an almost overt reference to the position held by Dr. Weizmann who, shortly after the close of the Biltmore Conference, had begun to criticize Ben-Gurion's interpretation of the commonwealth formula. Hadassah and the ZOA approved the Biltmore resolution; the National Board of Mizrachi in America did likewise; Poale Zion, whose delegates had fought for the resolution on the conference floor, naturally gave full approval. Thus, the Biltmore program became the official platform of the Zionist movement in the United States.

The Biltmore Resolution's Impact on American Zionism

From 1939 to 1942, American Zionism struggled with the ambivalence caused on the one hand by the increasing incompatibility of British policy with Zionist hopes, and on the other, by the need to cooperate with the British in the fight against the common enemy. After America's entry into the war, it began to dawn on the Zionists that it was now possible to suggest a political alternative to full cooperation with the British. The Biltmore program was the alternative toward which American Zionism had been groping ever since it had become clear that the liaison with Britain, as defined by the Mandate, had failed. The resurgence of truly political Zionism with emphasis on statehood was evoked by an interesting concurrence of elements: the state of mind prevailing in America, certain political facts, strategic considerations, and the realization that the Nazis were waging a war of annihilation against European Jewry.[6] American Zionists began to develop a political approach that can be termed "Jewish statism." Some of the factors that combined to bring this approach to the fore were the euphoric visions of the postwar world resulting from the prevalent view that democratic America's participation in the war was a kind of noble, anti-fascist crusade; the realization that the United States would play a central role in the postwar world; the assumption that at the end of the war, American forces would be spread throughout the world. This would mean that Palestine would no longer be an exclusively British problem (it was erroneously assumed that it would become a joint Anglo-American problem). Then there was the illusory hope that millions of Jews might be saved, which would force the victorious nation to seek a solution for them through mass emigration from Europe and settlement in Palestine.

Reliable reports of the horrors taking place had begun to appear in the press. Not only Zionists but Jews in general felt the need for a political reaction to Nazi brutality in Europe and to Britain's restrictions against Jewish immigration into Palestine. Until now, their frustration and anger had found no echo in the activities of the Jewish and Zionist establishments. The commonwealth slogan, however, provided American Jews with an emotional response to the painful dilemma caused by their inability to act to save European Jewry in that it offered more than just activist slogans and gestures of despair.

The Biltmore progam also indicated a way out of the profound perplexity with regard to Zionism's stand toward Great Britain. Although far from inciting to revolt, the program nevertheless deviated from the conciliatory approach hitherto maintained. At the same time, American Jewry felt that the commonwealth concept would be considered entirely legitimate by the American public in general, as it coincided with the idea of a free, democratic, postwar world. It is interesting to note in passing that the resolutions of the Biltmore Conference seemed almost deliberately to ignore the contemporary international scene. The fact that in the spring of 1942 Palestine was caught between the Nazi armies in North Africa and those in the Caucasus in no way marred the vision of the future.

The Biltmore program cannot be evaluated in accordance with rational criteria: there could probably have been no less appropriate time to adopt a political plan for the future of Palestine than May, 1942. The program must rather be measured by the role it filled for Zionists the world over, for Jewry in general, and for the Jewish community of Palestine in particular—an emotional role designed to restore pride in Jewish nationalism. With American Jewry having suddenly become the largest sector of the Jewish people, American Zionism had to react by throwing its full weight into the political struggle. The commonwealth, the return to the original Zionist concept of the Jewish state, became the political watchword that created a new set of priorities for Zionism—and Jewry—in the United States. For the first time in many years the aim of the Zionists was clear, and activities began to acquire a momentum of their own.

As the various Zionist groupings adopted the Biltmore program in the autumn of 1942, their goal had become clear, but the issue at stake was how to reach that goal. The progam itself was only the first of many drastic adjustments and changes that would have to be introduced, and, essentially, it posed more questions than it answered. How and by whom would it be implemented? What should be the interim policy toward Great Britain and how would that policy manifest itself in practice? What would be American Jewry's status and how should that Jewry be activated? The crystallization of Zionism's political aim threw a harsh light on the abyss that separated the movement's objectives from the instruments and forces it could marshal to realize those objectives. As it sought the answers to the above questions and many others, as it tried to marshal its forces, American Zionism would be rocked by further power struggles, with strong individuals vying for ascendancy; the rift between Chaim Weizmann and David Ben-Gurion would sharpen until eventually both would leave the American scene to a new, indigenous leadership.

The Struggle Between Titans

The relationship between Chaim Weizmann and David Ben-Gurion constantly veered from admiration to opposition and confrontation, on both the personal and the political planes. When Weizmann was reelected to head the World Zionist Organization in 1935, a partnership evolved with the Jewish Labor Movement in Palestine that both he and Ben-Gurion recognized as essential in view of the needs of the hour. But Ben-Gurion noted then that although Weizmann was a great man, there were certain internal issues that he did not fully understand. He was also, according to Ben-Gurion, prone to make mistakes—but because of his personal status and his influence with the British, he was of great importance to the movement.[7] As the official British attitude toward Zionism changed in the late 1930s, however, Ben-Gurion's attitude toward Weizmann also changed and he became more and more fearful that Weizmann would make erroneous political decisions.

Ben-Gurion's approach to the "problem of Weizmann" was to keep his political activities under close surveillance—something he tried to do through Berl Locker in the London office of the Jewish Agency. He recognized the need for Weizmann's leadership, but was determined to counteract his conciliatory approach to the British. Early in 1941, their differences rose to the surface when it became clear that the plan for a Jewish unit in the British Army had failed. Ben-Gurion was in London at the time, but, quite naturally, had played a subordinate role in the negotiations. He was convinced that Weizmann had not made a strong enough case and therefore blamed him for the failure, also claiming that Weizmann, believing in secret diplomacy, ignored the power inherent in public pressure. To some extent these differences were only an intensification of differences that had existed throughout the years; on the other hand, they were exacerbated by the frustration and helplessness of the Zionist leadership in the face of Britain's hostility.

At the end of 1941, when Ben-Gurion returned to the United States and began to embark on a series of political actions, Meyer Weisgal urged Weizmann to hasten his own return. Weizmann had been invited to America in the name of President Roosevelt to study certain aspects of the production of synthetic rubber. On the very day in February 1942 that he was to board a plane, he was informed that his son, a pilot in the RAF, was missing in action. He did not leave England until more than a month later, and in the interim Weisgal did everything he could to rally pro-Weizmann forces.[8] Before discussing this third wartime visit to the United States, however, certain events of Weizmann's previous visit must be mentioned, as they had direct bearing on the relationship between him and Ben-Gurion.

Early in 1941, Weizmann went to the United States and Moshe Shertok came to London to replace him in the Agency office there.[9] Upon his arrival in America, Weizmann immediately contacted non-Zionist organizations such as B'nai B'rith and the American Jewish Committee, as well as influential individuals, and invited them to an "exploratory conference" that was approved by the Office Committee of the Emergency Committee on the 24th of April, 1941. This inaugurated an ongoing exchange of views dealing with a proposal to reorganize the Jewish Agency and with postwar plans for Jews who, for some reason, would be unable to go to Palestine. Weisgal was the moving force behind these discussions, which he kept going even after Weizmann returned to London.

Weizmann also initiated a series of talks with American statesmen in the attempt to convince them to recognize Palestine as the solution to the problem of European Jewish refugees. He had lengthy discussions on this issue with Vice-President Henry Wallace; Sumner Welles, Under-Secretary of State; Henry Morgenthau, Secretary of the Treasury; and others. With the Zionists, Weizmann bent his efforts toward the creation of a political fund of some half a million dollars. He returned to England early in July after having visited fourteen Jewish communities—three of them in Canada. Encouraged by the goodwill he had found, but depressed by the mediocre leadership of most of the communities, Weizmann promised to return to the United States as soon as possible. He planned to convene two conferences, one to unify America's Zionists under a single roof and another, consisting of both Zionists and non-

Zionists, to reorganize the Jewish Agency. He had the full support of Stephen Wise, Louis Lipsky and Nachum Goldmann; when he left the country, entrusting realization of his plans to Meyer Weisgal, these men transferred their support to his faithful deputy. In fact, it was Weisgal who defined the "almost elementary common denominator" of both conferences: "the building up of Palestine."[10]

When Ben-Gurion came to the States in November 1941, it was his second wartime visit, too. For quite some time he had been at odds with large sectors of official Zionism. In April 1940, he had demanded that the Jewish Agency Executive call for intensification of the struggle against British policy in Palestine. He proposed protest demonstrations and a declaration of non-cooperation with the mandatory power in Palestine that would keep the country in a constant state of unrest. But even in Mapai, his own party, only Eliahu Golomb and Berl Katzenelson supported him. The Jewish Agency in London also rejected this kind of activism. However, just at this time the "phony war" became terrifyingly real. Hitler unleashed his massive "Blitzkrieg" into the Low Countries and France. Ben-Gurion's exhortation to fight the war as if there were no White Paper and fight the White Paper as if there were no war, acquired new and more immediate significance. From this point on, Ben-Gurion's power in the Zionist movement increased steadily. This, coupled with his views on Great Britain, made a clash between him and Weizmann inevitable.

In America, though, it was not all clear sailing for Ben-Gurion. He hoped to open an office in Washington that would become the central arena for political activity, but obviously the Emergency Committee would not give him a free hand on territory it considered its own. It was decided at a meeting of the Office Committee on January 5, 1942, that such an office would be opened in Washington by the Emergency Committee, and would be the only recognized Zionist office in the capital. At the same meeting, Stephen Wise was authorized to appoint a small "steering committee' to coordinate political activity. Thus, Ben-Gurion was not only prevented from heading a Washington office; whatever action of a political nature he might decide to undertake would have to be subordinated to decisions of the Emergency Committee. Nevertheless, he arrived at an agreement with the Emergency Committee which, although curtailing his independence to some extent, did not keep him from holding important meetings and discussions in Washington, New York, and other places. Agreeing to report his activities to the three-man steering committee, Ben-Gurion proceeded to work on the three problems that were his primary concern: the conduct of Zionist policy in America, how to influence American public opinion in support of Zionism, and how to strengthen the Zionist movement.

The outcome of the Biltmore Conference is sufficient indication that Ben-Gurion's program for political action bore fruit. He was much less successful, however, in his attempts to unify fragmented American Zionism—or even to bring the Mapai-oriented Poale Zion to adopt an activist Socialist-Zionist program. He was rather more successful with Hadassah, where he convinced a majority of the leadership to relinquish their separatist tendencies, as we have seen in their rejection of the binational state and approval of the Biltmore program.

Collision Over the "Jewish Army Committee"

Ben-Gurion's attitude to the Jewish Army Committee precipitated a head-on collision not only with some of the members of the Emergency Committee, but with Weizmann as well. Convinced that authorized Zionist bodies had to refuse all cooperation with the Committee because it was an outgrowth of the dissident Irgun Zvai Leumi, Ben-Gurion was furious to discover that members of the Emergency Committee were negotiating with Joseph Brainin. A personal friend of Weisgal, Brainin was acting as the Jewish Army Committee's go-between with Weizmann. Early in 1942, Weisgal and Brainin prepared an agreement providing for cooperation between the Zionists and the Committee. Weizmann, in England at the time, affixed his initials to the agreement in the name of the Zionist movement, and Pierre van Paassen initialed it in the name of the committee. Ben-Gurion took steps to nullify the document even before it would be brought to the Emergency Committee for final approval, and convinced the Hadassah representatives to veto it. The idea, therefore, came to nought, but this did not placate Ben-Gurion.

Both Weizmann and Ben-Gurion recognized the political and symbolic importance of a Jewish fighting force, but they differed sharply over how to work for it and with whom. Weizmann was impressed by the influential people who supported the Army Committee in America and believed that their names could be used effectively in his talks with the British. Ben-Gurion saw nothing but good publicity and effective fund-raising behind the Committee's work in America. Believing that as an irresponsible group that refused to accept Jewish Agency discipline they endangered Palestine's Jewish community, he felt everything should be done to expose them. This was implicit in his negative attitude to Emanuel Neumann, and did not help to ingratiate him with some of the American Zionist leaders. Ben-Gurion was unable to overcome the mistrust of Neumann which, no doubt, stemmed from the latter's membership in the anti-Labor General Zionist "B" faction during his years in Palestine. In addition, he felt that the general ineptitude of the Emergency Committee's leadership gave Neumann excessive control of the apparatus and made it relatively easy for him to hamper realization of Ben-Gurion's progam for American Zionism.[11]

Ben-Gurion expected the Emergency Committee to begin to implement the Biltmore Conference decisions immediately. Above all, he hoped that the Zionist forces would now make a concerted onslaught designed to win favorable public opinion and he proposed an immediate goal: getting one million American Jews to sign the Biltmore platform to prove the massive support it elicited. What other action could make as strong an impression on offical London and Washington? Dr. Wise supported the proposal, feeling that it would also be American Jewry's first organized reaction to the Nazi atrocities in Europe. But the majority of members of the Emergency Committee rejected the idea.[12]

From Ben-Gurion's entries in his diary it is quite apparent that he felt himself very much alone in the United States. Aware that he antagonized many of the Zionist leaders by trying to settle some of the chronic differences among them, he nevertheless forged ahead, his sense of responsibility to the Jewish people urging him on.[13] When Weizmann returned in April 1942, Ben-Gurion felt his isolation even more severely. With his prestige and dominating presence, Dr. Weizmann was the official interpreter of Zionism in America, a situation that Ben-Gurion sincerely believed was fraught with danger for the movement. He finally decided to bring the issue to a head and on June 11, 1942, he wrote to Weizmann saying:

> Since you came here you have acted entirely on your own, consulting and cooperating from time to time with people of your personal choice as one does in his private affairs. . . . [I]t seems to me that some of the things you have said and done so far are not very helpful to our cause.
>
> You are aware, no less than I, of the gravity of the hour. The threat of a Nazi invasion in Palestine is not yet over. The White Paper is still the official policy of Great Britain. The Colonial Office is as hostile as ever. . . . The State Department is not always averse to following the Foreign Office in matters concerning Zionism and Palestine. The British Ambassador in Washington is the father of the White Paper. The internal Zionist situation here is rather delicate . . . relations with large and numerous Jewish bodies in America, outside the organized Zionist movement . . . require careful and purposeful dealing. America is more and more becoming a decisive factor. We are only at the beginning of our task here and it is not an easy one. More than ever common counsel, concerted action and collective responsibility are indispensable . . .
>
> You know well, I hope, my high personal regard and deep friendship for you. You know, too, perhaps, that I don't care very much for formalities. But unless the Executive and the Emergency Committee with your wholehearted support can assure the necessary common and united action, I really don't see how our work can properly be done, or what use I can be here, or how I can share responsibility.[14]

Ben-Gurion's letter does not go into detail about which issues Weizmann chose to deal with on his own. There is every reason to assume, however, that he had in mind a meeting between Weizmann and Sumner Welles where the latter was asked to arrange an official discussion with State Department personnel, and several meetings that Weizmann had with Lord Halifax, Britain's ambassador to Washington. He had also had a half-hour meeting with President

Roosevelt, whose reaction to the Zionist program for the future contained little more than banal rhetoric—although Weizmann reported to the Office Committee on the 8th of July, 1942, that the President had been interested and sympathetic. Then, of course, there were countless meetings with Jewish leaders—non-Zionist as well as Zionist—and with heads of various organizations.

Divergent Interpretations of the Biltmore Program

The major issue dividing the two men, however, was their divergent interpretations of the Biltmore program or, as Judge Levinthal, president of the ZOA, at the time put it: "Weizmann's Biltmore" and "Ben-Gurion's Biltmore." Ben-Gurion's commonwealth formulation presupposed a total change of orientation, as a result of which the main weight of political work would be transferred to the United States. He believed that a Jewish state would be established essentially by a decision of the American government, which would then force the British to accept it. Weizmann maintained just the opposite: the Jews of America and the United States government would give Churchill the support necessary to enable him to solve the problem of Palestine in the direction desired by the Zionists. Ben-Gurion saw the United States as the decisive force in the Middle East in the immediate postwar period, whereas Weizmann believed that Great Britain would continue to play the role of major superpower in the area, with the active support of the United States.

Weizmann's response to Ben-Gurion's letter—which he referred to as an "inexplicable document"—was a rather ironic statement to the effect that the gravity of the current situation had not escaped his attention. He utterly rejected the contention that he acted on his own, writing: "I have spent considerable time in consultation with members of the Executive, the Emergency Committee and available members of the Actions Committee." Somehow, Ben-Gurion was absent from all those consultations.[15]

After receiving this letter, Ben-Gurion wrote to Stephen Wise as chairman of the Emergency Committee and asked him to "arange an informal meeting of American Zionist leaders and members of the Zionist Executive in New York." He stated that "unless this disastrous situation can immediately be remedied, no other course will be left for me than to ask the Executive and the Actions Committee in Palestine to call for his [Weizmann's] resignation."[16] Wise called a meeting on a rather informal basis, inviting Nachum Goldmann, Hayim Greenberg, Judge Levinthal, Louis Lipsky, Robert Szold, Meyer Weisgal, Weizmann and Ben-Gurion to his private study on the afternoon of June 27, 1942. Ben-Gurion opened the session, saying, "I am not going to tell you how painful for me is the statement which I am going to make. Perhaps when I am finished you will understand why I had to make it . . ." He then reported the contents of the letter he had sent to Weizmann and Weizmann's reply. Ben-

Gurion then challenged the statement in Weizmann's letter that he was "charged with the responsibility of conducting Zionist political affairs," saying,

1. Dr. Weizmann is not authorized to act alone.
2. It is not in the interests of the movement that he act alone. I certainly would not raise this issue on constitutional grounds now, but I do consider it harmful, expecially now, that Dr. Weizmann should act alone.

Ben-Gurion went on to say that since Weizmann's arrival in America they had met five times. Each time Ben-Gurion reported what he had done and asked what Weizmann wanted him to do next, to which he had received no reply. Weizmann had not reported on any of his own activities.

After reviewing specific issues on which Weizmann had acted on his own, Ben-Gurion noted that on many occasions Weizmann's reports were "unduly optimistic. He identifies personal position and personal courtesies with political courtesies . . ." Ben-Gurion then proceeded to touch on what was really the crux of the problem: American Jewry, the American public, the American government, and their influence on achieving the aims of Zionism.

> Before Dr. Weizmann's arrival I asked myself: is it necessary that I should remain? . . . I asked the Executive. They said I should remain and I came to the conclusion that it was necessary. . . . It is my view—I may be wrong—that America is even more important than England, though I do not think that we should write off England. England, whatever happens, will be a great power after this war. We can work in England, but America is different—it is the decisive power, and the political work in America is of decisive importance. . . . If America says a word they will have to heed it. Political work is not merely talks with the government. [There must be a] strong, united and purposeful movement in America—and America must stand together with world Zionism—without the support of America our work cannot be done. We need strong, consistent, purposeful guidance.
>
> To win American Jewry we must know what we want, and we must know what they are and mobilize them, as far as we can, behind our purpose. As far as the American government goes, we must convince the key men in America that Palestine is the real solution for a large problem, or we have nothing to do in America. We must believe we can do the work and have faith in the justice and practicability of Zionism as a large-scale solution. It is not enough that you Americans alone should do it. The Jewish people must speak to the American government. World Zionism must talk to America. It is my conviction that Dr. Weizmann cannot do this alone and that we cannot do it without Dr. Weizmann.

And then, to the shocked surprise of all present, Ben-Gurion called for Weizmann's resignation from the presidency of the World Zionist Organization—unless some accommodation could be found.

Dr. Weizmann did not take this lying down. His reply combined both defense and attack. He characterized the contents of Ben-Gurion's speech as

> misinterpretation, misunderstanding, and in a great many cases, mis-statements. The *leitmotif* of the whole business is that I am acting alone. I am not aware of it. I have never taken upon myself either to initiate a policy or even to execute it after its initiation, on my own. In London we worked with those colleagues who were present. Every step, good, bad, or indifferent, was discussed and debated and a decision agreed upon. Then, when I had to go to see someone, in most cases I went alone. I faithfully and honestly, according to the best of my ability, reported the interview. I do not consider this acting alone. . . . I always insisted on somebody being in London from Palestine, whether it was Moshe (Shertok) or Ben-Gurion, but we always thought there must be a living link between us and Palestine. I therefore reject *in toto*—absolutely reject—that I have been acting alone. . . . When Moshe Shertok was in London there was never a shadow of misunderstanding. It began with the advent of Ben-Gurion in Palestine when I was not there. What are the points of variance? If it were rationalizing something which may be a difference in conception, it ought to interest you. But the whole construction of these charges, I am genuinely sorry to have to say, is painfully reminiscent of purges. . . . I shall not swerve because I think that is the right way. I shall be collegial. If in most cases I choose to see people alone, or sometimes go with another, that must be left to my discretion.
>
> Having said that I consider the whole chapter of charges as unfair in equity and in justice, I shall turn your attention for a few minutes to the real differences which are at the bottom. Ben-Gurion has considered for two-and-a-half years that the Army is the single problem of Zionism. Everything else in comparison with that fades into insignificance. I do not share the view even now that Zionism fails or falls on the question of the army.
>
> Never did I share the view, and I think that Ben-Gurion has put it in a more restrained way today, that the world begins and ends with America. I think we should do our level best—as much as it is in our power to do—to get England and America to cooperate on our problem. Eden, the Foreign Secretary, is not a particular friend of ours and with all my naiveté, I have not lost sight of it. A great many of his friends advise us to try to activate American interest in Palestine. America alone cannot do it. Without England we cannot do it. It is most important to have this explained here and to work for it systematically and regularly.
>
> I did not know that another member of the Executive was always sent

to England to watch that I should not make mistakes. Ben-Gurion does not know what I talk to Lord Halifax about, but he is worried. That is his usual state. I reported. Either the report must be accepted, or I am a liar, or I am incapable of giving an accurate statement. But I am not going to be subject to these particular strictures or whims of a man, or men, who are trying to frame up a case out of imaginary grievances for political assassination.

Needless to say, the statements made by Weizmann and Ben-Gurion elicited a reaction from those present. Most of them, of course, had been aware of the differences that had separated these two powerful personalities—differences that had periodically surfaced but on the whole had been kept in check through the years; the depths of animosity that flared up on this occasion, however, was something of a shock. On the whole, each man who took the floor avoided direct reference to the issues on which Weizmann and Ben-Gurion differed, and attempted to suggest an organizational setup that would enable the Zionist movement to continue.[17]

For some time Weisgal had been urging Weizmann to establish an office of the President of the World Zionist Organization in the United States to be composed of the members of the Executive resident in the country, as well as three or four leading figures of the American Zionist movement. The suggestion had been waived, very likely because of the hesitancy on the part of the American leadership to give "outsiders" formal status, but now that the dissension between Ben-Gurion and Weizmann had become a matter of public knowledge, Weizmann's supporters advocated establishment of such an office as a partial solution. The idea was modified and rather than an office of the President, it was proposed as an ad hoc committee of the Jewish Agency executive members present in the United States. Its purpose would be primarily to coordinate the work of Ben-Gurion and Weizmann, attempting to bridge their animosity by frequent exchanges of information which might make it possible to reconcile their divergent political outlooks—or at least provide a modus vivendi.

Ben-Gurion was violently opposed to the idea, but, except for the occasional support of some of the leading Hadassah women, was, as we have seen, quite isolated. This did not keep him from undertaking political tasks. He was among the first to sense the growing influence of British policy on the American Department of State. Felix Frankfurter informed him—and Weizmann as well—that President Roosevelt was under increasing anti-Zionist pressure not only from the State Department, but also from his military advisers. The President, according to Frankfurter, had refrained from meeting with Ben-Gurion, because "in the present situation in Egypt, Palestine, Syria and Arabia, he feels that the less said by everybody of all creeds, the better." Despite his objection to a "committee of the Agency Executive," Ben-Gurion agreed to appear at a meeting of such a body with Dr. Weizmann early in August, where both men would report on their activities. From the standpoint of Nachum Goldmann and Louis Lipsky who convened the meeting, there were two objectives: one was to make a last attempt at reconciliation between Weizmann and Ben-Gurion; the other was to establish the ad hoc committee as a fact.[18]

In essence, not only was there no reconciliation—the two men did not exchange a single word throughout the session—there was also no meeting of minds. Each expounded his approach to current issues and his attitude towards the functioning of the committee itself; they remained far apart. The conclusion reached by Weizmann and his supporters was that if Ben-Gurion refused to cooperate within this new framework, he should be forced to leave the country as soon as possible. It is quite conceivable that Ben-Gurion himself contributed not a little to this feeling as, in his desperate concern for the physical safety of Palestine, he did not always seek the most diplomatic methods of telling the Americans—Zionists, Jews and non-Jews—that he felt they were not doing enough. But his prime concern was to try to jolt American Jewry to play an active role, a political role inspired by a political objective, rather than to permit it to lapse into the passive role implicit in the behind-the-scenes diplomacy conducted by Weizmann. The more he learned about the Zionist and general political scene in America, however, the more convinced he became that he could not work there the way Weizmann had worked in England during the First World War, and he decided to return to Palestine. Frustrated as he was, however, Ben-Gurion was not ready to leave the country without having a final word.

Ben-Gurion's Vision of the Future

A special meeting of the Office Committee was called for the afternoon of 17 September, 1942.[19] In addition to representatives of the ZOA, Hadassah, Poale Zion and Mizrachi, Israel Mereminsky (envoy of the Histadrut to the US) and Louis Segal of the Farband (a fraternal organization associated with the Labor Zionists) were invited. Nachum Goldmann, Arthur Lourie and Emanuel Neumann were present, as was Weisgal, whose invitation was apparently extended by word of mouth. Weizmann did not attend. Ben-Gurion—for whom the War Department had secured passage on the Clipper for the following day—opened the session with expressions of regret that ". . . the President of the Zionist Organization cannot be present."

He then embarked on a discussion of Zionist policy and how it should be conducted. He stated that above all, Zionism must realize that the Yishuv represented the Jewish people, morally speaking, and it was up to the Yishuv more than to any other Jewish community in the world to prepare a Zionist solution for the Jewish problem and the problem of Palestine. This was a political task and demanded a political solution. As a result of the war, it had been impossible to maintain normal relations within the Zionist movement. Regular communications were cut off and even the Executive could not meet normally—the representatives in London and Geneva were unable to meet with the Executive in Jerusalem and the convening of a Zionist Congress was impossible.

Saying that he had been sent to America by the Executive to interpret Palestine and explain the policies of the Executive and the Small Actions Committee, Ben-Gurion expressed his hope that despite the technical difficulties, the American movement would send people to Palestine as frequently as possible. Contact with England and sections of the movement in other parts of the world should be further developed as well. Then he spoke of Great Britain, and the recent appointment of Lord Moyne to the post of Assistant Secretary of State for the Middle East as extremely ominous. Lord Moyne had made the first antisemitic speech to be delivered in the British Cabinet for the past twenty years.

Speaking of a Jewish army, Ben-Gurion said that he still hoped and believed that it would materialize. He said that certain probabilities had to be taken into account, including the possible break-up of the British Empire and the emergence of other great powers. He was one of the first to recognize that both America and Russia would have a stake in the Middle East and something to say about its future. Thinking in terms of analogies with the First World War was misleading. It was probable that this time England, Russia and America would first settle things together and then call a peace conference. A Zionist solution was not something to be prepared for a peace conference, but was a process which should be begun at once and which must be completed before such a conference would take place.

> There are certain facts we must create, the major ones being:
> 1. No matter what, we must continue in America, in London and in Palestine to press for a Jewish army;
> 2. Palestine should become both a supply base and a strategic base for the Allies in the Middle East. There will be armies there for the decisive assault and there must be as many Jews in the fighting forces as possible;
> 3. As soon as the war is over the maximum number of Jews will have to be brought to Palestine, and America can help with this. Thousands of Jews converging on Palestine will in itself have a powerful influence on public opinion.

Ben-Gurion then described his new conception of Zionism's role, which would no longer be to bring about the gradual growth of the Jewish population in Palestine, but rather to transfer some two million Jews there in a single operation. After the war there would be new means of transportation; millions of civilians would be moved from one country to another, millions would have to be resettled and fed by government action. New, unprecedented problems would arise that would require new, unprecedented solutions. What would have to be done for the Jews would be a relatively small matter. Two million

Jews could be settled in Palestine as a governmental project in connection with a large public works plan, also government-financed.

It seemed to Ben-Gurion that after the establishment of Palestine as a Jewish commonwealth, Zionism's job would be finished. The task then would be to build Palestine, and for this the Jewish people were eminently equipped. The task of political Zionism was to secure the necessary governmental power to facilitate the agricultural and industrial development of the country. America, which had previously been a provincial power, was maturing and becoming politically independent. America, with a changed Russia and friendly China, had no such anti-Zionist bias as had evolved in British governmental circles. He did not want to give the impression that winnng America over was an easy job, but neither was the Zionist objective an easy one. Working with profound internal conviction, with mental and moral courage, with perseverance and a fixed purpose, the cause would be won. Zionism, according to Ben-Gurion, was sui generis and must not be conceived in terms of analogies but in terms of a real, large, one-time solution of the Jewish problem. Such a sweeping conception, he believed, would win America, and what was the current political task in the country.

The following day, Ben-Gurion boarded the Clipper for a long, roundabout flight back to Palestine.

Weizmann Leaves America Disillusioned

Ben-Gurion's departure might seem to have left Weizmann free to act however he saw fit, but that was hardly the case. First of all, Ben-Gurion left a legacy behind; his final session with the leading figures of American Zionism had been truly inspiring and had introduced them to a new way of thinking that was all-important for the months ahead. And then, Ben-Gurion was returning to his power-base; he could probably be more effective from Palestine than from any place else. Weizmann, on the other hand, was suffering from poor health and trying to divide his time between his scientific responsibilities and Zionism. It was becoming increasingly apparent that he was irresolute and sometimes inconsistent. He failed to elicit the enthusiastic support he had anticipated.

Soon after Ben-Gurion left, Nachum Goldmann decided to try to activate the American "branch" of the Jewish Agency Executive that had been proposed as a solution to the Weizmann–Ben-Gurion dispute, but had remained dormant as long as the latter was in the United States. To Goldmann and a few others, this seemed the ideal body to work with Weizmann in an advisory capacity. In addition to the long-standing members of the Agency Executive—Weizmann, Goldmann and Lipsky—the plan was to include Wise, Silver and Levinthal to represent American Zionism. It was also decided that Moshe Shertok would be asked to come from Palestine for a given period. Weizmann and the men who supported him never felt quite certain as to whether Ben-Gurion would make good his threat to demand Weizmann's resignation; they therefore made a point of sending frequent favorable reports of his activities to members of the Executive.

Following Ben-Gurion's report to the Executive—in which, significantly, he refrained from asking for Weizmann's resignation—the members of the Executive decided to ask Weizmann to come to Palestine for consultation.[20] He refused on the grounds of ill health, and at the same time suggested that Shertok come to America. In the cable sent on October 22, 1942, in which he asked that Shertok come, he also requested approval of the establishment of the American branch of the Agency Executive. Ben-Gurion was quite aware that this was a way for Weizmann to build a power-base in America and, at the meeting at which the Executive approved the Biltmore Resolution, he convinced them to refrain from endorsing the formation of an Agency "branch" in the United States. Shertok refused the invitation to America as he had to be in London just then.[21] Weizmann tried to convince Shertok to continue to the United States from London, and Shertok asked the Political Committee of Mapai to decide whether he should go or not. The Political Committee gave its approval. Ben-Gurion, incidentally, considered this a personal betrayal on the part of Shertok, who thus inadvertently became entangled in the Weizmann–Ben-Gurion dispute. The relationship between Ben-Gurion and Shertok never returned to what it had been before this incident.[22]

Contrary to Ben-Gurion's suspicions, although Shertok went to the United States and participated in a number of discussions with Weizmann, both in Washington and elsewhere, he refused to support the establishment of an American branch of the Executive. Weizmann, of course, was disappointed, blaming Ben-Gurion for having biased the Palestinian members of the Executive. Through the medium of Meyer Weisgal, as always, Weizmann then tried to organize a political committee of American Zionists to work directly with him. At its meeting on the 7th of January, 1943, the Emergency Committee finally agreed to appoint a five-man political committee, on a party basis. The committee was to be subordinate to the Emergency Committee— but after three meetings it was disbanded. The Office Committee as a whole, it was decided, would be the political committee and together with Dr. Weizmann would deal with important political matters.

Ben-Gurion had been altogether correct when he analyzed Weizmann's approach as deriving from his experiences in England during the First World War. Following that pattern, late in 1942 Weizmann asked Sumner Welles to arrange official talks with the American government about the postwar future of Palestine. His objective was to prepare the ground for an all-encompassing political program acceptable to the highest echelons of government. He explained that he was starting with the American Department of State as there were indications of the Department's willingness to enter into discussions, whereas the British government was not yet prepared to discuss postwar problems. Welles appointed Wallace Murray to represent him at several talks held by people of the Middle East section of the State Department with the

Zionist delegation headed by Dr. Weizmann. As should have been expected, the results were most discouraging, particularly to Weizmann, who had expected at least some sort of statement based more or less on the Balfour Declaration.

After two years of bitter experience, Weizmann nevertheless totally misread the situation in the Middle East section of the State Department. A report from the US representative in Cairo reached Washington just when the Zionists were engaged in talks there. The report recommended abstaining from all decisions that would change the basic situation in Palestine until the war was over, indicating that pro-Zionist declarations would adversely affect the prospects for an Allied victory.[23] With the obvious failure of his policy of working through high governmental officials, the refusal of the Executive to approve the establishment of an office in America and the flagging support of most of the American Zionist leaders, Weizmann asked Shertok to inform Jerusalem that he wished to be relieved of all responsibility for political affairs in America and everywhere else.[24]

Ben-Gurion had left America determined to translate the Biltmore program into a militant political program to be aggressively pursued by the Zionist movement, and he succeeded in convincing the Jewish Agency Executive and the Small Zionist Actions Committee to adopt his activist approach. Weizmann, on the other hand, left America eight months later, still believing in the gradualist, conciliatory approach that had succeeded during the First World War. Thus, the two outstanding leaders of world Zionism both returned home—one to London and one to Jerusalem—and left Zionism in America to fight its battles alone.

Notes to Chapter 5

1. See S. L. Hattis, *The Bi-National Idea in Palestine during Mandatory Times*, Tel Aviv, 1970, pp. 256–76.

2. A. Goren (ed.), *Dissenter in Zion: From the Writings of Judah L. Magnes*, Cambridge, Massachusetts, 1982, introduction, p. 47.

3. Those who advocated a binational state were never in the majority in Hadassah, but they held some of the most important positions in the movement (from the author's interview with Rose Halperin on August 17, 1971).

4. Minutes of OCEC meeting, September 19, 1942.

5. For Szold's speech, see *New Palestine*, November 6, 1941. It was also issued as a pamphlet called *Zionism: Its Cardinal Principle*, Washington D.C., 1942. In a letter to the author written on June 29, 1971, Szold stresses that the reference was to Weizmann.

6. Nevertheless, concern for European Jewry, although it appears as Point 2 of the Biltmore Declaration, is no more than a one-sentence message of hope to fellow Jews in Hitler-dominated Europe, with the prayer that they will soon be liberated.

7. D. Ben-Gurion, *Letters to Paula and the Children*, London, 1971, pp. 109, 113.

8. N. Rose, *Chaim Weizmann, op cit.*, pp. 370f.

9. For discussion of Weizmann's projected trip and interim arrangements in the London office of the Agency, see minutes of Executive of Jewish Agency in Jerusalem, February 23, 1941.

10. See Weisgal's letter to Weizmann, April 17, 1941, CZA, Z5/1215.

11. See Ben-Gurion's letter to Shertok, February 8, 1942, BGA.
12. See minutes of OCEC, June 3, 1942.
13. See Ben-Gurion's diaries, *op cit.*, 1942.
14. Ben-Gurion's letter to Weizmann, June 11, 1942, CZA, Z5/1219.
15. Weizmann's letter to Ben-Gurion, June 15, 1942, CZA, Z5/1219.
16. Ben-Gurion's letter to Wise, June 19, 1942, CZA, Z5/1219.
17. Minutes of meeting in Wise's study, June 27, 1942.
18. See minutes of "Committee of the Agency Executive," August 3, 1942.
19. For Ben-Gurion's speech, see minutes of special meeting of OCEC, September 17, 1942.
20. Cable from Agency Executive to Weizmann, October 19, 1942, and from Weizmann to Agency Executive, October 22, 1942 (Weizmann Archives).
21. Jewish Agency Executive meeting, November 15, 1942.
22. From Sharett (Shertok) diaries, November 23, 1953 (as published in *Ma'ariv* on May 17, 1974), in which he discusses Ben-Gurion's attitude toward him during the 1950s.
23. See Hoskins Report to Secretary of State, FRUS, 1943, vol. IV, pp. 747–50.
24. Weizmann's handwritten letter to Shertok dated March 30, 1943, where he blames his failure on Ben-Gurion, CZA, Z5/1217.

6

The Crucial Year

We must build upon the broad and secure base of public sentiment, the approval of public opinion which in the final analysis determines the attitude and action of governments in democratic society. With all my supreme admiration for the great personalities who are our friends, and for the significance of great personalities in the world crisis today . . . I still say unto you, what the Psalmist said long ago: 'Al tivtechu bi-nedivim.'—Put not your trust in princes.

ABBA HILLEL SILVER, 1944

A True Turning-Point

THE PERIOD 1943–44 represented a crucial turning-point in the history of American Zionism. As a result of changes that took place then, the majority of the Jews of America recognized Zionism as a political movement that offered the solution to the Jewish problem. The Emergency Committee was completely reorganized under a new, dynamic leadership that considered as its major task the consolidation of all of Jewry into a political influence group—a lobby. The lobby's purpose would be to convince the Allied powers to incorporate the principles of the Biltmore program into postwar agreements and treaties.

At the time of the Biltmore Conference the previous year, the horrifying news of the systematic annihilation of European Jewry had intensified awareness of the need to mobilize the support of American Jewry and of non-Jewish public opinion. Frustration at the inability to help was growing; there was rising anger at the British government for closing the gates of Palestine, and at the American government for its do-nothing policy. The Biltmore program had been the Zionist answer then. Now, a year later, the Zionists and their supporters, spurred by confirmation of the mass murders being perpetrated by Hitler's forces, were determined to make the world aware of their answer: a Jewish commonwealth in Palestine.

Other forces, too, were propelling the Zionists toward more militant action, among them the growing popularity of competing groups that had succeeded in attracting public attention. Such groups, particularly the delegation sent to

122

PLATE 9.   Abba Hillel Silver, chairman of the American Zionist Emergency Committee.

America by the Irgun Zvai Leumi, were drawing sympathetic sectors of the general population as well as Jews who sought an immediate emotional outlet. Engaging in propaganda for the formation of a Jewish army and later for rescue of European Jewry, the Irgun was equally vehement in its attacks on Great Britain and on the inactivity of the recognized Jewish and Zionist bodies. At the opposite pole, an outright anti-Zionist group called the American Council for Judaism was gaining momentum. For the first time in many years, and largely due to developments in the international arena, the Zionist movement was being attacked by an American Jewish group.

In addition, a previously unrecognized external factor began to impinge on Zionism and Jewry. With America's increasing involvement in the war, with oil becoming more and more important, the United States was viewing the Middle East with new interest. This had a twofold effect: first, aware of the danger inherent in America's new interest, American Jewry tended to close ranks behind Zionist militancy as expressed in the Biltmore program; second, confrontation between organized Zionism and the American government became inevitable. In this unprecedented confrontation, the Zionists scored their first success and learned an important lesson in the tactics and strategy of political warfare.

These events shook American Zionism out of the inertia and stalemate of the first war years. Under its new dynamic leadership, the Emergency Committee emerged as an active political body and American Zionism became an aggressive influence group.

Inadvertent Catalyst

The Jewish Army Committee in America, founded by emissaries of the Irgun Zvai Leumi, the "maximalist" offshoot of the Revisionist movement, acted as an inadvertent catalyst in the transformation of American Zionism. Conducting an independent "foreign policy" and advocating the use of force against the British, the Irgun was a clandestine organization in Palestine. It espoused armed struggle to achieve Zionist objectives, and rejected the methods of the Revisionists as too moderate. Abroad it also engaged in underground activities: whereas until the war the Revisionists were in contact with the Polish and Romanian governments and with official bodies in other Eastern and Central European countries—primarily for the purpose of organizing means of transporting Jewish refugees, the Irgun sought connections with the military, hoping to give its people military training and find sources for the purchase of arms. For their own reasons, the Poles were not loathe to cooperate.

The Irgun sent representatives to Yugoslavia and the Scandinavian countries to collect money and disseminate propaganda. An office was opened in Paris that attempted, primarily through the press, to replace the organization's British-fostered terrorist image with the image of a national liberation movement. The Irgun, maintaining that it represented all of Jewry rather than any single Jewish party, refused to be identified with the Revisionists and Jabotinsky. The Paris office closed after its unsuccessful attempt to convince the 1939 Zionist Congress to declare an active struggle against Great Britain and demand the immediate establishment of a Jewish state. (As a symbol of national resistance to foreign domination, the organization used posters of William Tell, the Swiss national hero.)[1]

As the threat of war increased, the Irgun decided to send a delegation to the United States, the only neutral Great Power. At first the delegation's objectives were limited to political action directed toward opening Palestine's gates to Jewish immigration; at the same time it planned to recruit support for illegal *aliya* and mobilize public opinion in favor of the activities of the Irgun itself.[2] The "American Friends of a Jewish Palestine," formed by the delegation in 1939, was primarily meant to raise funds for illegal immigration; its sponsors included both Jews and non-Jews and their activities centered mainly around publicizing their own existence. In 1940 Jabotinsky arrived in the United States, bringing with him his lifelong idea of a Jewish army; the "American Friends" incorporated the Jewish army slogan into their propaganda.

Jabotinsky's book, *The War and the Jew*, had just appeared in England and he now embarked upon an intensive drive to acquaint the American public with his ideas. But he met with the implacable opposition of the various Zionist organizations, as well as of other Jewish bodies which objected to his activities on two major grounds.[3] They maintained that he was fighting for a cause that had outlived its day as he was invoking both the methods and concepts of the First World War; secondly, they objected to the fact that he worked independently of the Zionist institutions, refusing to accept their discipline and denying their right to speak in the name of all Zionists. Jabotinsky indicated that he might be ready to seek some sort of modus vivendi, but at the time of his sudden death in August 1940, no reconciliation had yet been achieved.

In the meantime, the Irgun emissaries—Shmuel Merlin, Y. Ben-Ami, A. Ben Elieger, Ery Jabotinsky, A. Raphaeli, Yirmiahu Halperin, and their leading figure Hillel Kook, alias Peter Bergson, their overseas commander—had all gathered in the United States. For the next eight years they would engage in intensive, highly sophisticated propaganda and fund-raising activities, but always as a fringe group. Severed from their people in Palestine as war spread throughout the world, ostracized by the Zionists in America, they worked entirely independently and developed their own political line. They were young men, most of them in their twenties, and became "Americanized" very quickly, adopting techniques and tactics appropriate to the American scene. Bergson was undoubtedly the dominant figure among them, and most of their activities were undertaken by what became known as the "Bergson Group," a name that served both as camouflage and identification.

Their internal struggle with the Jewish establishment elicited a unique ideological development intended to bridge the duality Zionism created in the Jewish people. They attracted Jews who could not accept Zionism because they did not accept the European definition of nationality as a cultural–ethnic entity that surmounted frontiers and political divisions. These Jews considered themselves American: as long as they were integrally part of their country, they did not see themselves as a group with political rights to separate national sovereignty. The Irgun emissaries proposed a solution for this dilemma: Jews throughout the world who are not or do not choose to be nationals of other states, constitute the Hebrew nation and Palestine is their national territory. Assimilated, non-Zionist Jews could thus support the activities of the Irgun delegation. The majority of American Jewish organizations, however, bitterly attacked this ideological approach as undermining the unity of the Jewish people.

Early in 1941, the Bergson Group initiated its campaign for a Jewish army that would fight under the Allied command. To avoid a head-on clash with the Jewish and Zionist establishment, they started quietly, organizing small "parlor meetings" of "friends" in private homes. They tried to organize a pressure group of Jews and non-Jews to convince the American government to support the demand. It was their belief that a Jewish fighting force was the most effective way of counteracting claims that Jews had not taken up arms against Nazi Germany, and would also ensure the right of Jews to be heard when the time came to determine postwar settlements.

The vociferous Jewish and Zionist opposition to all action taken by the Bergson Group led the latter to work in innovative ways, using unconventional methods.[4] As a "nonsectarian" body, they were able to tap large reserves of goodwill among anti-Nazis and liberals, Jews and non-Jews. At the time, the American public had many levels of pro- and anti-British sentiment, of pro- and anti-isolationist sentiment, of radicals, conservatives, clericals—all looking for causes. As long as the cause came under the heading of democratic action and purported to improve the lot of the "underdog," it could elicit public support.

Appealing to public figures to support the Committee for a Jewish Army, the Bergson Group succeeded in accumulating an impressive list of sponsors who agreed to have their names appear on the Committee's letterhead. Included in the list were journalists, writers, scientists, cinema stars, most of whom simply lent their names. Some were helpful in fund-raising, but only a few became actively involved. Although they gave the impression of a powerful organization, in actual fact all that existed was a small nucleus of active people who were responsible only to themselves. The "Army Committee" and other committees subsequently formed by the Bergson Group, were essentially "front" organizations. They employed effective propaganda methods never before used by Jewish or Zionist organizations, publishing spectacular advertisements in the daily press calling for the formation of a Jewish army and a Hebrew state. Famous names generally appeared as sponsors and a form was attached to be sent in together with a contribution. Mass meetings and large gatherings were arranged, always under the sponsorship of well-known people from the world of arts, politics and religion.

The propaganda was effective, but organizationally the Bergson Group had little success. It never became a membership movement and had branches only in New York, Philadelphia, Chicago and California. Its support came primarily from a small group of Jews of European origin, some second- and third-generation assimilated Jews, and a spattering of disgruntled Yiddishists and Zionist "dropouts." The assimilated Jews—few over the age of 40—had previously participated in liberal or radical activities, but never in organized Jewish life.[5] Hitler managed to undermine their self-confidence, however, as he lumped all Jews together; given an attractive cause, their Jewishness now came to the fore. The outstanding figure among these new adherents to the Bergson Group was probably Ben Hecht, playwright and Hollywood scriptwriter, who became a major spokesman for the Irgun in America. Such Jews sought some kind of expression for their newfound identification that would not necessitate involvement in the petty, uninspiring manifestations of Jewish organizational life. In working for the Bergson Group, these newly awakened Jews saw themselves—loyal Americans—as proclaiming their right to stand up and fight back.

The non-Jews who signed up as supporters were courted for the prestige they lent. During the 1940s Pierre van Paassen, who for a time headed the Jewish Army Committee, was a highly popular intellectual and writer. His name alone served as a rallying point for several of his fellow writers. William Green (head of the AFL), Philip Murray (head of the CIO), the theologian Reinhold Niebuhr, the popular radio commentator Lowell Thomas, all announced their support of the Jewish Army Committee, as did several important congressmen. People of this calibre were capable of keeping the issue before the public in the press and radio, within the organized trade union movements and even in the halls of Congress. A congressman with a large Jewish constituency would read an impassioned statement (usually prepared by one of the Irgun's members) in support of the Jewish army, into the Congressional Record, after which thousands of copies would be distributed throughout the country.

With characteristic boldness, the "Committee" took over an ambassadorial residence in Washington D.C. initially called the "Jewish Army House" and then the "Hebrew Embassy." The group made its first public appearance on the 4th of December, 1941, at a large assembly convened in Washington. The chairman declared as the objective the mobilization of a Jewish army of 200,000 people to be recruited from Palestine's Jewish community and from among Jewish refugees who had escaped to England and the Soviet Union. The army would be legally established, with its own flag and insignia, and would fight alongside the soldiers of the Allied forces. Under the High Command of the Allied powers, the Jewish force would have the same rights as the men from Nazi-occupied countries who were fighting in the armies of the free world. Just a few days after this meeting America entered the war, which meant that such propaganda no longer exposed the Jewish Army Committee to accusations of warmongering. On the 5th of January, 1942, *The New York Times* carried a full-page advertisement under the banner headline: "Jews fight for the right to fight!" On May 13, 1942, a nationwide conference was held in New York and throughout the year there were mass meetings, press conferences, sessions with military and governmental personnel, and more advertisements in the press.

Several things combined to create the impression of highly successful activity, although actual success was achieved almost exclusively on the propaganda level. As a small, homogeneous group of young people solely and fanatically devoted to furthering their cause, the Bergson Group had a great advantage over the leaders of other Jewish and Zionist bodies, for whom public activity was usually secondary to considerations of job and family. The Irgun people lived modestly and were single-mindedly devoted to their cause. Furthermore, they were not subordinate to any higher authority; their decisions could be vetoed only by their acknowledged leader—Peter Bergson.

On the whole, the group acted on the basis of consensus; there were times, however, when the commander, Bergson, would summarize a discussion and then state that he had decided on a different course of action than the one proposed by the rest . . . and his decision was accepted as final.

The Irgun emissaries were able to make the impact they did on the American public primarily because the inactivity of the recognized Jewish and Zionist organizations had created a void. That void, which the Bergson Group seemed to fill, was painfully apparent from 1940 to 1943, when the leadership of American Jewry seemed to have no answer to the harrowing plight of Europe's Jews. The Bergson Group did seem to have answers, to offer direction and focus. The very idea of a Jewish army had a satisfying ring to militancy about it, but at the same time was unlikely to hurt Britain or the United States. It was therefore acceptable to both Jews and non-Jews.

The Bergson Group and Organized Zionism

Bergson and the Jewish Army Committee began to appear more and more frequently on the agenda of the Zionist Emergency Committee. In May 1941, Bergson approached Stephen Wise and asked for a cessation of organized Zionism's attacks against the Irgun. Wise agreed on condition that the Irgun accept the discipline of the authorized Zionist institutions, a condition which Bergson, of course, would not accept. At the same time, demands for unified action were becoming more insistent on the part of rank-and-file Zionists, as they found it hard to comprehend the issues that kept the two groups apart. A few branches of the ZOA even passed resolutions calling for the formation of a Jewish army. Neumann and Weisgal in particular felt that some form of cooperation would have to be found to avoid serious internal disarray. Weisgal convinced Nachum Goldmann, Lipsky and Weizmann, as described in the previous chapter, to formulate the draft of an agreement, but although Weizmann had already initiated it, it was scrapped at the insistence of Ben-Gurion and the Hadassah leadership. For Ben-Gurion the Jewish army was central to the concept of Jewish sovereignty; it was therefore inconceivable for him to leave it in the hands of the Irgun members who, in his opinion, had "removed themselves from the fold of the nation."

Meyer Weisgal and Judge Levinthal decided nevertheless to continue to negotiate with the Jewish Army Committee, but in the name of the ZOA. At the same time, the Emergency Committee began, with some hesitancy, to publicize the idea of a Jewish fighting force. For the first time it printed full-page newspaper advertisements, and in February of 1942 it held a mass meeting in New York's Carnegie Hall to call for the formation of a Jewish army. Neither the Emergency Committee nor the Bergson Group brought about the establishment of a Jewish army in 1942, but there is little doubt that the aggressive militancy of the Committee for the Jewish Army galvanized the organized Zionist movement into undertaking activities it might otherwise never have considered. The Bersgon Group's dynamic assault on public opinion sharply underscored the ineffectivity of the Emergency Committee and the danger that it was losing the support of America's Jewish masses. The heads of the Emergency Committee realized that only by organizing for bold political action could it counteract the powerful Irgun propaganda machine and, more important, transform the Biltmore program into a political fact.

American Council for Judaism

At just about the same time, the Zionists came under attack from another quarter altogether. Certain elements of the Reform movement began to exhibit pro-Zionist tendencies; this quickly elicited protest from a rather large group of Reform rabbis who organized to counteract the trend. Early in June 1942, ninety rabbis met in Atlantic City to crystallize a non-Zionist program for Reform Jewry.[6] Following the lead of the rabid anti-Zionist, Rabbi Morris Lazaron of Baltimore, the Zionist movement and the idea of a Jewish army were devastatingly attacked. The rabbis issued a proclamation repudiating Zionism and political nationalism, claiming that Judaism's role in the world was an exclusively spiritual one.

No organized Jewish group in America had ever before publicly proclaimed an anti-Zionist stand, although individuals—even some important ones—had done so. In the autumn of 1942, those Reform rabbis were the moving spirit behind the formation of the American Council for Judaism, which had as its objective the consolidation of anti-Zionist Jewish sentiment. In other words, they declared war on Zionism, just when general frustration was building up over the inability to help Jews abroad. They gathered a coterie of well-known anti-Zionists such as Lessing Rosenwald, Chairman of the Board of Directors of Sears-Roebuck, and C. H. Sulzburger, publisher of *The New York Times*. With funds made available by some of its affluent supporters, the American Council for Judaism launched a concerted attack on the Zionists. It published articles and pamphlets, sent letters to influential individuals, chose anti-Zionist speakers to address gatherings of non-Jews, and even began to organize local branches. Stressing Judaism's spiritual-religious role, the Council described the Zionist movement as unpatriotic in that it demanded dual loyalty from its adherents. In time they rather overplayed their hand and forfeited their credibility in the eyes of the public (among other things, they claimed that the Zionists raised money for use of a foreign government and interpreted the Zionist ideology to mean that all American Jews would be expected to move to Palestine). Their hopes to attract four million American Jews were never realized; their constituency remained primarily rabbis and wealthy Jews of German extraction.

But the Council for Judaism, too, was an inadvertent catalyst for American Zionism and roused a fighting spirit on the part of the Emergency Committee. Objectively speaking, the Council had chosen an inauspicious moment for recruiting anti-Zionist sentiment. American Jewry was awakening to the magnitude of the holocaust in Europe, and the Zionists realized that the time had come to crush their Jewish adversaries. They published sharply worded articles[7] and a militant pro-Zionist statement signed by almost a thousand Conservative, Reform and Orthodox rabbis from all parts of the country. They intentionally fostered internal polarization by declaring the Zionists to be "whole, positive Jews," and the members of the Council for Judaism "marginal, minimal Jews." Essentially the effect was positive in that Jews were compelled to take a stand, to clarify their identification. In conjunction with the Zionist parties, the Emergency Committee formed regional public relations committees with the clearly defined objective of fighting the anti-Zionist enemy from within.

In the course of preparing bulletins, arranging public meetings, rallying local pro-Zionist rabbis and engaging in other practical activities in the various communities, Zionism went beyond the usual bounds of fund-raising and preaching to the converted: large segments of the "silent Jewish majority" were drawn into the fray. By September of 1943, over half the rabbis who had helped found the Council for Judaism had abandoned it, and the Council itself remained an insignificant splinter group.

Impact of the Holocaust

Although by 1942 the desperate situation of the Jews in Europe was becoming known, Zionist leaders continued to believe that interim solutions of a temporary nature would necessarily detract from the cardinal principle of the centrality of Palestine. Thus, to a great extent the struggle over the fate of Europe's persecuted Jews was left in the hands of the American and the World Jewish Congress. Because Stephen S. Wise and Nachum Goldmann were leading figures in both organizations, as well as recognized Zionist leaders, a strange dichotomy was created. While the congresses undertook sporadic rescue activities, the Zionist movement ignored short-term programs and devoted itself to building and strengthening the national home. Dr. Wise and

Dr. Goldmann both served Jewry faithfully in this dual capacity, but were often forced to seek ways of reconciling the organizations they headed.

The Emergency Committee continued to concentrate on "Zionist affairs." When the World Jewish Congress organized a mass protest meeting in New York's Madison Square Garden on July 21, 1942, it was with some hesitation, and over the outright objection of the president of Hadassah, that the Emergency Committee decided to participate. In convincing the Zionists to take part, Dr. Wise felt it necessary to make it clear in advance that the meeting would not demand a Jewish army or a Jewish state, but would protest the atrocities against the masses of Jews in Central and Eastern Europe and demand that Great Britain and America take action to ensure that the Jews of Palestine would not meet a similar fate.[8]

As American Jewry learned more about what was happening to Jews in Europe, it began to press its representative organizations to "do something." The Irgun delegation, too, became even more vociferous, established an Emergency Committee to Save the Jewish People of Europe, and thereby increased the pressure for action. On 6 December, the Office Committee of the Emergency Committee met to discuss cables received from the London and Jerusalem offices of the Jewish Agency and from the Va'ad Leumi in Palestine. All the communications demanded urgent action to prevent the mass murder of Europe's Jews. There were specific requests that the Emergency Committee ask Roosevelt to warn Germany and other Axis countries that mass murder would elicit severe reprisals. Other requests were for help in evacuating children from Nazi-occupied areas to neutral countries, and others asked that representatives be sent to the occupied areas to discuss the rescue of children by the Red Cross. It was suggested that the Joint Distribution Committee and the World Jewish Congress be approached to send representatives to Stockholm and Istanbul to try to transfer children from the conquered territories. The Jewish Agency Executive in Jerusalem asked for the Emergency Committee's support in an appeal to Roosevelt, Churchill, Stalin and Smuts to make every effort to rescue Jewish children and to suggest that Jews be exchanged for German civilian prisoners.

The cables clearly reflected the desperation and helplessness of those who sent them; unfortunately, those receiving them in America were no less confused and helpless. It was finally decided that a subcommittee of the Emergency Committee together with the American Jewish Congress would decide within 48 hours on a program of action in which other Jewish and non-Jewish organizations would be asked to participate. It was agreed to approach the Joint, the National Council of Jewish Women, and the US Committee for Care of European Children headed by Marshall Field—Eleanor Roosevelt was its honorary president. In the name of the Emergency Committee, Meyer Weisgal was asked to prepare the program of action. Weisgal's point of departure was that America had gone to war with the Axis powers to wipe out Nazism and everything it advocated and represented. It was therefore not enough to stress the fact that the Jews were suffering more than any other people in Occupied Europe: America must be made to realize that the Jews were victims of genocide because of their abnormal position as a nation without a homeland. At the same time, the general public must be made aware of the one and only solution—Palestine as a Jewish homeland—that would make a recurrence of genocide impossible. As to the present, his conclusion was that very little of practical value could be done to help the Jews in Hitler's hands apart from giving Jews everywhere the hope that their position would be normalized after the war.

In view of the foregoing, Weisgal proposed a program for practical Zionist action, adequately funded and with an efficient apparatus for implementation. Non-Jewish America had to be convinced that the overwhelming majority of Jews in the United States supported the concept of a Jewish commonwealth as the one constructive solution to the Jewish problem, and that an Allied victory—although a sine qua non—was just the first step on the way to a solution. The core of Weisgal's program was the proposal to call a conference at which representatives of all American Jewry would confirm their overwhelming support of Zionism's postwar program.

Thus, the Zionist movement adopted a general strategy aimed at gaining maximum support in the United States for a postwar Jewish state in Palestine. Its perception was that the opportune time for this would materialize right after the war. The world international order would be fluid and the status of Palestine again come under consideration. At that point the Zionist movement should be ready to wield all the influence it could muster for the diplomatic struggle on postwar political settlements. The early reports on mass atrocities in Europe only fortified this trend. The more American Zionists learned about the assembly line mass murders, the more they worked for the realization of the postwar goal of Jewish statehood.[9]

The American Jewish Conference

In January 1943, with the approval of Dr. Weizmann and the Zionist leaders, Henry Monsky, president of B'nai B'rith, called a meeting of representatives of 34 Jewish organizations. All but two of the organizations agreed to participate in an overall Jewish conference to formulate a program of action to meet Jewry's postwar needs. This was Monsky's own personal initiative, inspired by his resentment at the bilateral negotiations between the Zionists and the American Jewish Committee—which had, in fact, broken down; a desire to show B'nai B'rith's lead in creating a united American Jewish delegation to present Jewish demands at a forthcoming peace conference; and his own Zionist convictions on the need to establish a Jewish commonwealth. Monsky's position as head of one of the largest Jewish organizations in America—which was considered neutral on ideological issues, including that of political Zionism—ensured that the initiative was favorably received by the majority of

Jewish communal leaders, as well as by their Zionist counterparts. For the latter it came as a windfall, resolving the question of how to convene an American Jewish assembly to marshal the Jewish community at large (including the non-Zionist organizations) behind the Biltmore platform.[10]

Following initial criticism of the Monsky initiative, the Emergency Committee determined to transform the projected conference into a forum expressing the overwhelming support of American Jewry for the Biltmore program. After deciding that the conference would be held at the Waldorf Astoria in New York from 29 August to 2 September, 1943, the organizing committee determined the constituency: 500 delegates, 375 of whom would be elected directly by a regional conference of local Jewish communities and the remainder appointed by national organizations.[11]

The Zionists stressed the democratic nature of the conference in the hope of publicly discrediting anti-Zionist forces by showing them to be in the minority. By refusing to participate in the conference, a body such as the American Council for Judaism exposed itself to the scorn and castigation of the Yiddish and Ango-Jewish press. Attributing great importance to the results of the elections for conference delegates, the Emergency Committee established a national coordinating committee to work for the Zionist candidates. The strategy proved extremely effective: 340 of the 379 elected delegates were from the Zionist parties, and their influence was even more pervasive as the delegates formed "blocs" based on organizational, religious or social affiliation and the Zionist presence in most of the blocs was conspicuous.[12]

As planned, the American Jewish Conference held its first session on the 29th of August at the Waldorf Astoria Hotel in New York, and it soon became apparent that Palestine was the only issue over which there was disagreement. Judge Joseph M. Proskauer of the American Jewish Committee expressed the hope that the conference would deal only with issues on which consensus could be reached. As an example of such an issue, he spoke of the pioneering work being done in Palestine—for which there was massive Jewish support. The content of the first speech delivered by a Zionist, Stephen Wise, was more surprising. Dr. Wise refrained from mentioning the Jewish commonwealth, limiting himself to a denunciation of the British White Paper policy.[13] Another non-Zionist, Israel Goldberg of the Jewish Labor Committee, further strengthened the "moderate" line by emphasizing the need to permit Jewish immigration into Palestine, naturally saying nothing about the commonwealth. All the speakers emphasized their agreement on the need to annul the White Paper and open the gates of Palestine.[14]

The second evening of the conference was devoted to Palestine, but then, too, the Zionist speakers did not mention the Biltmore program or the commonwealth. Delegates began to suspect that their leading spokesmen might have agreed to refrain from explicit mention of the Zionist program in return for non-Zionist support of the demand that the British open the gates of Palestine to Jewish immigration. And indeed, some time before, Wise, Lipsky,

Nachum Goldmann and Meyer Weisgal had come to the conclusion that rather than alienate the American Jewish Committee entirely, it was preferable to seek consensus on several principles. They were certain that in the future the Standing Committee, to be formed on the basis of relative delegate strength at the conference, would deal with the Palestine issue as the Zionists wished. Pursuant to this compromise Weisgal, general factotum of the conference, had excluded Abba Hillel Silver, who was known as leader of the "maximalist" Zionists, from the list of speakers. At the insistence of Emanuel Neumann, and after some internal party juggling, Silver was eventually asked to speak. His stirring pro-commonwealth address wrought a complete change in the conference atmosphere. The delegates were electrified, gave Silver a standing ovation, and their fervent expression of support determined the tenor of the resolution on Palestine.[15]

In his speech, Silver dismissed the "thick blanket of appeals to Jewish unity" as a ploy to evade the basic problem—Jewish national homelessness. This was the "principal source of our millenial tragedy," from the times of the dispersion until the current Nazi onslaught. In Silver's view, the only solution was to normalize the political status of the Jewish people by giving them an autonomous base in their national and historic home.[16]

Regarding the question of immigration to Palestine as a means of rescue—an issue which could unite American Jewry—Silver declared that it could not constitute a viable option unless Jewish political rights to the country were recognized. "Our right to immigration in the last analysis is predicated upon the right to build the Jewish commonwealth in Palestine. They are interlinked and inseparable." It was demonstrated once again that for the great majority of Zionists, leaders and laymen alike, rescue and Palestine constituted a single, indivisible issue whose resolution lay in the creation of a Jewish common-wealth.

Even among the Zionists, however, there was some doubt about the wisdom of taking an unequivocal maximalist stand. Some of the ZOA representatives warned against eliciting adverse reactions from the British and American governments; there were also differences of opinion with respect to the exact interpretation of the term "commonwealth." Certain pro-Zionist rabbis called for moderation and compromise. Proskauer maintained that maximal demands played into the hands of the enemies of Zionism and therefore endangered both Palestine and world Jewry. He made a plea for Jewish unity as the need of the hour, but most of those who took the floor supported the Zionist stand as expressed in the Biltmore program. In a tremendous wave of enthusiasm, the pro-commonwealth resolution was passed two days later by 480 votes, with 16 abstaining and the four American Jewish Committee delegates voting against. It is misleading to see this as a "conspiracy" to force the Zionist program on American Jewry: the Zionists found a receptive ear for their proposals. This was another stage in the mutual process of "Zionizing" American Jewry on the one hand, and Americanizing Zionism on the other.

The resolution catapulted the Zionist movement to the forefront of American Jewry. A democratic roll call of representatives of the Jews of the United States had transformed Zionism from a marginal to a central phenomenon in Jewish life. Within the Zionist movement itself the maximalist approach was thereby reinforced and the commonwealth was legitimized as the political goal of all efforts. The first stage of the Biltmore program had thus been accomplished: American Jewry had been won over. It now remained for the Zionist movement to convince the American people and the American government to support the program.

The American Jewish Conference was disbanded after choosing an Interim Committee (the projected Standing Committee) consisting of 51 members in addition to electing Israel Goldstein (president of the ZOA), Stephen Wise (chairman of the Emergency Committee) and Henry Monsky (president of B'nai B'rith) as co-chairmen.

Rescue versus a Jewish Commonwealth?

Both contemporary and present-day studies castigate the Zionist leadership in general, and Abba Hillel Silver in particular, for paying too high a price for the Zionist victory. Some sectors of American Jewry—Zionists among them—claimed that Silver and his supporters had sabotaged a unique opportunity for unifying American Jewry. Even before the conference convened, the Union of Orthodox Rabbis and Agudath Israel withdrew on grounds of insufficient representation. A month after the conference had taken place, the American Jewish Committee resigned from the Standing Committee. Other non-Zionist organizations such as the (Reform) Union of American Hebrew Congregations, the Jewish Labor Committee, and the National Council of Jewish Women harbored reservations about the Palestine resolution, or disapproved of it outright.[17]

The American Jewish Conference did not develop into a "democratic" umbrella organization for American Jewry. In view of the community's character and conflicting ideologies, it cannot be stated with any certainty that the conference would ever have taken on this role. By many it was regarded at best as a loose, ad hoc, coordinating body, and that was the way they wanted it to remain. Silver and his supporters were aware that these views were prevalent, particularly among the non-Zionists, and he criticized his opponents sharply for fortifying themselves behind what he called "a wall of philanthropy and *shtadlanut.*" "Are we forever to live a homeless people on the world's crumbs of sympathy, in need of defenders, forever doomed to thoughts of refugees and relief?"[18] Silver negated any sort of unity which would mean forfeiting Jewish statehood for the sake of "peace" with the non-Zionists.[19] "If I agree with certain people," he declared, "that is unity. If I ask them to agree with me, that is disunity."[20] He approached the delegates over the heads of their organizations, and succeeded in enlisting their support. The split in the community led eventually to widespread support for a Jewish state.

Another, far more serious charge has been leveled against Silver and his circle: Zionist emphasis on the struggle for a Jewish commonwealth effectively stymied any chance of creating a united American Jewish front for the rescue of European Jewry. Although, with the logic of hindsight, there may appear to be some truth to this claim, it would be difficult, given the American Jewish organizational maze, to imagine the American Jewish Committee (AJC) or the National Council of Jewish Women acting, even for the purposes of rescue, in the unorthodox and "irresponsible" manner of the "Bergson boys" or even Silver himself. Recently, an even graver issue has been raised: If the American Zionists could harness Jewish efforts nationwide to transform the American Zionist Emergency Council after August 1943 into a political and public relations device of an effectiveness seldom surpassed in American influence group politics, why then was a comparable drive for the rescue of European Jewry never attempted?

As demonstrated above,[21] the American Zionist leadership, as early as the end of 1942, concluded that hopes for any immediate rescue of European Jewry were unrealistic. The Jews were trapped between the murderous Nazi persecution on the one hand, and Allied apathy and reluctance to assist them on the other. At this stage, American Zionists did not differentiate greatly between the twin targets of rescue and Jewish statehood.[22] These had merged into one Jewish national goal: a Jewish commonwealth in Palestine which could serve as a guarantee that the tragic events of the period would never recur. As for the various opportunities for rescue that occurred during the following years, the Zionist movement regarded them as falling within the province of its "twin" organization—the AJC, which had been established by Zionists in the 1920s as the main instrument for political campaigning on behalf of persecuted Jews outside Palestine, and later served as the national Jewish response to the Nazi peril. The AJC's activities were not always approved of by the Zionist movement, and more than once there was conflict between the two bodies.

Thus, throughout the 1920s, 1930s and 1940s, there evolved a duality within American Zionism. On the other hand, the movement did not cooperate in efforts to alleviate the condition of Jews outside Palestine but concentrated solely on the upbuilding and strengthening of the Jewish national home and—after the Biltmore Conference—on the political battle for a postwar Jewish commonwealth. At the same time, however, the AJC—and later the WJC—were engaged in combating antisemitism both within and outside the United States, and assisting persecuted Jews. The Zionist organizations were ipso facto part of the AJC and their leaders also headed the latter body. This duality found particular expression in the person of Stephen Wise, who himself served simultaneously as chairman of the AJC and the Emergency Committee for Zionist Affairs (ECZA). Wise insisted time and again that ECZA "limit itself to purely Zionist problems."[23]

Like most organized Jewry in the United States, the American Zionist leadership failed at times to measure up to the magnitude of the catastrophe and misread the signs where rescue was concerned.[24] Seemingly, it could not imagine that Jewish suffering at its apogee—mass murder—might rule out the possibility of realizing the Zionist solution to the "Jewish problem." On reading the documents of the period, one gains the impression that it was felt there would always be enough survivors to establish a Jewish commonwealth, which would guarantee that such a tragedy would never recur.[25] Once reliable news of the extermination process had been released in November 1942, some attempts were made to mobilize public opinion by mass protests, to lobby officials and to organize plans for rescue, but in the prevailing atmosphere, in which the war effort was regarded as the first priority, little was achieved. Many non-Jews received news of the Holocaust with disbelief. Roosevelt made sympathetic statements but refused to take any action.[26] Without any real power to change US policy, the American Zionist leadership, seeing events in Europe through the perception of Jewish history in the Diaspora, a chain encompassing two thousand years of hatred and murder, saw the only real solution in the creation of a Jewish state.[27] It regarded the two actions—rescue and the struggle for the Jewish commonwealth—as one. As Meyer Weisgal phrased it in his early report on rescue possibilities: "One flows from the other and there is no distinction between being Zionists and being Jews."[28] So every action taken in the direction of achieving a Jewish commonwealth was seen and understood as an act toward a solution for the Jews of Europe.

America Crystallizes its Middle East Policy

At this point it is necessary to return briefly to the period immediately preceding the conference. The publicity that accompanied the advance preparations projected the significance of the conference far beyond the Jewish community; it had important reverberations in American governmental circles. At first, there were quasi-official warnings against the idea of convening such an all-Jewish conference or, more specifically, against the adoption of "extremist" decisions on the subject of Palestine.

After America's entry into the war, all political questions became subordinate to military considerations. Britain's cardinal tenet that Arab goodwill was vital for the war effort was adopted wholly by the American War Department, and stated bluntly to the Zionists: The Arabs may not be reliable, but they are a power which must be appeased, and, terrible though this may be for the Zionists, they must "take it in good part." This principle continued to guide American and British military and political thinking throughout the war.

Early in 1943, a change had taken place in the Middle-East policy of the United States. Whereas previously America had been a "back-up" force in the area, assisting its allies logistically, the country now had direct military, economic and political interests there. When its army entered North Africa, the

United States all at once became a power in the world of Islam, with millions of Moslems in Morocco, Algiers and Tunisia under its rule.[29] Another focal point of American influence became the Trans-Iranian railway: more than 25,000 American soldiers and civilians were involved in transporting huge quantities of American equipment to the Soviet Union over this railway. Then there were the growing interests of the oil companies; after giving Ibn Saud a generous loan in 1943, the American government became a party to those interests. In addition, Saudi Arabia was the only non-belligerent country to receive equipment under the "lend-lease" agreement. In view of its burgeoning interests and responsibilities in the Middle East, America faced many new problems. Among the major ones were the national aspirations of the Arabs and, in this context, America's relations with her allies—France and Great Britain. In the same context the American government could no longer avoid taking a clear stand with regard to Palestine.

Of course, the most immediate and overriding interest was to win the war. The Middle East Supply Center, originally established by the British to coordinate distribution of military supplies, soon became the regional agency for distribution of American lend-lease equipment such as armored vehicles and planes, which were crucial for the victory at El Alamein. The United States began to exploit this to make further political inroads in the region. With respect to the national aspirations of the Arabs, the Americans formally adhered to the Wilsonian principle of the right of self-determination for all peoples, which meant that the Department of State and other American agencies were free to oppose British and French imperialism, at least in their informal relations with Arab leaders. On the spot, however, it was hard to implement this idealistic approach and the deeper the Americans penetrated the region, the more dependent they became on the policies and methods of the powers that had preceded them there. In North Africa, they supported the French colonial regime (even when it represented the Vichy government). In the Middle East, America depended on the policy set down by British statesmen and diplomats.

As to oil, at the beginning of 1943 there was widespread concern over the increasingly popular theory that America's oil reserves were dwindling dangerously. That spring, under the direct order of President Roosevelt, an international conference was called to discuss the problem. As a result, the United States formed the Petroleum Reserve Corporation,[30] the above-mentioned loan and lend-lease were arranged for Saudi Arabia and a permanent American minister was posted to Jedda.

In the past, the inconsistencies of American policy in the Middle East as a whole, and in Palestine in particular, had often seemed due to internal pressures rather than to any pre-planned foreign policy. But now, just as political Zionism was becoming a factor in the United States, this growing American interest in the Middle East reinforced the consistent policy of the State Department that had always viewed Zionism as a political danger. The rise of American prestige in Saudi Arabia, together with the growing national consensus that its oil was a vital national interest, led the State Department to discourage British attempts to arrange a "deal" between the Zionists and Ibn Saud in December 1942.[31]

Ethnic groups in America had often attempted to exert political pressure, particularly during wartime, to further the national aims of their countries of origin. Trying to stave off pressure from the Jews, the State Department made good use of the Council for Judaism's claim that the Jews were not a nation, and that the Zionists represented only a small fraction of Jewry. The British did their part: with little pretense at subtlety, they made several outright attempts to "balance"—in other words, to counteract—Zionist propaganda in America.

Toward the end of 1941, shortly before America entered the war, Palestine's High Commissioner, Harold MacMichael, and the British Foreign Office transmitted a memo to the American Department of State that included the following statement:

> Viewed from certain aspects, the industry and powers of organization displayed by the Jews in bringing the political structure of the community in Palestine to its present highly elaborate form induce a feeling of admiration. Nevertheless the effort as a whole cannot be cleared of the charge that it has been misdirected to the creation of a national-socialist state [sic!] rather than a national home. Those who direct Zionist policy ignore everything that is not consistent with their own ideas and plans; and to realize these ideals and plans they adopt dangerous means and measures.[32]

After America entered the war, the British changed their line and claimed that the Zionists were sabotaging the war effort. In October 1942, Sir Ronald Campbell, minister at the British embassy in Washington, informed Under-Secretary of State Sumner Welles that Jewish "extremists" were trying to buy arms for use against the British. The British government encouraged the Arabs to launch an anti-Zionist campaign in the United States to neutralize the impact of the Zionists. Ambassador Halifax suggested asking the government of Iraq to activate its embassy in Washington for the same purpose. A similar suggestion was made to the Saudi government, as recorded in Cordell Hull's memoirs.[33] Freya Stark, a renowned archaeologist and "Arabist," a kind of "Freya of Arabia" who had lived with the Bedouin and studied their customs, agreed to clarify the British Foreign Office position with newspaper editors and senators. She also tried to convince non-Zionist and anti-Zionist Jews to join the British in their fight against Zionist aspirations, even suggesting that they formulate an alternative proposal for settling Jews outside of Palestine.[34]

American reports from the Office of War Information in Cairo[35] and from Beirut indicated that the indigenous population of the Middle East was disturbed by what was considered America's pro-Zionist tendency and its implications for postwar settlements. Disenchanted as they were with the

British and the French, the people of the region were doubly interested in America's postwar plans. These and other reports gave the British a basis for accusing the Americans of exacerbating the problem of Palestine; the United States accused British agents of spreading the word that America was helping the Jews to take over the country.[36]

Such reports also encouraged the Mid-East section of the State Department to conclude that the President could now be convinced to agree to issue a declaration together with the British openly opposing the dissemination of wartime Zionist propaganda in the United States. The excuse for such a declaration would be the damage to the American war effort in the Arab and Moslem world that such propaganda could cause. When the Foreign Office and State Department learned of the plans for an American Jewish Conference which the Zionist movement hoped to use to further pressure the American government over the issue of Palestine, they feared serious repercussions.

The Anglo-American Declaration

Throughout the first half of 1943, representatives of the American government in the Middle East deluged the State Department—and through it President Roosevelt—with conflicting reports about the situation in Palestine. Harold B. Hoskins, a Lebanese-born American who had headed several special missions to the Middle East for the Office of Strategic Services, and also served as the State Department's liaison with the President and the joint chiefs of staff, tried to convince Roosevelt to take an unequivocal anti-Zionist stand. He claimed that the extremist demands of the Jews were undermining America's relations with the Arabs whose antagonism, he warned, would soon be uncontainable.

The President asked General Patrick Hurley (who was on his way to Iran) to send reports directly to the White House of talks he held with local leaders in Cairo and Palestine. After meeting with both Arab and Jewish leaders, Hurley reached the conclusion that there was no danger of confrontation until the war was over, but that "an eventual showdown is inevitable" unless extremism were checked.[37]

These reports of two on-the-spot observers are only a small sample of the divergent points of view that buffeted the President as he tried to clarify his own position. Finally, however, he reached a decision, and in June he approved the draft of a declaration on Palestine prepared by the Department of State. It closely reflected the views of Hoskins. America's ambassador to London then gave the draft to the British Foreign Minister, Anthony Eden, stressing that the time had come to put an end to this "serious distraction from the war effort." The declaration was drafted in the name of the United Nations and the plan was to have all the Allied powers announce the final version, as agreed upon by the Americans and the British.

The declaration read in part that as it is

> . . . undesirable that special viewpoints should be pressed while the war is
> in progress . . . the United Nations have taken note of public discussions
> and activities of political nature relating to Palestine and consider that it
> would be helpful to the war effort if these were to cease. Accordingly, the
> United Nations declare it to be their view that no decision altering the
> basic situation of Palestine should be considered until after the conclusion
> of the war. When the matter is considered, both Arabs and Jews should be
> fully consulted and their agreement sought.[38]

The British requested the addition of a clause to the effect that the British
government had ". . . no intention of permitting or acquiescing in any changes
brought about by force in the status of Palestine or the administration of the
country . . ." The clause was accepted by the Americans.

Roosevelt and Churchill approved the declaration and it was decided to
publish it simultaneously in London and Washington on the 27th of July.[39] But
as the date approached, it became apparent that trouble was brewing: the
Foreign Office in London received a cable from Halifax asking for a week's
delay, during which time efforts would be made to secure the support of the
War Department. He added that the Zionists in the United States already knew
about the declaration and were taking steps to prevent its publication.[40]

Indeed, at that very time, one of the most dramatic developments in the
history of American Zionism was under way. Utmost secrecy had surrounded
all discussion of the joint declaration until the beginning of July when Moshe
Shertok (Sharett), head of the Jewish Agency Political Department, was in
Cairo. From authoritative British sources, he had heard that His Majesty's
Government was about to issue a definitive statement on Palestine and he
immediately flew to Ankara. Turkey being neutral, he could transmit
information from there to the Jewish Agency Executive in London for
verification. The following week, a cable was sent to Stephen Wise in America,
alerting him to this new danger. Deeply concerned, Wise decided to broach the
subject with President Roosevelt, whom he was scheduled to see on 22 July. He
sent Dr. Weizmann an encouraging report of the meeting, although he still had
gnawing doubts. On the 23rd of July, he wrote to the President in a vein he had
never before used with the "chief":

> I cannot make it too clear . . . that any statement insisting upon or even
> urging avoidance of public discussion of claims and Jewish hopes in
> Palestine would evoke country-wide Jewish protest with reverberations
> throughout the English-speaking world.[41]

The Zionist leadership sought to clarify just what was happening. When
they approached Sumner Welles, he tried to reassure them by saying that he

had managed to prevent any statement from being issued which, of course, only increased their suspicions. Samuel Rosenman, Roosevelt's speech-writer and close assistant, gave the impression that the President had told Wise that a statement would be issued jointly with the British, but that from the Zionist point of view it would be innocuous. This was hardly reassuring, and Nachum Goldmann went to see Isaiah Berlin, observer on Jewish affairs at the British embassy in Washington. Berlin felt that if what Rosenman said was true, no protest should be forthcoming, as it would only annoy the President. Interpreting this as direct confirmation that a statement was indeed imminent, the Zionist leaders turned to the group of Jews who held influential positions in the capital: Ben Cohen, Felix Frankfurter and David Niles.[42]

At that point, the Current Affairs section of the State Department informed the press that a declaration about Palestine was being prepared. It was through this channel that Herbert Bayard Swope, correspondent and public relations man whose Jewishness had been awakened by the reports of the Holocaust in Europe, heard about the statement. Studying its contents, he came to the conclusion that it was extremely damaging to Jewry and he decided to inform both Felix Frankfurter and Bernard Baruch, renowned financial adviser to several American presidents. Swope, Frankfurter and Baruch met and agreed that in addition to all its other drawbacks, the proposed statement would foster antisemitism in the United States, and they decided to approach Henry Morgenthau Jr., Secretary of the Treasury. Much disturbed, Morgenthau promised to do his best to prevent publication of the declaration.[43]

Nachum Goldmann and Stephen Wise approached Morgenthau at about the same time; the day before the declaration was scheduled to be announced, it had become an open secret and was being opposed from several different directions at once. The combined pressure of Morgenthau, Swope and Rosenman was effective, and on the very day set for the announcement, a week's postponement was decided upon. Other factors also influenced the decision: Hull had been trying to elicit the support of the War Department, believing that if it declared Zionist propaganda a threat to the Allied war effort, a joint American–British declaration deferring discussion and solution of the Palestine problem until after the war would be more acceptable. When he realized that he could not elicit the War Department's unequivocal support since Stimson, the Secretary of War, regarded the military situation in the Middle East as relatively stable, Hull, too, had turned to Rosenman.[44]

Rosenman responded to the Zionist leaders primarily by trying to convince them to modify their tone. He asked Wise to try to put a stop to the abrasive propaganda of the Jewish Army Committee, which had published a full-page advertisement during Churchill's recent visit to Washington which read, "Mr. Churchill, drop the Mandate." On the 30th of July, the *New York Times* had published a statement by Moshe Shertok that caused great consternation in American military and intelligence circles. As Shertok headed the Political Department of the Jewish Agency, his statement that the Jews of Palestine were capable of "deeds of despair if driven to extremes of exasperation by a decision to persevere in what is to them a cruelly unjust policy" carried considerable weight. Rosenman now requested Wise and other leading Zionists to assure the President that such intransigent statements would not appear in the future. His third message from the State Department and the President was a request to cancel the projected American Jewish Conference.

Dr. Wise explained that he had no control over Bergson and the Irgun delegation and therefore could not guarantee cessation of their propaganda for a Jewish army. Nor could he undertake an obligation in the name of Moshe Shertok. With respect to the American Jewish Conference, however, something might be done; cancellation was unlikely, but it might be possible to tone down the tenor of the Palestine resolution. On 12 August, Wise and Goldmann brought the request that the Conference be cancelled to the Office Committee. It was turned down by an absolute majority of those present. Only Wise and Goldmann voted in favor, and they now had only one hope of demonstrating their good faith to leaders of the administration in return for the scrapping of the joint declaration: a non-militant statement with respect to Palestine.[45] As we have shown above, they made every attempt to uphold what they considered their end of the bargain. They were thwarted by the position taken by Silver and his supporters and by the brilliance with which Silver stated the case for militant Zionism. As a result of Wise's willingness to play down the demand for a Jewish state, Silver became convinced that he no longer had heart for the fight and decided to depose him as leader of American Zionism.[46]

There were even more far-reaching implications to the outcome of the struggle against the joint declaration. This was the first head-on clash between American Zionism and the government. It was shown convincingly that American Jewry, mobilized in support of Zionism, could win out over the President and the heads of America's governmental agencies.

Inadequacy of the Emergency Committee

The joint declaration, and the actions undertaken to avert its publication, had the effect of "shock treatment" on the American Zionist leadership and the Emergency Committee. Once again they realized how unprepared they were to deal effectively with a crisis; they still had no efficient mechanism with which to counter hostile political moves. The successful outcome of their encounter with officialdom could not be attributed to their own ability to act quickly and competently. It was due to newly awakened Jewish awareness on the part of assimilated Jews in high governmental positions and to the government's sensitivity to public opinion, particularly in a pre-election year. The Zionist leaders had acted individually, each exploiting his own prestige and utilizing his own contacts, but they had none of the power of an organized political influence group. Yet, this basic weakness notwithstanding, it had been shown quite clearly that when properly executed, an appeal to the goodwill of both

Jews and non-Jews in government and in the media could influence the direction of American policy. The leading Zionists thus became less fearful of confrontation with the government than they had been, and the "activist" stand, with Abba Hillel Silver as its outstanding advocate, was thereby vindicated.

The two lessons learned from the success of the struggle to prevent publication of the joint statement led to a complete overhauling of the Emergency Committee. Silver's remarkable performance at the American Jewish Conference presaged the major and most significant change that would be wrought.

During August of 1943, behind-the-scenes forces were set in motion to hasten the reorganization of the Emergency Committee. A group that included Emanuel Neumann, Meyer Weisgal and other active Zionists began, with Weizmann's approval, to look for ways of involving Silver more directly in the work of the Emergency Committee, as a first step toward revitalizing the entire American Zionist movement. At first he was suggested as a candidate for the presidency of the ZOA, which was to have its national convention in mid-September. In that capacity, were he to follow in Judge Levinthal's footsteps, he would almost automatically become chairman of the Emergency Committee's Office Committee.[47]

Silver himself was not very enthusiastic about the idea as he had little desire to become involved in the petty internal politics that plagued all the Zionist parties, and the ZOA in particular. He wanted to be in a position to deal with the tremendous challenges that faced all of Zionism and all of Jewry, and in his view this meant a complete reorganization of the Emergency Committee. There were also many in the ZOA leadership who recognized Silver's charismatic brilliance but felt that he would be a hard man to work with. They proposed Dr. Israel Goldstein, a less combative, less controversial, figure as candidate for president.

Just a few months earlier Dr. Wise, together with Louis Lipsky and Dr. Weizmann, had asked Silver to take a more active public role in the movement. Silver, therefore, was under the impression that Wise agreed with him about the need to reorganize the Emergency Committee and inject new life into the ZOA. On 10 February, Wise wrote to Weizmann, saying:

> I assume that you will make it clear to Dr. Silver how glad all of us would be if he were to take over the too onerous duties of the chairmanship of the Emergency Committee. He could do the work and do it exceedingly well, as all of us know. The work should come into the hands of a younger and stronger man—and he is the man . . .[48]

While Silver's supporters convinced him nevertheless to agree to be candidate for the ZOA presidency, Wise apparently realized that more was now at stake than just a revamping of the Emergency Committee: the question involved the very leadership of American Zionism, something Wise was not yet ready to relinquish. He saw the issue as a personal struggle for dominance between himself and Silver, and in August of 1943 wrote to Nachum Goldmann:

> I was perfectly willing to step out from the Chairmanship, but although Silver could hardly bring himself to believe it, there are still people in and outside the Zionist movement who, curiously enough, imagine that my name means something in American life. I shall show my fellow-Zionists that I am not to be shelved . . . that I will exert my authority as Chairman of the Emergency Committee, with Silver, of course, as cooperative Co-Chairman . . .[49]

Electioneering for Silver and Goldstein rose to fever pitch as the date of the convention approached. On 2 August, Wise called a small group of active Hadassah and ZOA members together, in the hope of averting a split at the convention. As it was generally known that Silver was not pressing for presidency of the ZOA, but was more interested in being given responsibility for Zionist political activity in America, they decided to negotiate with those who were pushing his candidacy. Promising in Dr. Goldstein's name that the movement's political activities would be run by Silver as head of the ZOA's Political Committee, the latter's supporters were asked to agree on a single candidate for president—Israel Goldstein.[50] Agreement was reached in three areas:

1. Personnel: it was confirmed that Dr. Silver would be called upon to lead political work, and Dr. Goldstein would be unanimously chosen as ZOA president.

2. Guidelines for political action were drawn up: the American Zionist movement would coordinate its work with that of the Jewish Agency Executive, which had full authority in questions of policy; the ZOA would cooperate with all other groups involved in political activities; and the necessary changes to expedite political work would be brought about by mutual agreement among all bodies involved in such work.

3. Practical implementation: it was agreed that Silver would be elected either chairman of the Emergency Committee or of its executive body, with responsibility for directing political activities. The ZOA convention would choose a seven-man Political Committee to determine its internal policies in the spheres of public relations and political activities, said committee to be authorized in emergency situations to give directives to ZOA members on the Emergency Committee and other bodies, without waiting for instructions from the movement's Executive Committee.

This agreement signaled a change in the political set-up of American Zionism and above all, it led to the reorganization of the Emergency Committee. It invested Silver with the leadership of Zionism's political activity, but even more important, it broke the stranglehold of the conservative leadership that had "muddled through," but had outlived its effectivity. Dr. Wise had no alternative but to "swallow" the agreement reached between his (and Dr. Goldstein's) supporters, and those who supported Silver. On the 9th of August, Silver was appointed as Dr. Wise's co-chairman on the Emergency Committee, and at the ZOA convention a "Zionist Proclamation on Political Action" was put through by the pro-Silver forces. It promised that steps would be taken to transform the Emergency Committee—with full ZOA support—into an effective political pressure group; it declared the independence of the Emergency Committee, promising the ZOA's financial support and its full cooperation in public relations.

On 26 August, the Emergency Committee plenum changed the name of the Office Committee to "Executive" Committee, thus creating room for two chairmen. Dr. Goldstein nominated Silver to be chairman of the Executive Committee; he was elected unanimously. So it came about that one day before the date on which the joint American–British declaration was to have been issued, and only a few days before the opening of the American Jewish Conference, Silver and the Zionist activists who supported him undertook to transform American Zionism into a body capable of mobilizing the Jews of the United States for the struggle to realize Zionism's declared aim—a Jewish commonwealth in Palestine. With his talent for leadership, strong convictions and powerful personality, Silver was indeed the right man to lead the Zionist movement into a new era.

Notes to Chapter 6

1. For policy in international relations, see D. Niv, *Battle for Freedom, The Irgun Zvai Leumi*, Tel Aviv, 1965 (Hebrew), from p. 120. Also see author's interview held on March 5, 1970 with Dr. Raphaeli-Hadani, who was the Irgun's emissary in the European countries. The text can be found in the Oral Documentation section of the Institute of Contemporary Jewry.
2. Author's interview with S. Merlin, June 8, 1978.
3. *New Palestine*, June 21, 1940.
4. Author's interview with Hillel Kook, March 17, 1971.
5. See Teller, *Strangers and Natives, op. cit.*, p. 203.
6. For description of preparations, see Halperin, *The Political World of American Zionism, op. cit.*, pp. 81–3.
7. For the effect on movements of conflict with rival groups see, for example, D. Truman, *The Governmental Process*, New York, 1951, p. 209; E. Hoffer, *The True Believer*, New York, 1958, p. 336; C. Wendell King, *Social Movements in the U.S.*, New York, 1956, p. 78.
8. Minutes of OCEC meeting, July 8, 1942.
9. Wyman, *The Abandonment of the Jews, op. cit.*, pp. 160f.; D. H. Shpiro, "American Zionist Leaders and the Rescue of European Jews—November–December 1942," *Yad Vashem Studies*, vol. XVI, Jerusalem, 1984, pp. 376–79; Halperin, *op cit.*, pp. 148, 220–21.
10. The international organizational causes which brought Monsky to convene the conference were clarified to the author by Bernard Postal, former National Public Relations Director of

B'nai B'rith, in his letter of September 28, 1976. See also M. Kaufman, *Non-Zionists in America, op. cit.*, pp. 84–104, and Halperin, *ibid.*, pp. 219f.

11. See "The American Jewish Conference, Its Organizations and Proceedings of the First Session" (AJCOP), New York, 1944.

12. Some non-Zionist organizations declared their support of the Biltmore program in advance. See Halperin, *op. cit.*

13. AJCOP, p. 74.

14. *Ibid.*, pp. 57–8, 67–76, 87–98; Halperin, *op. cit.*

15. For a description of the enthusiasm with which the commonwealth resolution was passed, see Carl Alpert in the *New Palestine* of September 10, 1943; letter from Goldmann to Shertok of September 16, 1943, CZA, S25/237; and report by Lourie to Lauterbach dated September 2, 1943, CZA, Z4/10207 IV.

16. AJCOP, *op. cit.*

17. Wyman, *op. cit.*, pp. 162–70.

18. *Ibid.*

19. Kaufman, *op. cit.*, pp. 98–102.

20. I. L. Kenen, *Israel's Defense Line, Her Friends and Foes in Washington*, Buffalo-New York, 1981, p. 13.

21. Wyman, *op. cit.*, pp. 170–2.

22. *Ibid.*, pp. 175f.

23. This started as early as February 1940 and continued throughout the war. See Shpiro, "American Zionist Leaders and the Rescue of European Jews," *op. cit.*

24. Penkower, *The Jews were Expendable, op. cit.*, pp. 144f.; Wyman, *op. cit.*, pp. 174–7.

25. Shpiro, "American Zionist Leaders and the Rescue of European Jews," *op. cit.*, pp. 378f.

26. Urofsky, *A Voice That Spoke for Justice, op. cit.*, pp. 319–25. Urofsky also discusses the controversy over Wise's reaction to the Riegner telegram and his supposed dependence on his personal relations with Roosevelt, binding him to the need for action. Urofsky concludes that Wise and the other Zionist leaders, were not silent, but they had no way of pressuring the government and possibly relied too much on Roosevelt's humanitarianism.

27. Wyman, *op. cit.*, pp. 174–7.

28. Shpiro, "American Zionist leaders and the Rescue of European Jews," *op. cit.*, pp. 378f.

29. P. Baram, *The Department of State in the Middle East 1919–1945*, Philadelphia, 1978, pp. 298f.

30. See B. Schwadron, *The Middle East Oil and the Great Powers*, Jerusalem, 1974, pp. 443–52.

31. Baram, *op. cit.*, pp. 260–8.

32. FO 371/31378 E2026, October 16, 1941.

33. Cordell Hull, *Memoirs*, New York, 1948, p. 1513.

34. F. Stark, *Dust in the Lion's Paw*, autobiography 1939–1946, London, 1961, p. 176.

35. Military Intelligence Division WDES, I. G. No. 3040 from G 2 USA FIME, April 4, 1943 (OSS Document No. 23057).

36. *Ibid.* A report dated March 15, 1943, quotes excerpts from the internal Haganah journal *Eshnav* in which high mandatory officials are accused of organizing protest demonstrations against both the United States and the Jews of Palestine; SDF 867 OL/1846.

37. For report of his meeting with Ben-Gurion, see minutes of Jewish Agency Executive, April 4, 1943. See also Pinkerton to Hull, April 17, 1943, FRUS, 1943, vol. 4, pp. 771f.

38. FRUS, 1943, vol. 4, p. 785.

39. Memorandum of Minister of Foreign Affairs to the Cabinet W P (43) June 26, 1943, CAB 66/38. Winant, July 2, 1943, FRUS, 1943, vol. 4, p. 800. The contents were sent to Kirk, American ambassador in Cairo, with instructions to distribute it immediately after official publication among all the diplomatic representations in the Middle East, in the hope it would allay the fears of the local population; FRUS Conferences, p. 678.

40. Halifax to Foreign Office, July 27, 1943, FO 371/35036 E4347.

41. Wise to Roosevelt, July 23, 1943 (Wise Papers).

42. See the recollections of Isaiah Berlin, "Zionist Politics in War-Time Washington: A Fragment of Personal Reminiscence," *The Yaacov Herzog Memorial Lecture*, delivered at the Hebrew University of Jerusalem, October 2, 1972. The official report dated August 9, 1943, is in FO 371/35037 E5043.

43. Isaiah Berlin's report, *ibid.*; see also the Morgenthau Diaries, FDRL, pp. 207–22.

44. Baram, *op. cit.*, p. 292.

45. See Weisgal's letter to Weizmann, August 13, 1943 (Weizmann Archives).

46. Urofsky, *A Voice That Spoke for Justice, op. cit.*, p. 339.

47. Neumann, *In the Arena, op. cit.*, p. 188, and author's interview with him; also see Weisgal's report to Weizmann dated August 11, 1943 (Weizmann Archives).

48. Wise's letter to Weizmann, February 10, 1943 (Wise Papers).

49. Wise's letter to Goldmann, August 4, 1943 (Wise Papers).

50. See Weisgal's report to Weizmann dated August 11, 1943, *op. cit.*, and record of Neumann–Boukstein conversation that took place on August 2, 1943 (Silver election file, Neumann Archives).

7

From Emergency Committee to Emergency Council

Jewish public opinion throughout the country must be mobilized for political action. Those who have the responsibility for formulating American foreign policy must be made to feel it.

ABBA HILLEL SILVER

Restructuring the Executive and the Plenum

AT THE same meeting at which the Emergency Committee decided to change its name to the "American Zionist Emergency Council," a new structure was suggested for both the Executive Committee and the plenum.[1] Silver's decisive approach was immediately apparent in the speed with which the proposed changes were implemented. Determined to transform American Zionism into a political influence group with the Emergency Council spearheading action and giving clear political direction, he hoped to restructure the council in such a way that it would rest on a secure foundation of public support.

To overcome the inefficiency and wasteful duplication of effort that had been caused by lack of professional personnel and vague definition of tasks, Dr. Silver suggested forming committees with clearly defined responsibilities and authority. Each committee was to be headed by a member of the Executive, and would include at least one representative of each of the Zionist parties that constituted the council. The committees were to hold regular meetings, would have full authority to initiate action based on directives issued by the Executive, and would have to report to the bi-weekly Executive Committee meetings. Fourteen such committees and departments were set up under professional direction. The full Emergency Council was enlarged to 26 members and the Executive to 12. In accordance with the internal agreement reached in the ZOA, Wise and Silver alternated as chairmen of the Executive Committee. The New York office was expanded and toward the end of 1943, a permanent office was opened in Washington.

PLATE 10.   The "Silver Team." From left to right: Leon Shapiro, Dr. Silver; Harold P. Manson; Abe Tuvim.

PLATE 11. Dr. Silver planning the Palestine Resolution together with the leaders of Congress. From left to right: Congressman McCormic, majority leader; Dr. Silver; Congressman Sol Bloom, chairman of the Foreign Affairs Committee; Congressman Martin, minority leader.

PLATE 12.   The AZEC delegation to the Democratic Convention in Chicago. First row from left to right: Leo Sac, Dr. Israel Goldstein, Dr. S. Wise, Herman Shulman. Second row: Harold P. Manson, Elihu D. Stone.

The following committees were set up: Community Contacts, American Palestine Committee, Christian Clergy, Labor Relations, Mobilization of Intellectuals, American Jewish Religious Forces, Research, Publications, Press and Radio, Special Services and Events, Contact with Postwar Planning Groups, Postwar Political Planning, Economic Resources, Finance and Personnel.

The success of the reorganization depended upon the choice of appropriate personnel to direct the subcommittees. Much thought was therefore given to appointing people with the necessary experience and connections such as Meyer Weisgal to head the subcommittee for Special Events, Emanuel Neumann to head the committee dealing with Economic Resources, and Robert Szold to be in charge of Postwar Planning. Henry Montor, director of the United Palestine Appeal, became the administrative head of the Emergency Council.[2]

Lack of funds to finance activities had also plagued the Emergency Committee from its very first days. Convinced that soliciting for a special political fund such as Dr. Weizmann had proposed in the past was not the solution, Dr. Silver believed that it was entirely legitimate to allocate money for the Emergency Council from the national funds.[3] Just as these funds financed the Jewish Agency's political work in London and Palestine, so a given proportion of the monies collected in America should be allocated for political work in the United States. Silver put his considerable influence to bear on the ZOA and the national funds and secured a regular allocation. The Emergency Council's Executive Committee asked for 500,000 dollars to cover the year starting in October 1943. The request was approved, and from then on the Council was financially independent.[4]

Community Contacts

The committee responsible for Community Contacts was the instrument through which the Emergency Council hoped to achieve countrywide grassroots support. Initially, this meant forming a network of local Emergency Committees which would be autonomous with respect to other local bodies and would comply with directives from the national Emergency Council. Thus, they could react with speed and efficiency such as would have been impossible to achieve if they had had to work through bureaucratic organizational channels. Local committees were established not only in the larger metropolitan centers, but also in smaller places that were important by virtue of their influential representatives or senators.

Representatives of each Zionist party were on the committees, as well as individuals influential on the local scene. Some of the latter were not formally members of the Zionist movement, but wanted to take part in the struggle against the White Paper. For the sake of efficiency the committees were kept relatively small, usually not exceeding twelve members. Each committee had a chairman and a public relations director, although sometimes both positions were adequately filled by the same person.[5]

Particular importance was attached to forming direct contact with the senator or representative from the area, not only to create goodwill, but to increase the amount of information about Palestine, the British Mandate and Jewry that members of both houses of Congress would have available to them. This was sometimes done through individual contact and sometimes through large affairs organized in the congressman's honor.[6] Silver had a longer range object in mind than only preparing the ground for an eventual congressional resolution: he hoped to establish a permanent body of important congressmen who would not only vote for a pro-Zionist resolution, but would constitute a dependable support group, fully acquainted with the issues involved. Such a group had existed for many years in the British House of Commons. To this end, the various Emergency Committees had to develop good relations with their local political leaders, whether they repesented the opposition or the party in power. Silver tried to implement this two-party approach—a major innovation he introduced—on both a national and local scale.

The local committees also tried to have their municipal councils and state legislatures adopt pro-Zionist decisions, frequently formulated by the Emergency Council's subcommittee on Community Contacts. Activity in this direction was particularly intense at the end of 1943 and early in 1944, in the hope that the American Congress would take a stand against the White Paper's total ban on Jewish immigration into Palestine, scheduled to take effect on 31 March, 1944.[7]

Each local committee was instructed to create an apparatus capable of initiating rapid public reaction should the need arise. This was done primarily through special teams in each place that were prepared on short notice to organize the writing and sending of thousands of letters and telegrams to governmental officials and congressmen. Guidelines sent by the Community Contacts Committee in New York to all the local committees included several possible versions of texts to be used when speed was essential and various levels of public opinion had to be mobilized. Among those to whom the different versions were addressed were Christian clergymen, Jewish war veterans, trade union members, servicemen's wives or parents, etc.

In addition to maintaining constant contact with the various local Jewish organizations and societies, the committees in each place had to be prepared to distribute petitions and organize mass meetings, in coordination with efforts undertaken on a national scale. Thus, it would become apparent to the policy-makers in Washington that the Jewish reaction was not a random sporadic phenomenon but a planned, integrated effort supported by masses of Jews throughout the country.

As the long-range political goal was to demonstrate the support of the Jewish and non-Jewish public for the commonwealth idea, the Emergency Council prepared a ramified plan for sending information and educational material to the local Emergency Committees with carefully outlined directives for use. Information about British policy in Palestine, the dangers of the White Paper and the situation of European Jewry was made available to the individual Jew as well as to the Jewish religious and social institutions in each community. Discussions centering on these and other pertinent issues—including the futility of looking upon charitable and welfare activities as basic solutions to the problems European Jewish survivors would face after the war—were held in countless clubs and centers all over the United States. In other words, all resources were directed to educating the people to accept Zionism's solution to the Jewish problem.

Educational and propaganda activities among non-Jews required more thorough groundwork as vast sectors of the American urban and rural population had never even heard of the British Mandate, the White Paper or the Holocaust. It was particularly vital to reach the many agencies that dealt with postwar planning and problems of peace. The Foreign Policy Association and the Free World Association both had active local branches in many parts of the country, and they were the targets of much of the educational work done by the local Emergency Committees. Educational and propaganda activities were also aimed at labor organizations, church groups, press and radio.

In addition to political and educational tasks, the local committees were invested with responsibility for "vigilance." In other words, they were constantly on the lookout for hostile propaganda in the local media; the Community Contacts Committee in New York as well as the people on the spot prepared immediate rebuttal and refutation. The New York office also received copies of everything that appeared locally—whether favorable or unfavorable—that might be of interest of the Emergency Council at some future time.

The key role of the local Emergency Committees was constantly stressed, and the New York office supplied the local leadership with vast quantities of up-to-date information, guidelines for action and background material. On the other hand, the national Emergency Council gave the committees a free hand when it came to implementing decisions: the personal involvement, loyal commitment and independent initiative of the local leaders was unquestionable. A sampling of the subject-matter covered in the material sent to the Emergency Committees throughout the country in the course of 1943–44 includes:

1. Appropriate occasions for letters and wires to congressmen, and suggested texts;
2. Reprints of pro- and anti-Zionist articles, accompanied by suggestions for ways of reacting in each case;
3. Information about events in Palestine and the Middle East;
4. Copies of lectures and speeches by Wise and Silver;
5. Speeches by congressmen on Palestine and related subjects;
6. Suggested ways of counteracting the propaganda of the Bergson Group;

7. Distribution of informational material among policy-makers, in university libraries, to the press, etc.;

8. Background material for articles to be submitted to the local press;

9. Reports on the situation of European Jewry;

10. Plans for demonstrations, conferences, etc.;

11. Material to be used in preparation for confrontation with anti-Zionists; and

12. Suggested formulation for pro-Zionist resolutions in state legislatures.

Harry Shapiro, head of the Community Contacts Committee in New York, maintained close contact with the local Emergency Committees,[8] and every six months the heads of the local committees met to hear reports of political activities and to plan the work for the future. The number of local committees grew quickly. By January 1944 there were more than 200 of them already functioning, and a year later there were 380 committees in 76 states and localities.[9]

Spreading out into the communities and working through local personnel proved highly effective. Almost immediately after the committees were formed, they were asked to contact local congressmen in preparation for the proposal to pass a congressional resolution in support of the commonwealth. Responses came in from a wholesale grocer in South Dakota, from a department store in a town in Texas, from an insurance company in Atlanta, Georgia, from a lawyer in a small city in upstate New York, from an office equipment shop in a town in Arkansas, to mention only a few of the many hundreds who undertook to carry out this important work. Report after report arrived at the New York office of meetings with senators and representatives and the responses elicited.

This approach to the congressmen on home vacation by members of their local constituencies proved more effective than lobbying that took place in the capital itself.[10] Its significance would become clear during the period between 1944 and 1948 when the struggle for the Jewish state reached a climax. The issue of Palestine was finally brought to Congress for decision and 411 of the 535 legislators voted in favor of the establishment of the Jewish commonwealth. In addition, 39 of the 48 States and hundreds of municipal councils passed pro-Zionist decisions.

For the Zionism movement, these activities meant not only greatly expanded arenas for action, but important accretion of personnel. The circle of people engaged in intensive Zionist work grew from a few dozen at the beginning of 1943 to several thousand by the beginning of 1944.[11] Silver's contention that support for Zionism must be built from grass roots rather than imposed from above was more than vindicated by the success of the local Emergency Committees. The very first "guideline" issued to the local committees spelled out this approach:

We must keep in mind that all of our political activity has as its objective the mobilization of the public opinion of the American people. The government in Washington, if it is inclined to take a certain line of action with regard to the White Paper or Palestinian matters generally, must feel that there is a very substantial public opinion on this subject throughout the country. National political leaders follow the lead of their local constituencies. If they are made to feel that the American people is interested in this subject, that fact will play an important part in helping them to make up their own minds.[12]

Naturally, not all local activities were unmitigated success stories: there were problems—to mention only a few—of personnel, of vested organizational interests and divergent approaches to matters of principle. On the whole, however, the important educational and political work done within the Jewish and non-Jewish communities was the basis for effective political action on a national scale.

American Palestine Committee

As the local Emergency Committees gathered momentum, they infused new life into the American Palestine Committee, the non-Jewish support group that Emanuel Neumann had reconstituted in 1941. The APC was encouraged to form branches in local communities alongside the Emergency Committees. The Emergency Council appointed Herman Shulman as its liaison with the APC and allocated 55,000 dollars for the year starting October 1943.[13]

In the hope of interesting large numbers of non-Jews in the American Palestine Committee, 10,000 personalized letters were sent to selected individuals throughout the country. Only about ten percent of the recipients responded, but as field-workers began to function in a number of geographical areas, membership grew. By the end of 1944, 10,000 people were organized in 75 branches of the APC. On the whole, the APC membership came from the professional strata and people active in local or national public life. The local Emergency Committees shared technical and office facilities with APC branches, and were always ready to supply background material, speakers, informational brochures, etc. There was little danger of duplication of work since the APC appealed to segments of the population that were generally inaccessible to the Zionists. Geared to react swiftly on the political level, the local APC branches usually sought the support of the community's most influential non-Jews, thereby preparing the ground for Zionism's future struggle in the American political arena.

Under the able chairmanship of Senator Robert F. Wagner, the APC held annual dinners in Washington at which prominent Americans spoke on themes related to Jewry, the postwar world and Palestine. One of the committee's earliest activities was the preparation of a declaration entitled "The Common Purpose of Civilized Mankind" dated the 2nd of November, 1942—the 25th anniversary of the Balfour Declaration. Presented to President Roosevelt by Senator Wagner, the declaration, reconfirming support of the Jewish national home and signed by over two-thirds of the senators and close to 200 members of the House of Representatives, was distributed in many thousands of copies.[14]

Unlike the Emergency Council, the American Palestine Committee laid stress on immediate humanitarian concerns, looking upon the Jewish commonwealth as a future objective, a goal to be reached in the postwar world.

The Christian Clergy (Christian Council for Palestine)

The potential latent in the Christian Council for Palestine was not exploited until after the reorganization of the Emergency Council. Composed entirely of Christian clergymen and led by Professor Reinhold Niebuhr and Dr. Henry A. Atkinson, this group was formed as the focus for clerical support of Zionism's struggle. In addition, these men were best qualified to help counteract the classic Christian justification of Jewish distress as legitimate "punishment" for not having acknowledged Jesus as the messiah; they also could activate local clergymen to exert a pro-Zionist influence in their churches and in society as a whole.

When started in December 1942, the Christian Council had 400 members; by 1944 it already had a membership of 2,500. Like the American Palestine Committee, the Council distributed information bulletins based on material supplied by the Emergency Council, sent speakers to campuses, churches and social clubs throughout the country, and gave a staunch support to all efforts designed to help alleviate the distress of European Jewry. Although not all the clergymen advocated the creation of a Jewish commonwealth in Palestine, they unanimously agreed that the White Paper was an "inhuman document." They also believed that the Jews should not be prevented by administrative order from becoming a majority in Palestine if sufficient numbers of them went there and found ways of making their absorption economically feasible.

The Christian Council, too, thought more in humanitarian than in political terms, but was nonetheless an invaluable ally. The Emergency Council appointed Rabbi Philip Bernstein as its liaison with the council, and initially allocated 15,000 dollars for this work. To the world at large, however, this organization of Christian clergymen appeared entirely independent of official Zionist bodies, both on the local and the national scene.[15] This was essentially true. The pro-Zionist bent of the Christian Council, and the American Palestine Committee as well, was not artificially stimulated by the Zionists: the Emergency Council simply served as a conduit for channeling a tradition of pluralistic tolerance ingrained in American culture. Expressions of support were entirely sincere and were occasionally accompanied by spontaneous effusions of original thinking.

The mobilization of pro-Zionist Christians had a positive effect on certain Jews who had previously hesitated to come out publicly in support of Zionism.

This non-Jewish support reassured them; it made them less vulnerable to accusations of dual loyalties or un-American activities. Nevertheless, the extent of Christian endorsement should not be exaggerated: a large portion of liberal Protestant America remained hostile to the idea of Zionism.[16]

Labor Relations

The Emergency Council had to be rather circumspect in order to reach the Jewish workers, the majority of whom—some 500,000—were organized under the loose umbrella of the Jewish Labor Committee, which prided itself on maintaining neutrality and permitting membership of both Zionists and anti-Zionists. In the spring of 1944, to circumvent the Jewish Labor Committee, the Zionists formed the American Jewish Trade Union Committee for Palestine under the chairmanship of Max Zaritsky, well-known head of the United Hatters Union. Philip Murray, president of the CIO and William Green, president of the AFL, were chosen to serve as honorary chairmen of the new committee. The most important Jewish trade unions sent delegates to the founding conference, where they declared as their objective acquainting organized labor with American Jewry's Zionist aspirations. The committee had no formal bond with the Emergency Council: indeed, it declared openly that it would give the Zionist movement as much assistance as possible, but would not become part of it.

Both the AFL and the CIO were favorably disposed toward Zionism. During the 1930s and 1940s Zionist functions were about the only occasions at which their two leaders, Green and Murray were willing to appear on the same platform. At its national convention in 1944, the AFL went on record as favoring Zionist aspirations in Palestine; the following month the CIO national convention demanded that the American Congress approve a resolution to establish a Jewish commonwealth in Palestine. These pro-Zionist acts were almost as beneficial for the trade unions as for the Zionists as the labor movement was often rather isolated on the American scene; its alliance with a large and increasingly powerful sector of Jewry somewhat mitigated that isolation. For the Zionist movement, of course, the support of the unions was of inestimable importance.[17]

Mobilization of Intellectuals

The extremely difficult task of mobilizing intellectuals devolved upon a committee directed by Rabbi Milton Steinberg. Throughout the 1930s these elements had been dominated by the many and varied leftist circles, and it was not until World War II that Jewish intellectuals began to evince interest in Zionism as a solution to the Jewish problem. Rabbi Steinberg considered writers, journalists, radio commentators and the academic community as the committee's primary target groups. Persuading people in these professions was a long, slow process that required a good deal of intensive work on an individual basis. Small luncheons and teas were held by carefully selected hosts; a pro-Zionist literary "salon" met regularly at the home of a prominent author, Marvin Lowenthal. These efforts to make personal contact with influential intellectuals helped create a more positive climate in the arts, the media, and the academic world.[18]

Jewish Religious Forces

Chaired by Wolf Gold, this committee tried to involve the Orthodox religious community in Zionist activities. The Orthodox rabbis were organized in five vying factions; to the extent that they had lent support to pro-Palestine activities (this generalization excludes the membership of the Mizrachi), they had tended toward the Revisionists or the various front organizations of the Irgun.

The committee dealing with American Jewish religious forces attempted primarily to channel emotions roused by the plight of European Jewry into pro-Zionist activity. One of the outstanding projects undertaken by Rabbi Gold was the organization of an Orthodox Conference for Palestine and Rescue. Attended by over a thousand delegates representing several organizations from all parts of the country, the conference took place in January 1944. It passed resolutions condemning the White Paper and advocating the establishment of a Jewish commonwealth. Thus, with the conspicuous exception of Agudat Israel, the Orthodox community of the United States expressed its support of Zionism. When necessary it would mobilize hundreds of congregations, rabbis, women's organizations and, above all, its youth movement, "Young Israel," to engage in Zionist-inspired activities.[19]

Research Department

Perhaps the most important tools of any political influence group are the reports, studies, public opinion surveys, and other authoritative documentary material it can offer to sway the thinking of policy-makers. Aware of the abysmal ignorance about Palestine that prevailed in the American administration as well as in both houses of Congress, the Emergency Council established a Research Department to prepare scientifically accurate, basic information. The Lowdermilk Report discussed above was an excellent prototype for material to be issued by the Department.

Rose Jacobs, head of Hadassah's study group on Jewish–Arab relations, was appointed as chairman. Strategically this was a clever move, as Mrs. Jacobs brought with her the entire body of research, as well as some completed studies, that her Hadassah group had prepared. Dr. I. B. Berkson, who believed that the Research Department should be politically neutral, was actually its moving spirit. His long-range plan was to amass a series of monographs that would serve as the basis of Zionist claims at the peace conference which presumably would follow the war. His shorter-range objective was to prepare background material, position papers, etc., to bolster the Emergency Council's ongoing political activities. Of course, the Department's most important task was to supply a steady flow of material on the development of Zionist policy under the mandate, the progress being made in Palestine's Jewish community, and the situation in the Arab world.[20]

Publications

Louis Lipsky headed the Publications Committee, with Shulamit Schwartz-Nardi as its professional director. The committee's initial project was the publication of a monthly bulletin called *Palestine*. The first issue appeared in December 1943; its 15,000 copies were distributed to local Emergency Committees, the media, and governmental and academic circles. The editorial policy was to publish articles by internationally known Zionists such as Ben-Gurion and Weizmann, or by well-known non-Jews such as Dorothy Thompson, Freda Kirchwey, Richard Crossman, Sumner Welles and others of that calibre. The American Zionists who ordinarily wrote for such publications were rarely included, thereby making room for new names and new approaches.

The Emergency Council also subsidized publication of pro-Zionist books, among them *His Terrible Swift Sword* by Rev. Norman MacLean, *American Policy Toward Palestine* by Carl J. Friedrich of Harvard, and Pierre van Paassen's *The Forgotten Ally*. The Publications Committee issued reprints and pamphlets dealing with all aspects of Zionism.

At the end of 1943 and beginning of 1944, numerous articles were published attacking British policy in Palestine, among them Churchill's address to Parliament in May 1939 in which he impugned the White Paper. Reprints of sympathetic articles from the press were distributed as "Press Books," with essays on Palestine's Jewry's contribution to the war effort, its social and economic achievements, and the implications of the White Paper.[21]

Press and Radio

Directed by Harold Manson, this was one of the Emergency Council's most active and effective committees. The dependability of its material and the alacrity with which it reacted to events pertaining to Jewry and Zionism made it a preeminent informational source for both the Emergency Council and the media.

Most of the more responsible American papers reacted to news of the Holocaust in Europe with expressions of sympathy for the sufferings of the Jews. As a result of the efforts of the Committee on Press and Radio, this sympathy was expressed largely through castigation of Great Britain's White Paper policy and support for the establishment of a Jewish commonwealth. The

Jewish-owned *New York Times* was one of the few important daily papers that remained consistently anti-Zionist.

During the Second World War, the Yiddish press in America was still a force to be reckoned with. The 1944, one-third of all American Jewish families still subscribed to Yiddish newspapers, and it can be reasonably assumed that this reading public tended to be active in Jewish and Zionist affairs. Full-page advertisements began to appear in the largest English and Yiddish newspapers, containing statements by the Emergency Council, solicitations for signatures, and invitations to demonstrations and rallies.

Radio time was bought by the ZOA and the Emergency Council on 182 American and 50 Canadian stations. For 39 weeks in 1944, a series of 15-minute programs called "Palestine Speaks" were broadcast to 46 states by well-known figures from the entertainment world such as Eddie Cantor, Edward G. Robinson and Gene Kelly, who expressed their sympathy with Zionist objectives. The broadcasts, as well as the material prepared for the press, were beamed to different population strata; Jewish, non-Jewish, Zionist, non-Zionist, and even anti-Zionist.[22]

Special Services and Events

The Committee for Special Services and Events, directed by Abe Tuvim, was responsible for the organization of public rallies and received the largest allocation for the 1943–44 fiscal year—158,000 dollars. As Silver assumed an increasingly active role in the Emergency Council there was a marked improvement in the arrangements for mass meetings and protests, some of which drew 200,000 people.

This committee, together with those on research, publications and the media, constituted a formidable educational and propaganda apparatus that succeeded in reaching large sectors of the general, as well as Jewish, population. In addition, during 1943–44, the committees for Contacts with Postwar Planning Groups, Postwar Political Planning and Financial Problems prepared the groundwork for the intensive activities the Zionist movement would have to be ready to undertake as soon as the war ended.

The Washington Bureau

The American system of government almost seems designed to include pressure groups advocating every conceivable nuance of economic, political or social policy under consideration in any of the multifarious governmental agencies. Such groups function most effectively in the country's nerve center— Washington D.C. Since the establishment of the Emergency Committee for Zionist Affairs in 1939, many of its leaders had been aware that the lack of a Washington office seriously hampered Zionist political work. This lack was conspicuous during the intense activity initiated by the Zionists to block the joint declaration prepared by the American and British governments in the late summer of 1943.

Silver gave highest priority to a Washington Bureau, and immediately after assuming office in the Emergency Council, took steps to establish it. He visualized three main spheres of activity that would make the Bureau the pivot of a pro-Zionist lobby. The first sphere involved establishing contacts with governmental and congressional personnel to ensure the passage of a pro-Palestine resolution in Congress. Secondly, the Bureau would serve as a listening post and maintain contact with the many offices and agencies involved in planning Palestine's future. This would enable it to keep track of official positions and adjust its own activities accordingly. The Bureau's third major concern would be to counteract anti-Zionist propaganda emanating from certain British and Arab sources that were acquiring ever-increasing influence in Washington due to American oil interests in Saudi Arabia. The Bureau was manned by experienced Zionist leaders who were respected by both local Emergency Committees and important members of Congress; the staff was strengthened by a veteran Washington journalist who had thorough inside experience of the capital's political scene and put his knowledge at the disposal of the Zionist lobby.

The joint American–British declaration discussed above is an example of the work done by the Bureau, and one incident in that connection should be emphasized at this point. During the summer of 1943, local Emergency Committees began to canvass their congressmen for support. In this context, the editor of the *Detroit Jewish News* approached Illinois senator Arthur H. Vandenberg and was rebuffed. The senator wrote a detailed description of a discussion he had had with a colonel sent to him by the War Office to explain the damage support of Zionism would cause to America's Near-East interests. Learning that the "colonel" in question was Harold Hoskins, the editor immediately sent in a report that was transmitted to the Washington Bureau. In a matter of days, an intensive campaign was underway to expose Hoskins' true credentials: he was not a military man, nor had he been authorized by the War Department to approach congressional personnel; the pro-Arab bias of the material he was distributing had its source in specific economic interests (proof was furnished). It was also proven that during his visit to the Near East, he had refrained from contacting anyone representing Palestine's Jewish community or the Jewish Agency. His distortions and misrepresentations were analyzed and controverted. Exposed as an imposter and prevaricator, Hoskins lost credibility with many official circles in matters pertaining to the Near East.[23]

Another example of action taken by the Washington Bureau involved Senator J. W. Baily of North Carolina. When a local Emergency Committee in his state asked for his support, the senator responded with a nasty attack on American Jewry. The Bureau learned that a group called the Arab-American League for Democracy was distributing copies of Baily's answer to many senators and was even pressing to have it read into the Congressional Record.

Appeals to sympathetic senators elicited refutations and Baily himself backtracked, declaring that he was not really well acquainted with this delicate matter and had had no intention of creating dissension over a "religious" issue.

Like any other lobby, the Bureau's prime function was to further the interests of Zionism in the halls of Congress and the White House. This necessitated a ramified network of contacts with all levels of government, as well as constant telephone communication with Silver and others members of the Emergency Council in New York. The various tools for maintaining these contacts were given their ultimate test in 1944 in the course of the struggle described below to secure the passage of a pro-Zionist resolution in both houses of Congress.

The Political Front

Even before the Emergency Council was fully reorganized, preparations were being made to secure active support of the government. The first reports reaching New York from the Washington Bureau indicated that this would not be an easy task: key individuals in the capital were wary of taking an overt pro-Zionist stand for fear they would be accused of interfering with British policy or of adversely affecting military developments. Nevertheless, the new Emergency Council leadership was determined to try to elicit a clear statement of the United States government's position on the Palestine issue.

Between mid-October and mid-November of 1943, Dr. Silver made several trips to Washington. After meeting with the British ambassador as well as with influential members of the American government, he began to crystallize the direction political action should take.[24] He realized that President Roosevelt, influenced by British offical policy and by pro-Arab elements in the American State Department, was convinced that Palestine could not absorb a large Jewish immigration and therefore was not the solution to the problems the Jews would face after the war. Roosevelt also feared that an outbreak of Jewish–Arab violence would be detrimental to American interests. Silver learned, too, that the British were considering a "compromise" that would ostensibly ease the White Paper restrictions and thereby muzzle the Zionists. To offset such a possibility, American Zionism had to insist not only on the revocation of the White Paper policy but on the establishment of the Jewish commonwealth as well.

Dr. Silver's impression of what was going on behind the scenes in Washington was corroborated by a position paper prepared at President Roosevelt's request. It was intended to analyze the "new Zionism"—in other words, America's Zionist movement following the American Jewish Conference and its confirmation of the Biltmore program—in connection with the work being done by the President's committee for planning postwar foreign policy. Professor William Westerman of Columbia University, a known anti-Zionist, was asked to prepare it. Describing Zionism's attempt to unify American Jewry behind its new political slogan, Westerman exaggerated the importance of the American Council for Judaism and the American Jewish Committee, with the intention of proving that the Zionists did not truly represent the views of American Jewry.[25] He ruled out Palestine as a solution to the Jewish problem, declaring that the rapid growth of the Arab population made absorption of Jewish masses impossible. He also maintained that America, which did not restrict rescue efforts to the narrow parameters of political Zionism's plans for Palestine, was doing everything possible to help the European refugees.

Westerman's short-range proposals included temporary asylum in the United States and other "free" countries for those Jews who could escape from Europe. The long-range proposals were based on exclusively political considerations. Since 21 million Arabs were united in oposition to a Jewish state in Palestine, and since there was absolutely no proof that the majority of the Jews favored such a state, the administration should support the Jewish non-Zionists who advocated postwar rehabilitation of Jewish life in Europe; in everything connected with the complex problem of Jewish immigration into Palestine, the decisions of Great Britain, the mandatory power, must be respected. The Department of State should reconfirm its interpretation of the Balfour Declaration as favoring a national home for the Jews that would do nothing to prejudice the religious and civil rights of the country's non-Jewish residents. Westerman's final recommendation for America's Middle East policy was to flatly reject the demands of the Biltmore program that the Jewish Agency be given control of immigration and that a Jewish commonwealth be established in Palestine.[26]

This top secret document, intended only for the eyes of the highest policy-makers in the administration, was "leaked" to the Zionist leaders and confirmed their worst fears. Here was incontrovertible proof of the anti-Zionist approach being disseminated in and by the State Department. It was Silver's belief that this opposition should be met with a concerted onslaught on the part of the Zionists and that protest against the White Paper policy should be made in integral part of the commonwealth demand.

Silver had two reasons for proposing immediate political action, despite the revelation of hostility among government personnel. He was increasingly disturbed because certain elements that had supported the pro-Zionist resolution of the American Jewish Conference were consistently refraining from making their support public. And then, the Interim Committee formed to implement the conference resolutions was not functioning and the momentum engendered by the historic gathering was being lost.

On the 26th of November, 1943, the British Colonial Minister declared that 31,670 unused entry certificates to Palestine would remain valid for Jewish immigrants even after the expiration date fixed by the White Paper. Having eliminated the deadline, the British could now flaunt their humanitarian leniency, whereas in actual fact they had made it possible to extend the validity of the White Paper indefinitely. It was clear to Silver, Neumann and others that unless the full implications of the mandatory government's new tactics were exposed, public sympathy for militant Zionist action would be seriously diminished. Henry Montor, on the other hand, believed that an all-out struggle for Zionism's maximal political goals would create dissension and discord between the Zionists and non-Zionists. He therefore advocated stressing the more limited objectives—revocation of the White Paper and rescue of Jewish refugees.

Thus, once again, debate centered on two opposing viewpoints, one that advocated mobilizing Jewry around the minimalist common denominator—the struggle against the White Paper; the other that advocated inspiring Jewry to strive for the maximalist goal—the Jewish commonwealth. Silver's view prevailed and Henry Montor relinquished his post as administrative director of the Emergency Council. Local Emergency Committees also were affected by the decision favoring the maximalist position. Henceforth it would be impossible to include non-Zionists; only supporters of the Jewish Conference resolutions could be members of local Emergency Committees.[27]

* * *

Silver's political approach to Zionist work represented a new departure for large segments of Zionists and their sympathizers within the general Jewish and American public. From now on, American Zionism would not only attack Great Britain; it would have to engage in constant public confrontation with the American government and, above all, with the revered President. Compromise was impossible. Zionism would have to fight for America's support of a Jewish commonwealth in Palestine, and would have to convince the administration to insist that despite the stress and strain of war, Great Britain consent to work toward the same objective.

Dr. Silver, who since 1941 had been warning of the erosion of American policy, was more and more disturbed by Zionism's growing dependence on the Democratic Party and its president. He questioned the wisdom of leaving Jewry's fate to a few officials—no matter how highly placed—with whom Zionist leaders had traditionally curried favor. Knowing that in a democratic society public opinion plays a vitally important role in determining the stands taken by the government, he stressed well-organized, aggressive action based on widespread public support and recognition of the equal importance of the two major American political parties.[28]

Having accepted Dr. Silver's position, the Council turned its attention to Congress, hoping that direct pressure exerted on strategically placed senators and representatives from both parties would lead to decisive congressional action. In mid-December 1943, the local Emergency Committees were instructed to discuss the following issues with congressmen at home for the mid-winter holiday recess: the proposal that Congress reconfirm its decision of 1922 to support the establishment of a Jewish national home in Palestine; that it recognize the dire need for a homeland in which Europe's desperate Jewish refugees could find a haven; that Congress call upon the government to use its good offices to open Palestine to Jewish immigration and land purchase with a view to fostering the establishment there of a Jewish commonwealth. In other words, organized Jewry throughout the country was being mobilized to sound out congressmen and elicit their support for a resolution favouring the Biltmore program.[29]

Within the Emergency Council itself, however, it was not unanimously agreed that the time was ripe for such a resolution. Nachum Goldmann, whose World Jewish Congress office maintained close contact with governmental circles, predicted failure for a pro-Zionist resolution because of the opposition of the Executive branch. If the resolution were voted down or deferred, he believed the damage would be irreparable. Dr. Silver, on the other hand, was more optimistic: he felt that even if the resolution did not pass at once, the very fact that it was placed on the congressional agenda would force the adoption of a stand.

Having seen reports from the various community leaders of the reactions of their congressmen, he believed that there was a reasonably good chance of success. Other leaders favored immediate action, fearing that if the Emergency Council did nothing, the Irgun would fill the vacuum with noisy propaganda, as it had in the past. The Irgun's failure to achieve significant results would be attributed to the responsible Zionist organizations, as the public still tended to confuse the two bodies. Eventually, it was unanimously decided to authorize Silver to activate the mechanism necessary to introduce pro-Zionist resolutions into both houses of Congress.

Prospects seemed good, in view of the response of influential congressmen to the appeals of their local constituencies and considering the dominant position in both the House and Senate of the men who agreed to speak for the resolutions: J. M. Wright (Democrat from Pennsylvania) and Arnolf Compton (Republican from Connecticut) in the House of Representatives; Robert M. Wagner (Democrat from New York) and Robert A. Taft (Republican from Ohio) in the Senate.

On the 27th of January, 1944, Compton and Wright brought identically worded resolutions before the House and on the 1st of February, Wagner and Taft did likewise. The House Foreign Relations Committee headed by Sol Bloom, a Jew who represented the largely Jewish population of Brooklyn, conducted several hearings during the first half of February. Eight members of the Emergency Council testified before the Committee, reinforced by the impressive testimony of Walter Clay Lowdermilk, who described Jewish achievements in Palestine and the possibilities of exploiting the country's natural resources to enable it to support a large future Jewish population. Non-Zionists in the American Jewish Committee submitted a memorandum recommending that the United Nations (which at the time meant the Allied forces) hold Palestine in temporary trusteeship rather than try to form a Jewish commonwealth. A strong case against Zionism was made by the American Council for Judaism, which objected to the establishment of any political entity that would give Jews a state or commonwealth of their own. Lessing Rosenwald, president of the Council for Judaism, described the demand for Jewish statehood as a Nazi-inspired racist concept that would put Jews who lived outside of such a state—including American Jews—in an "equivocal" position.

For the first time, an Arab—Professor Philip K. Hitti of Princeton University—appeared before the Foreign Relations Committee and made an anti-Zionist plea. He claimed that he spoke in his own name only because, unlike the Jews, the Arabs in the United States were not organized in pressure groups or lobbies and had no means of rallying public opinion. His central thesis was that since the Arabs had not created the Jewish problem, there was no reason why it should be solved at their expense. Appealing to the conscience of the democratic world, he asked why, if the American legislators were so concerned over Jewish suffering in Europe, they did not amend the immigration quotas to permit the victims of the tragedy to enter the United States.

Warning that passage of the Palestine resolution would endanger Arab friendship for America, he asked rhetorically whether the United States would be ready to send an army to defend a Jewish commonwealth formed over the opposition of 275 million Moslems. Hitti was supported by the president of the Federation of Syrians and Lebanese in the Eastern United States.[30]

Most of the testimony, however, favored the resolution. Non-Jewish support coming from groups such as the American Palestine Committee and the Christian Council for Palestine and favorable statements by congressmen were written into the minutes of the committee hearings, as were many supportive letters, telegrams and editorials. By the end of February, there seemed little reason to doubt that the resolution would be brought to the House floor with a positive recommendation from the committee. But there was more to be reckoned with than the hearings of the House Foreign Relations Committee. Stimson was now willing to state that in view of Allied difficulties in Italy, the delicate negotiations with Saudi Arabia over an oil pipeline and preparations for the invasion of Europe, the military situation in the Middle East should not be jeopardized by a pro-Zionist commitment.[31]

On 2 March, in a letter to representative Bloom, Secretary of War Stimson summed up the contents of discussions he and Bloom had had prior to the House Committee hearings. Stimson reiterated the view of the War Department that without reference to the merits of the resolution, action on it should be suspended. Bloom was also aware of the tremendous pressure the British embassy was exerting on the Department of State to prevent passage of the resolution.[32]

At the same time, the Senate Foreign Relations Committee was conducting closed discussions on the Wagner–Taft Resolution. The Committee's chairman, Senator Tom Connally of Texas, invited General George C. Marshall, head of the joint chiefs of staff, to an off-the-record meeting that was attended by almost all the members of the committee. The General repeated the, by then, familiar claim that a pro-Zionist stand would endanger American forces in the region because troops badly needed on other fronts would have to be called upon to quell Arab riots. Reminding his audience of the potential threat to the Soviet Union's supply routes and to Iraq's oil pipeline, he also hinted at the possibility of an uprising of Moslem soldiers serving in Allied armies.[33]

Marshall's off-the-record testimony to the Senate Foreign Relations Committee was leaked to the Emergency Council, which transmitted its contents to Drew Pearson for publication in his popular column, the "Washington Merry-Go-Round."[34] In essence, Marshall's testimony was the result of a decision taken by President Roosevelt, Stimson and Under-Secretary of State Stettinius at a meeting convened on 19 February, 1944, by Breckinridge Long, assistant to the Secretary of State and the President's close confidante. It was decided at that meeting to "kill" the resolution in both houses primarily on the strength of statements issued by the War Department. If that did not suffice to stalemate further congressional action, the deathblow would be delivered by publication of the letter from Stimson to Bloom. Publication had been withheld, even though at a Cabinet meeting Roosevelt had pressed Stimson to make its contents public.

Now that Drew Pearson had revealed the story of Marshall's testimony, the President felt that Bloom and Connally would be unable to deal with the issue. He decided to publicize Stimson's letter to the effect that the War Department considered that further action on House Resolutions 418 and 419 would be prejudicial to the successful prosecution of the war (the original text read that "no further action . . . would be advisable at this time," but was amended in Bloom's handwriting to read that "further action . . . at this time would be prejudicial . . ."—which also cast light on Bloom's own position).[35] Thereupon all further debate over the House Resolutions was suspended.

This development in Congress exacerbated the already tense relationship between Dr. Wise and Dr. Silver. Their fundamental differences of approach became more and more apparent. Each advocated entirely different tactics: Wise was determined to maintain the good relations with the Roosevelt administration that he had nurtured for so many years. Not so Silver, who was convinced that "backstairs diplomacy" could only lead to a dead end. He believed that the administration was merely giving lip service in support of Zionist objectives and that unless pressed, would do nothing to rescue Jews, open the gates of Palestine, or support the establishment of a Jewish commonwealth.

Pursuant to his conception of what was best for Zionism, Wise worked on the external front, mainly through the Jewish Agency Executive, concentrating on contacts with the government and the President and largely ignoring the Washington Bureau. De facto, Nachum Goldmann was the embodiment in America of the Agency Executive and Wise transferred to him most of his own hard-won political contacts. Silver, on the other hand, concentrated on the internal strengthening of the Emergency Council with the intention of using it as a countrywide political pressure group.

1944 was an election year. Roosevelt, running for his fourth term, was in the uncomfortable position of having to appease an unfriendly Congress and at the same time make sure of the Jewish vote. He was also engaged in a crucial struggle to hide his declining health: there was constant public concern over his ability to withstand the rigors of a campaign, carry the war to a successful conclusion, establish international peacekeeping mechanisms, and restore the American economy to a peacetime footing.

From previous campaigns, starting with his first successful bid for the presidency in 1933, Roosevelt knew the extent of Jewish loyalty to him. Therefore, when early in 1944 Wise asked that he and Silver be invited to a meeting with the President in connection with the congressional resolutions, Roosevelt promptly fixed the date for the beginning of February. Suddenly, without consulting his co-chairman, Wise asked to postpone the meeting, having decided that it would be ineffective unless representatives of non-Zionist and anti-Zionist groups were present. Appearing without Silver, as part of a delegation meeting with the President in the name of all American Jewry, Wise could claim to represent all American Zionists.[36]

This placed the Emergency Council in an untenable position: at a session with the President, the anti-Zionists would not hesitate to come out openly against the commonwealth, thereby undermining the impression that the American Jewish Conference had spoken in the name of all Jewry. This would also enable Roosevelt to settle for a declaration in favor of continued Jewish immigration into Palestine, and permit him to evade all commitments with respect to the future of the country and of Zionist aspirations there.

Sources close to the President confirmed that he was indeed prepared to issue just such a declaration, one that would exclude all reference to the "Jewish commonwealth." Therefore it was decided to ask for a postponement of the meeting, in the hope that during the interim the resolutions would be voted on favorably in both houses of Congress.[37] Although this proved to be a vain hope, there was nevertheless some rather unexpected help from a candidate who wanted to be returned to the Senate in the forthcoming elections. Robert Wagner, chairman of the American Palestine Committee and senator from New York, a state with the largest concentration of Jews in the world, told Roosevelt of the avalanche of pro-Zionist letters he had been receiving from Jews and non-Jews all over America. At Wagner's suggestion, the President invited Dr. Wise and Dr. Silver to meet with him on the 9th of March. On that occasion, the Zionist leaders made it clear that American Jewry was awaiting a statement with respect to Palestine. They offered Roosevelt a draft which he modified in a way that he felt would make it more acceptable to the British. That very day, it was distributed to the press in the form of a presidential statement to Wise and Silver. It read as follows:

The President authorized us to say that the American Government has never given its approval to the White Paper of 1939. The President is happy that the doors of Palestine are today open to Jewish refugees, and that when future decisions are reached, full justice will be done to those who seek a Jewish National Home, for which our Government and the American people have always had the deepest sympathy and today more than ever, in view of the tragic plight of hundreds of thousands of homeless Jewish refugees.[38]

This was a cleverly watered down version of the text the Emergency Council leaders had suggested, and it left wide margins for interpretation, particularly by the enemies of Zionism. Ambiguously worded, the President's statement could readily have been interpreted to mean that although the United States had never approved the 1939 White Paper, it also had never disapproved it. It therefore could mean all things to all men, and thus was used by the State Department to reassure the Arabs privately that there was no real change in American policy,[39] which further convinced Silver that Zionism could succeed only by conducting its struggle in the inter-party arena of the American political scene. He attributed the blocking of the resolution in both houses of Congress to the army's fear of the deteriorating situation on the Italian and Balkan fronts, and to the negotiations taking place over the trans-Arabian oil pipeline. The introduction of these extraneous considerations, in Silver's opinion, had had the paradoxical effect of strengthening American Jewry's determination to fight against the White Paper and for the Jewish commonwealth.

The very fact that for the first time the United States had taken an independent stand on the Palestine question, one that differed from that taken by the British, was an important achievement, even if the statement itself was more equivocal than the Zionists had hoped for. In large measure, Silver felt that his insistence that unremitting pressure be exerted on the highest governmental echelons was vindicated—although this meant further polarization of the positions taken by himself and his co-chairman, Stephen Wise. The Emergency Council's Executive Committee fully supported Silver's viewpoint and at its meeting on the 23rd of March, 1944, decided to undertake additional public activities, even at the risk of annoying the administration.

Dr. Silver did not delude himself; he knew that in actual fact they had suffered a serious setback. The administration had revealed an anti-Jewish, anti-Zionist bias: in addition to "military" reasons adduced for supporting the White Paper, America's oil interests were superseding all other concerns the country might have had in the Middle East. On the 3rd of April, the Executive Committee of the Emergency Council held a lengthy meeting to review the situation and prepare its program of action for the coming months.

The political objectives of the Council were formulated in the clearest terms: a) to win the United States government's support of a Jewish commonwealth and bring about a decision, notwithstanding the fact that war was still being waged; and b) to make the government realize that the crystallization of a pro-Zionist policy was not only compatible with America's interests in the Middle East, but would significantly further those interests.

To pursue the above objectives, the following guidelines for action were established: 1) to continue efforts to secure a public declaration by the President on American policy concerning Palestine. Failing that, to convince the President to communicate such a statement to the British through diplomatic channels; 2) to encourage the President to appoint a representative who would be accessible to the Zionists and authorized to discuss their problems; 3) to continue the campaign to win support of the Republican and Democratic parties; 4) to secure a guarantee that no commitment prejudicial to Zionist aspirations would be part of a quid pro quo in a Saudi Arabian oil deal; and 5) to undertake action to secure the entry into Palestine of the maximum number of Jews—beyond the White Paper quota.[40] Although to some extent these guidelines represented a compromise between what became known in the course of time as Silver's approach and Wise's approach, they nevertheless marked a new departure in the political thinking of the Emergency Council.

The End of an Era

Toward the end of 1944, Silver had the opportunity to put into practice his bipartisan strategy on the grounds that, as the Zionists were not committed to either political party, they could gain political capital in an election year. That summer the Zionist political front shifted to Chicago, where the national conventions of the Republican and Democratic parties were being held. Silver calculated that it would be easier to obtain a strong pro-Zionist declaration which might subsequently be used as a lever on the President from the opposition candidate, Governor Thomas E. Dewey, and Arthur Lourie was sent to Albany to assist the governor in writing a pro-commonwealth statement which was then read at the Republican convention. Silver and Neumann, who were present at the convention, convinced the Republican leadership not only to accept a "free and democratic commonwealth" for Palestine, but also to condemn Roosevelt for failing to insist that Britain live up to the obligations of the Balfour Declaration and the Mandate. Silver then asked the Emergency Council to give public approval to the plank. Several among the ZOA leadership, including Stephen Wise and Israel Goldstein, as well as the leaders of Hadassah, who were all solid Democrats, did not wish to endorse a Republican platform which cast aspersions on the President. A modified Emergency Council endorsement was approved by a narrow vote.

At the Democratic national convention Wise, Goldstein and some of their colleagues were instrumental in obtaining the passing of the following Palestine plank:

We favor the opening of Palestine to unrestricted Jewish immigration and colonization, and such a policy as to result in the establishment there of a free and democratic commonwealth.[41]

Under election year pressure, President Roosevelt went a step further and sent a message through Senator Wagner to the October convention of the ZOA, personally reiterating the Democratic Party platform commitment:

I know how long and ardently the Jewish people have worked and prayed for the establishment of Palestine as a free and democratic Jewish Commonwealth. I an convinced that the American people give their support to this aim; and, if re-elected, I will help bring about its realization.[42]

The Zionists had won a minor victory. It was the first time in American history that planks on Palestine were inserted into national party platforms. However, it should be noted that in neither the Democratic nor the Republican plank was there a specific mention of a *Jewish* commonwealth in Palestine. Roosevelt, after strong urging by Zionists and Senator Wagner, stated that "efforts will be made to find appropriate ways and means of effectuating this policy [i.e., the Palestine plank] as soon as practicable." He did not state, however, how soon it would be "practicable," or if, indeed, it would ever be so.[43]

On October 13, 1944, Secretary of War Stimson declared that previous military objections to the Palestine resolution had been removed. The Emergency Council now needed only the assurance of the State Department that it would not block the bill. Silver, Wise, and Jewish Agency representative Nachum Goldmann met in November with Secretary of State Stettinius, who promised to inform them of the State Department's position within a few days. The Emergency Council minutes of November 21, 1944, record:

. . . Dr. Wise reported that Mr. Stettinius had telephoned him a few days ago and informed him that he had seen the President, who urged that nothing be done about the Bill at this time.[44]

Silver had previously agreed, at a 30 October Emergency Council meeting, that if the State Department was at all vague (and it was not) on the Palestine resolution, he would not recommend proceeding with it. However, it was also recognized that there was a large Zionist stake in the passage of the resolution at this time. For a year, the major part of American Zionist efforts had gone into securing passage of the Palestine resolution. If the project was abandoned, it would be a considerable blow for the Jewish community.[45] If the resolution was passed, on the other hand, the Emergency Council and the Zionists would have secured enormous propaganda value for their year's work, and a favorable postwar settlement on Palestine might be facilitated.

Silver, without consulting the Council, gave written authorization to Sol Bloom to force the Palestine resolution through the House Foreign Relations Committee and on 30 November, Bloom succeeded in obtaining its passage— with the retention of the word "ultimately" and the deletion of the word "Jewish" before "commonwealth." Thus, the resolution which was reported out of committee was in favor of the "ultimate" reconstitution of "Palestine as a free and democratic commonwealth." There was no mention of a Jewish state: the resolution could have been construed to support a binational, or even an Arab state. Even Lessing Rosenwald, president of the American Council for Judaism, gave it his approval.

In order to stop the passage of such a weak resolution in the Senate, Wise sent a telegram to Stettinius the evening before Silver's scheduled meeting with Stettinius and Wagner on the subject. The telegram stated that influential Zionist leaders would agree to a deferment of the resolution.[46] In the meantime, Silver continued to press for passage of the resolution in the Senate, maintaining that it had enough merit—it contained an implied condemnation of the White Paper—for its passing to be considered a propaganda victory for the Zionists.

An Emergency Council meeting was called on 7 December, after the House had passed its weakened Palestine resolution. Wise presided. Silver was away in Washington. With only seventeen members present, it was resolved to send a number of delegates to Washington that night and to request Silver to head the Emergency Council delegation which would inform Wagner and, if necessary, Senator Connally (chairman of the Senate Foreign Relations Committee), that the resolution could be left pending. When the delegation arrived, Silver refused to concur on the line of action to be taken. Instead, he insisted on pushing the resolution through the Senate committee, where it was blocked on the advice of the President and the Secretary of State.[47] The result of the divergent action taken by the two co-chairmen was a public split within the Emergency Council itself.

The Wise–Silver Split

From the outset of their co-chairmanship, Wise and Silver had been at odds with one another. While Wise believed that only wholehearted backing of the administration by American Zionists could secure endorsement of Zionist aims, Silver felt the government would only undertake pro-Zionist action if subjected to tremendous political pressure. Whether the administration was antagonized or not was immaterial, in his view. A decided lack of communication was discernible between the two co-chairmen, as well as between the Emergency Council's pro-Silver faction and those who upheld Wise. The actions which led to the collapse of the Palestine resolution provided the proverbial "last straw." Both Silver and Wise resigned their co-chairmanships, and the council was forced to choose between them. The two most powerful organizations—the

ZOA and Hadassah—supported Wise, while Mizrachi and Poale Zion backed Silver. Wise was reinstated.

Defending Silver at a meeting of the ZOA Administrative Council, Emanuel Neumann declared Silver innocent of a breach of discipline and emphasized that it was Wise who had breached council discipline by sending a telegram to Stettinius before Silver had met with him. Israel Goldstein, one of Wise's chief defenders at the meeting, did not deny Silver's past achievements, but declared that Silver should have abided by the will of the majority instead of insisting on his own way, and emphasized that access to the President remained essential. The meeting upheld Dr. Wise and the reorganization of the Emergency Council by a vote of 74 to 23.[48] The leadership of the World Zionist Organization also gave Wise strong support. Nachum Goldmann informed the ZOA Executive: "If this fight against the President and this policy of attacking the administration is continued, it will lead us—and I choose my words carefully—to complete disaster."[49]

A week later, Weizmann sent a letter regretting the "error" he had made in the choice of Silver as the Emergency Council's chairman. Wise quoted from Weizmann's letter when he wrote to David Niles, Administrative Assistant to President Roosevelt. Weizmann wrote concerning Silver's action on the Palestine resolution:

> It seems to me that the last step was ill-timed and generally superfluous. We were in the best possible position. Why was it necessary to tempt the gods? This over-playing of our hand leads us to no end of trouble, and this does not only relate to our affairs in the United States, but unfortunately also here. An ounce of restraint is worth more than a pound of invective.[50]

The Emergency Council continued to function without Silver. Mizrachi and Poale Zion agreed to retain their membership. Certain of Silver's supporters, however, resigned from key positions on the Council, including Executive Director Harry Shapiro and Harold Manson, Director of Information of the Washington Bureau. The two men, using their own personal funds, established a pro-Silver headquarters in New York City. Other staff members from the Washington Bureau, including Abe Tuvim and Harry Steinberg, quickly followed suit.

The pro-Silver faction formed the American Zionist Policy Committee on February 13, 1945. Its aim was to bring Silver back to the leadership by working through one specific organization—the ZOA. The Policy Committee pledged it would not interfere with the Emergency Council's work, but would attempt to "revitalize the democratic principle basic to our movement so that the composition and policies of the national administration shall reflect the great body of American Zionists."[51] The committee was officially headed by Charles J. Rosenbloom, treasurer of the United Palestine Appeal and former treasurer of the United Jewish Appeal. Emanuel Neumann, who remained a member of the Emergency Council, actively guided it. The committee was privately financed by a group of Silver's friends. It sent out literature to ZOA districts, as well as to local Emergency Council committees. Members of the Policy Committee also tried to engage in public debates with the "Wise–Goldstein" forces. Their goal was to channel existing widespread popular support for Zionist militancy into votes for Silver as the ZOA's president, at the 1945 ZOA convention.

Within a few days after Silver's resignation, the Brooklyn Zionist Region—the largest ZOA region—reaffirmed by a huge majority "our unshakable confidence in the leadership of Dr. Abba Hillel Silver and his policies . . ."[52] The Yiddish press urged Silver's reinstatement. Wise supporters were forced into public debates and the Emergency Council repeatedly had to issue memoranda to local Emergency Council chairmen, explaining its position on Silver. The memoranda stated that it was Silver himself who had resigned, and that he would be welcomed back as a *member* of the Emergency Council.

Two months after Silver's resignation, the Zionist movement was in such turmoil that Weizmann cabled Wise and Silver to find a way to resolve their differences. Silver demanded "conditions which will enable me to carry on the active political leadership of the Emergency Council." He also asked that Dr. Wise admit himself wrong on the reorganization of the Emergency Council.[53] Silver's conditions were rejected. However, the Executive Committee of the ZOA formed a committee under Judge Levinthal on April 1, 1945, to resolve the internal dispute without casting aspersions on Wise's leadership. In the meantime, the council continued action by means of a quiet approach to the President. David Niles, Administrative Assistant to the President, appears to have been the chief liaison between Wise and the executive branch of the United States government at this time. Through his efforts, Roosevelt met Wise on January 22, 1945, shortly before the President's departure for the Yalta Conference, but there was no apparent change in United States policy toward Palestine. The Zionists were told that any final decision on the Palestine issue would have to await the end of the war.[54]

After the Yalta Conference, Roosevelt met with Ibn Saud on board an American warship in the Suez Canal and assured him that he would never act against Arab interests and that the American government would consult both Arabs and Jews before making basic changes in its Palestine policy. The conversation was made public only after Roosevelt's death, and it thus came as a shock to the Zionists to hear of President Roosevelt's open remark to Congress on 1 March:

> Of the problems of Arabia, I learned more about the whole problem, the Muslim problem, the Jewish problem, by talking with Ibn Saud for five minutes than I could have learned in an exchange of two or three dozen letters.[55]

The ensuing widespread Zionist disillusionment with the Roosevelt administration was only partially allayed when Wise issued a statement on 16 March authorized by the President, claiming that the latter still upheld his 1944 pre-election pledge on the Palestine plank.

The San Francisco Conference, held between 25 April and 26 June, was the founding forum of the United Nations. Major international issues were slated to be discussed there. The Emergency Council decided not to appear at the San Francisco Conference as a separate entity, nor to have headquarters of its own there; rather, the council's representatives would work with the Jewish Agency and the American Jewish Conference.[56] In conjunction with the American Jewish Conference, the council sponsored 88 mass rallies calling for a Jewish commonwealth. Nachum Goldmann, however, cautioned against too much optimism over the conference. It was evident to him from both public and confidential information that the Palestine question, as such, would not be on the agenda.

> . . . to mislead Jewish public opinion to expect something, and then to shout we have been betrayed because these groundless expectations were not fulfilled is, to say the least, not a very responsible method of approach.[57]

Even though the nine representatives of the Emergency Council and the eleven-man delegation of the American Jewish Conference issued more than forty different statements on approximately 50,000 stenciled sheets in three languages to the UN delegates and the press corps, the general feeling among American Zionists was one of disappointment. No significant progress was made in relation to Zionist goals, and there was a strong feeling that an important, if not crucial, opportunity had been neglected.

The conference coincided with the first news reports from Europe on the liberation of the concentration camps by the Western Allies. On April 11, 1945, the American Army entered Buchenwald. Shocked beyond belief, the soldiers beheld stacks of naked, skeletal corpses piled ten feet high in storerooms, living inmates barely distinguishable from the dead, and bunks crowded with shaven-headed prisoners so emaciated that they appeared scarcely human.[58] Three days later, British forces liberated Bergen-Belsen in central Germany. Of the one-and-a-half million prisoners who had entered its gates, no more than fifty thousand had survived. Disease-ridden and starving, many inmates outlived the liberation by only a few days. During the following weeks, Dachau, Mauthausen and Theresienstadt were liberated amid similar horrific scenes.[59]

The news of these unprecedented atrocities flashed through the media worldwide as hundreds of newspapermen visited the camps. American Jewry, in common with Western society as a whole, was witness at last to the real meaning of the Nazi "Final Solution" as photographs and eyewitness accounts by soldiers, volunteers and journalists provided indisputable evidence of Nazi brutality. A Western correspondent began his dispatch on Belsen with the words: "It is my duty to describe something beyond the imagination of mankind."[60]

A growing feeling that Roosevelt had abandoned European Jewry led to increasing disillusionment with the Roosevelt administration and its adherents in the Jewish community—particularly Stephen Wise. This discontent affected both the Zionist leadership and the movement's rank and file. On 11 June, the president of Mizrachi, Leon Gellman, dispatched a letter to the Council which took the form of an ultimatum: Silver must be recalled and the council reorganized within two weeks. Gellman charged the Council with "the continuing failure to pursue more vigorous and militant policies," and sent the letter to the press even before the Emergency Council had received it. Hayim Greenberg, head of Poale Zion and acting chairman of the Emergency Council's Executive Committee, resigned on 19 June on account of the internal dissension,[61] and on 15 July, 1945, Silver was recalled to his former position on the Emergency Council, reinstating with him the officials who had resigned out of sympathy with his policy—Harry Shapiro, Harold Manson, Abe Tuvim and Harry Steinberg. Although Wise retained the title of co-chairman, the conditions under which Silver returned show the extent of his triumph. Among the resolutions the Emergency Council adopted were the following:

> All executive and administrative responsibility shall be vested in the Executive Committee of the Council. Dr. Silver shall be its chairman and Hayim Greenberg, Leon Gellman and Herman Shulman . . . shall be its Vice-Chairmen.
>
> The Chairman of the Executive Committee [i.e. Silver] will be Chairman of the Board of Officers.
>
> The Chairman of the Executive Committee shall have the right to name, with the approval of the Executive Committee, an Executive Director and other key members of the staff.
>
> The Executive Committee shall be enlarged by the addition of Mr. Louis Lipsky and Mr. Emanuel Neumann as members at large.
>
> . . . the ZOA shall designate its representatives on the Council with the understanding that two of its designees, and their special alternatives, shall be persons recommended by Dr. Silver; and that these two designees and their special alternates shall have freedom of action.[62]

Hadassah remained the only organization within the Emergency Council which refused to follow a pro-Silver line. Poale Zion and Mizrachi almost always supported Silver over Wise, and now at least half of the ZOA representatives to the council would most assuredly support Silver.

In October 1945, six months after Roosevelt's death, the Roosevelt–Ibn Saud correspondence was made public. The revelation shook the Zionist ranks, discredited Wise's tactics, and reconfirmed Silver's past denunciation of the

Roosevelt administration. It was clear now to the great majority of American Zionists and Jews at large that despite their success in mobilizing public opinion, they had not managed to convert the Roosevelt administration to a pro-Zionist position. An increased surge of militancy swept the Zionist ranks. The ZOA national convention, held in November, elected Silver president of the ZOA practically by acclaim. The rallying slogan was, "Put not your trust in princes."

In the trying times ahead, it gradually became axiomatic that the Zionist movement would work with the two major parties, would take up the cudgels to fight Great Britain's restrictions against Jewish immigration to Palestine, would try to come to grips with the oil interests, as well as attempt to win the new President's goodwill. As this new line of policy became entrenched, the Emergency Council—representing American Zionism—would develop into a powerful influence group on the American scene, ready to meet the challenges of the postwar world and, above all, to succor the brands plucked from the European inferno.

Notes to Chapter 7

1. See minutes of Executive of Emergency Council (hereafter, ECAZEC) dated December 13, 1943; also ECAZEC, October 5, 1943, and voluminous Silver–Neumann correspondence that began in September 1943 and dealt with all aspects of Emergency Council policy.
2. Minutes of last meeting held under name of Emergency Committee, September 20, 1943.
3. ECAZEC, October 18, 1943.
4. The exact figure budgeted for 1943–44 was $509,382.
5. D. Bierbrier, "The American Zionist Emergency Council: An Analysis of a Pressure Group," *AJHQ*, vol. LX (September 1970), p. 88.
6. Author's interview with Harold Manson (Oral Documentation Section of Institute of Contemporary Jewry). See also, *Guidelines for Local Emergency Committees* (henceforth, *Guidelines*), CZA, Z5/902.
7. Fink, *America and Palestine: op. cit.*, pp. 390–412.
8. Author's interview with Harry Shapiro, October 17, 1971 (Oral Documentation Section of Institute of Contemporary Jewry).
9. *Palestine Year Book* (hereafter, *PYB*), New York, 1945, vol. I, p. 368.
10. For the file of letters from local Executive Committees and responses of members of House and Senate, see CZA, Z5/402.
11. *PYB*, vol. I, p. 369; also "Reports on Community Contacts Submitted to the ECAZEC," May 15, 1944.
12. See *Guidelines, op. cit.*.
13. ECAZEC, October 5, 1943; October 18, 1943.
14. American Zionist Emergency Council (hereafter, AZEC), "A Report of Activities, 1940–1946," pp. 7–8; also "The Voice of Christian America," NYZA.
15. *PYB*, 1944, p. 372; also AZEC, "A Report of Activities," *ibid.*, and recorded discussion with Dr. Carl Herman Voss held on June 21, 1966 (Oral Documentation Section of Institute of Contemporary Jewry).
16. H. Fishman, *American Protestantism and the Jewish State 1937–1967*, Ph.D. dissertation, New York University, 1971.
17. See V. O. Key, *Politics, Parties and Pressure Groups, op. cit.*, p. 171, where he notes that "lobbyists also lobby each other."

18. Report by Fanny Cohen, secretary of Committee for Mobilization of Intellectuals, to A. H. Silver, December 12, 1943; also Emergency Council press release dated January 1, 1945, Press Release Box, NYZA.

19. ECAZEC, April 5, 1943. On the conference, see CZA, Z5/1213.

20. For Berkson's plans for the Department, see ECAZEC, January 13, 1944.

21. ECAZEC, November 15, 1943; and *PYB*, vol. I., p. 370.

22. Halperin, *The Political World of American Zionism, op. cit.*

23. At a meeting with Nachum Goldmann on October 28, Leary, one of the head of the Middle East section of the OSS, reported that Hoskins—whose conclusion that civil war was about to break out in the Middle East Leary considered highly exaggerated—was no longer working for the OSS (Goldmann report, October 28, 1943, Silver Archives). Hoskins remained active in the region, however, and in 1945 made his last attempt at intervention. On 10 March, 1945, he tried to defend himself to President Roosevelt against the attacks of the Zionists, still maintaining that implementation of the Zionist solution could be imposed only by the use of force; FRUS, 1945, vol. VIII, pp. 690f.

24. Minutes of Emergency Council, December 13, 1943.

25. "Studies of American Interests in the War and Peace. Territorial Series: Memorandum on the New Zionism and a Policy for the U.S.," October 19, 1943 (catalogued under No. T-G 68, in archives of Foreign Policy Association, New York).

26. *Ibid.* Copies of the text can also be found in the personal archives of various Zionist leaders.

27. ECAZEC, December 12, 1943; January 3, 1944.

28. ECAZEC, January 3, 1944. Also A. H. Silver, *Vision and Victory: A Collection of Addresses, 1942–1948*, New York, 1949.

29. See Yoel Gross's memorandum to heads of local Emergency Committees dated December 23, 1943, NYZA; also Feuer Report to the ECAZEC, January 3, 1944.

30. U.S. House of Representatives, Committee of Foreign Affairs, *Hearings before the . . . The Jewish National Home in Palestine*, Washington D.C., 1944, pp. III, 203, 204, 313–15.

31. P. Baram, *The Department of State in the Middle East, op. cit.*, p. 293.

32. Stimson to Bloom, March 15, 1944 (Bloom Papers, New York Public Library—autobiographical file; henceforth, Bloom papers). See also memo of conversation between Sir Ronald Campbell, minister at the British embassy in Washington, and Adoph Berle; FRUS, 1944, vol. V, p. 562, and other protests, *ibid.*

33. Assistant Secretary of War John McCloy prepared a lengthy survey of all possible reasons against passage of the resolution in the Senate, to be presented by a relatively low-level War Department official, not by General Marshall; FRUS, 1944, vol. 5, pp. 575f. See also Stimson diary.

34. On Drew Pearson's journalism and influence, see O. Pilat, *Drew Pearson: An Unauthorized Biography*, New York, 1973.

35. Stimson to Bloom, March 17, 1944 (Bloom Papers), including Bloom's handwritten corrections to Stimson letter of March 2, 1944.

36. ECAZEC, January 31, 1944.

37. ECAZEC, February 7, 1944.

38. ECAZEC, March 13, 1944; also *New York Times* of March 9, 1944.

39. Baram, *op. cit.*, p. 288.

40. ECAZEC, April 3, 1944 (morning and afternoon sessions).

41. *New York Times*, October 16, 1944.

42. F. E. Manuel, *The Realities of American-Palestine Relations, op. cit.*, p. 312.

43. *Ibid.*; J. B. Schechtman, *The United States and the Jewish State Movement: The Crucial Decade, 1939–1949*, New York, 1966, p. 41.

44. AZEC minutes, October 30, 1944.

45. AZEC minutes, November 9, 1944; November 21, 1944; October 30, 1944.

46. *Independent Jewish Press Service* (Bulletin), January 5, 1945, p. 6.

47. AZEC minutes, December 7, 1944.

48. AZEC minutes, December 20, 1944; *New Palestine*, January 19, 1945.

49. Schechtman, *op cit.*, p. 86.

50. Weizmann to Wise, December 26, 1944; Wise to Niles, January 8, 1945 (Wise Papers).

51. *Independent Jewish Press Service*, July 27, 1945, pp. 9f.

52. Interviews by the author with Harold P. Manson, April 4, 1971; Harry Shapiro, May 16, 1971; also see H. P. Manson, "Abba Hillel Silver. An Appreciation," reprinted from *In the Time of Harvest. Essays in Honor of Abba Hillel Silver on the Occasion of his 70th Birthday*, New York-London, 1963.

53. AZEC Executive minutes, April 3, 1945.

54. N. Goldmann, "Jews at San Francisco," *New Palestine*, April 13, 1945; E. Elath, *San Francisco Diary*, Tel Aviv, 1971 (Hebrew).

55. For an official transcript of the conversation, see memorandum of conversation between Ibn Saud and Roosevelt, February 14, 1945, FDRL. For a full description of the meeting, see J. Bishop, *F.D.R.'s Last Year*, New York, 1975, pp. 584–6.

56. AZEC minutes, April 16, 1945.

57. Goldmann, "Jews at San Francisco."

58. J. W. Jacobson, "The Day Buchenwald was Freed," *New York Times Magazine*, April 7, 1946, pp. 28f.

59. D. Sington, *Belsen Uncovered*, London, 1946.

60. W. Laqueur, *The Terrible Secret*, London, 1980, p. 2; see also P. Berben, *Dachau: The Official History 1933–1945*, London, 1975; P. Tillard, *Mauthausen*, Paris, 1945; L. Sacher, *The Redemption of the Unwanted: From the Liberation of the Death Camps to the Founding of Israel*, New York, 1983.

61. AZEC Executive minutes, June 11, 1945.

62. AZEC minutes, May 30, 1945.

63. L Feuer, "Abba Hillel Silver: A Personal Memoir," *AJA*, vol. XIX (November 1967), p. 123.

Conclusion

HISTORICAL hindsight is a mixed blessing. On the one hand it informs today's evaluations and conclusions with the wealth of knowledge that has been amassed about yesterday's events. On the other hand the eye looking back forty or fifty years may easily be deceived. Tendencies and trends, methods and procedures that might have had revolutionary import in the 1930s and 1940s may be commonplace in the 1980s and 1990s. Is it not self-evident that American Zionism, a political movement, would use the normally accepted tools of American political life to achieve its ends? Exploitation of the media, mobilization of public opinion, formation of a "lobby"—these have become banal means regularly employed by all special interest groups. But on the eve of the Second World War none of this was self-evident or banal for American Zionism. The Zionist movement then was totally unprepared to meet the challenges thrust upon it by the world situation.

Understanding the metamorphosis that occurred in American Zionism between the years 1933 and 1945 is the key to understanding the crucial role American Jewry played in the struggle for the establishment of the Jewish state and for its survival. During those years the Zionist movement was transformed into an organized, American-style political entity. Although the transition was marked by recurrent crises, a vigorous, unified political influence group emerged. It mobilized reserves of pro-Zionist sentiment and initiated public action supported by Jews and non-Jews, as a result of two decisive developments: the mass murder of Jewry in Nazi-occupied Europe, and America's new status as an international power with growing interests in the Middle East.

The transformation of the Zionist movement in America from a loosely organized social body of well-intentioned Jews into a militant political force necessitated an unequivocal definition of the movement's strategic goal and of the tactics to attain that goal. In the period between the two world wars, American Zionists had found it convenient to indulge in "practical," quasi-philanthropic Zionism devoid of national, cultural and political dimensions. The individual member thus suffered no conflict between his obligations as a Jew and his obligations as an American. When the Nazis created masses of homeless Jews, "refugeeism"—a term coined by Abba Hillel Silver—became the primary expression of American Zionism. Palestine, it was argued, was the main haven for the Jewish refugees. The American Jew thus reiterated altruistic concern for his European kin while remaining aloof from any personal involvement that might expose him to suspicions of harboring dual loyalties. But the publication of the White Paper in the spring of 1939 and the outbreak of war in September of the same year changed the situation drastically.

American Jewry was shaken. The community and the Zionist movement within it found themselves helpless: their charitable support of Jewish Palestine and the needy Jews of Central and Eastern Europe for many years had obviously failed to solve either the immediate or the longer range problems of Jewish existence. Clearly there was need for a more far-reaching and definitive solution than the one strived for thus far. The only answer to Nazism and to Britain's refusal to permit free Jewish immigration into Palestine was a return to political, "Herzlian" Zionism. Consequently, after much soul-searching, the Zionist movement began to press for realization of its political goal—the Jewish commonwealth.

The commonwealth formula became acceptable to the majority of American Jews primarily because it seemed to offer a solution to the terrible plight of Jewry at the time and because the American public could accept it as fitting into the vision of a utopian, free, democratic postwar world in which the United States would play a central role. American Jewry, now the largest and strongest Jewish community in the world, would have to take upon itself the realization of the only comprehensive solution to the Jewish problem—the establishment of a Jewish state. It was just as obvious that the Zionists would have to place themselves at the forefront of American Jewry and ensure that the United States, the strongest power in the world in the 1940s, would lead the postwar world toward the desired goal.

With America's entry into the war late in 1941, the Emergency Committee—and its successor the Emergency Council—became the recognized spokesman for the American Zionist movement. As such, its immediate problem was one of tactics: how to overcome American Jewry's helpless frustration with regard to the deteriorating situation of Europe's Jews; what new modes of action would afford an outlet for the emotions stirring in American Jewry and, more important, would lead to positive results. Those who were attracted to the various committees formed by the Irgun Zvai Leumi delegation found an emotional outlet but soon discovered that little could be done beyond venting anger. Most people turned to the Zionist and Jewish establishment for leadership. That establishment was woefully unprepared, but realized that the awakening then taking place on the American Jewish scene was attended with tremendous potential power. To harness this power for the purpose of influencing American policy on Palestine it would be necessary to act as a pressure or influence group.

American Zionism had never conceived of itself in such terms, although some of its leading figures had concluded soon after war broke out that Zionist policy could be conducted effectively only through the exercise of public and political influence. Emanuel Neumann, Abba Hillel Silver, Meyer Weisgal and Ben-Gurion fought against the traditional position of veteran Zionist leaders, who prevented the transition to influence-group political activity and continued to rely on behind-the-scenes personal dealings with governmental power-brokers. The internal struggles and dissension that resulted from these two different approaches continued to hamper effective action until the full impact of the Holocaust and American Jewry's mass approval of the commonwealth program in late 1943 tipped the scales in favor of public political action.

With the adoption of this new tack, a new leadership came to the fore, dominated by Dr. Abba Hillel Silver. The Emergency Council was reorganized and, lead by Dr. Silver, it issued directives for political activity which enabled it in a relatively short time to wield widespread influence on American public opinion and governmental circles. The first directive was to "return Zionism to its political basis." This was more than a new slogan: it reflected a basic change in strategy. American Zionism now recognized the need for a political solution achieved through political means, based on a consensus of the majority of Jews in the United States. The age-old principle of "all Jews are responsible for one another," which in the past had prompted the Jews of America to provide generous aid for their needy brethren overseas, now assumed the form of political responsibility that sought a fundamental and definitive solution to the problem of Jewish suffering. Supported by the Jewish community in general, the Zionist leaders were able to exert effective political pressure on the American government, while simultaneously stressing that their activities were a legitimate expression of America's political system.

The second directive for political action was to broaden the base of Zionist support. By the end of 1942, the leaders of the Emergency Committee already knew that Zionism needed the support of more than just its own members in order to acquire political influence in the United States. A consensus had to be created that would enable the committee to act in the name of all American Jews. American society expects American organizations to function democratically, and in this respect the Zionist movement in the United States had conformed. Because Zionist policies were determined by majority rule, more than once dissenters within the fold of Zionism had ignored differences and closed ranks. Acceptance of the "Biltmore program" was an outstanding example of this phenomenon, and it paved the way for the American Jewish Conference to approve the program, again by democratic consensus. This consensus enabled the Emergency Council to speak in the name of American Jewry as a whole and, even more important, the council had been given a franchise to work within various Jewish frameworks throughout the country. Another aspect of this process of "democratization" was that thousands of members and their local leaders could now take part in activities that had previously been the province of only a few individuals.

A further highly significant change introduced by Silver was the adoption of a bi-party policy. Throughout the twelve years of Roosevelt's presidency—and even before this period—American Jewry gave the Democratic Party overwhelming support. Understanding the American scene, Silver was convinced of the need to rid American Zionism of its one-party affinity and secure the support of both major parties—particularly after the 1942 congressional elections when the Republicans nearly gained control of the Senate. He was aware of the many advantages of inter-party competition for the goodwill of the Jews, and his instructions to the local Emergency Committees constantly stressed the desirability of overcoming the one-party monopoly. In consonance with this principle, both a Democrat and a Republican sponsored the motions on Palestine brought before both Houses of Congress early in 1944. Later, when the Palestine resolutions were stalemated in Congress, Silver and Wise headed representative Zionist delegations to the Republican and Democratic national conventions respectively, and consequently both conventions passed resolutions in the spirit of the Biltmore program.

The Emergency Council conducted activities in a style that was totally different from that of its predecessor, the Emergency Committee. It made vigorous incursions into the general Jewish community, drew thousands of local Jewish leaders into the circle of Zionist activists, and transformed the Council into the national headquarters for Zionist political activities. Dr. Silver was the central figure, with Neumann as his chief adviser. Silver's personality, oratorical ability, acumen and courage galvanized a devoted group which worked tirelessly at his side. Together they engineered the process that transformed American Zionism from a well-intentioned but politically passive group of individuals into a highly motivated nucleus promulgating a revolutionary program with mass appeal. They were not afraid to adopt the innovative tactics introduced by the Irgun Zvai Leumi's American committees, nor did they fear the reaction of the gentile community. As the Second World War was drawing to its close, Zionist leaders realized that increased militancy strengthened rather than weakened their support within the Jewish community.

By 1944, the men leading the Emergency Council were well acquainted with the American political arena. They understood that a relatively small group of people capable of achieving unified action and of channeling all resources and energies in a single direction could achieve their desired aims within the American political system. The council had become such an influence group, acting decisively and consistently, despite the different conceptions held by Wise and Silver regarding the role the Zionist movement should play on the American scene.

With Neumann and Silver came a new reading of America's social and political map, upon which they formulated the new character of Zionist activity in America. They viewed America as an active, pluralistic society which expects ethnic and religious groups, as well as other groups, to take an active part in public affairs on behalf of their causes. From the end of the 1930s, they had insisted on the Jewish state as the solution for Jewish problems—a position which took on new significance to the American and Jewish public as information about the fate of Europe's Jews and the inaction of the Allied powers became generally known.

The demand for practical political activity on behalf of world Jewry, coupled with a hard-line approach vis-à-vis the British, seemed more realistic than Rabbi Wise's hope that Jewish suffering would end with the victory of "good over evil" under Roosevelt's leadership. Dr. Wise and his adherents, who feared that too "loud" a Zionist or Jewish activism might encourage antisemitism, believed that Zionism's interests could best be served by bringing personal influence to bear on those who held power. Thus, the American Jewish community was faced with a choice between two kinds of internal political leadership: one advocating personal intervention in high places, and the second—organized communal political activity for specific political goals.

In the final clash between these strategic approaches at the end of 1944 and in early 1945, the majority of American Zionists opted for communal political activity under the leadership of Abba Hillel Silver and the Emergency Council. As an influence group, the council had already set in motion distinctly American democratic processes to further its struggle for the establishment of a Jewish state. It enjoyed the active support of the overwhelming majority of American Jewry. Beyond that, it established patterns of identification and action that organized Jewry in the United States has been following for over four decades.

Bibliography

The historical sources upon which this study is based can be divided into three categories:

   I.   Archival sources:
         A. Organizational archives
         B. Minutes
         C. Government archives
         D. Personal archives
         E. Archives of Zionist personages
         F. American personages
  II. Oral documentation
 III. Printed sources:
         A. Speeches, documents, memoirs and pamphlets
         B. Monographs and studies
         C. Periodicals and newspapers
         D. Articles

I. Archival Sources

A. Organizational Archives

1. The central archival source for the history of American Zionism in general, and the activities of the Emergency Committee and Emergency Council in particular, are the Emergency Committee's files; the minutes of the plenary sessions, the Office Committee and other committees; and an extensive collection of the various internal and external publications and correspondence in the New York Zionist Archives.

2. The New York Zionist Archives are largely complemented by section Z5 of the Central Zionist Archives in Jerusalem, containing the files of the American office of the Jewish Agency, in addition to a wealth of material on the activities of the Emergency Council and its ties with Zionist and Jewish organizations and institutions, as well as with the American government. This section also contains numerous files from the early years of the Emergency Committee.

3. Other sections of the Central Zionist Archives prominent in this study are section Z4—the files of the Zionist Executive in London, and section S25—the files of the Political Department of the Jewish Agency Executive in Jerusalem, containing material of great importance on various aspects of the Emergency Committee's activity, primarily with regard to its connections with the Zionist Executive in Palestine and in London. Documents from the following archival sections of the Central Zionist Archives were also used:

> Z6 Archives of Dr. Nachum Goldmann's personal office;
> Z5 American section of the World Zionist Organization, Jerusalem;
> A-322 Papers of Rabbi Morton Berman (head of the local Zionist Emergency Council, Chicago).

B. Minutes

The following minutes were studied during the compilation of this work:

1. Minutes of Jewish Agency Executive meetings, located in the Central Zionist Archives.

2. Minutes of the Zionist Executive in Jerusalem, located in the Central Zionist Archives.

3. Among the archives of the Zionist organizations of America, those of the Hadassah women's organization are especially important as they include, inter alia, complete transcripts of the minutes of the organization's national board meetings. The archives are kept in Hadassah's central headquarters in New York.

4. Documents concerning the activities of the committees established by the Irgun Zvai Leumi delegation in the United States (the "Bergson Group"), at present in the Jabotinsky Archives in Tel Aviv, and the Palestine Statehood Committee Papers, in Yale University's Sterling Memorial Library (manuscript group number 690), were carefully scrutinized. Extensive use was also made of the large collection of documents in the possession of Shmuel Merlin, who served as the general secretary of the committees.

C. Government Archives

1. *United States.* In order to examine the stand of the American administration and its ties with the American Zionist movement, the American Department of State (SDF) files dealing with Palestine were scrutinized. These files are housed in the National Archives in Washington, and in the Historical Division of the State Department.

Also examined were the minutes of the meetings of the US joint chiefs of staff for the years 1941–45, and the minutes of the combined chiefs of staff (of the United States and Great Britain) during World War II. These records illuminate the military aspects of the American position, adopted against the background of the war, and the role accorded to the Middle East in America's defense strategy.

Extensive use was also made of another collection which enhances our understanding of the US position during the war years: the records of the Office of Strategic Services. All of these documents are housed in the Modern Military Records Division of the National Archives in Washington D.C.

Additional archives central to the study of the period are those of President Roosevelt at Hyde Park. These archives contain not only the President's papers, but also those of his close colleagues. Especially useful were the papers of Henry Morgenthau, Jr. (particularly the diary), Samuel Rosenman and Harry Hopkins.

2. *Great Britain*. An understanding of the position, actions and responses of the mandatory power during this period was gained through the study of the files of the British Foreign Office, the Cabinet and the Prime Minister, which are kept in the Public Records Office in London.

D. Personal Archives

This type of archive proved crucial for a full understanding of the personal side of the political activity, and was therefore used extensively. Some personal archives are housed in public libraries and archives, while others are kept by the individuals themselves.

E. Archives of Zionist Personages

1. David Ben-Gurion Archives—Institute of Ben-Gurion Heritage at Sdeh Boker (originals in the Israel Defense Force Archives).

2. Papers of Dr. S. Goldman (a few files turned over to the Central Zionist Archives by H. Halkin).

3. Letters of Stephen S. Wise (originals at Brandeis University and photocopies of selected documents in section A243 of the World Zionist Organization Archives). Both sources were utilized.

4. Weizmann Archives—Yad Chaim Weizmann, Weizmann Institute, Rehovot.

5. The Harold P. Manson Files—Dr. Abba Hillel Silver Archives, The Temple, Cleveland, Ohio.

6. Dr. E. Neumann Archives—Dr. Neumann's office, New York.

7. Files of Robert Szold (in Mr. Szold's possession at time of research; subsequently turned over to the World Zionist Organization Archives).

8. Dr. Abba Hillel Silver Archives, The Temple, Cleveland, Ohio.

9. Meir Passov—Zionist Activity files (in his possession).

F. American Personages

1. Papers of David Niles (kept by Professor Sacher, Brandeis University).

2. Papers of Professor William Westerman—Butler Library, Columbia University, New York.

3. Papers of Sol Bloom—New York Public Library.
4. Stimson Diaries—Yale University, New Haven.
5. Robert Wagner Papers—Georgetown University, Washington D.C.

II. Oral Documentation

The following persons, who took an active part in the events under discussion, were interviewed. The interviews were recorded; most are stored in the Oral Documentation Section of the Institute for Contemporary Jewry, The Hebrew University, Jerusalem.

Akzin Binyamin
Eilat (Epstein), Eliyahu
Epstein, Judith
Ben-Gurion, David
Berlin, Isaiah
Berman, Morton
Cohen, Benjamin V.
Cohen, Miriam
Gelman, Leon
Goldstein, Israel
Halperin, Rose
Harris, Lucien
Jacobson, Charlotte
Kook, Hillel ("Peter Bergson")
Kulitz, Zvi
Levinthal, Louis

Littel, Franklin
Lourie, Arthur
Manson, Harold
Merlin, Shmuel
Nardi (Schwartz), Shulamit
Neumann, Emanuel
Passov, Meir
Passow, I. David
Shapiro, Harry
Sternstein, Joseph
Szold, Robert
Torczyner, Jacques
Turover, Dennis
Weisgal, Meyer
Voss, Carl Herman

III. Printed Sources

Abbreviations used in the Bibliography

AJA   *American Jewish Archives*
AJH   *American Jewish History*
AJHQ   *American Jewish Historical Quarterly*
EAJ   *Essays in American Jewish History to Commemorate the Tenth Anniversary of the Founding of the American Jewish Archives under the Direction of Jacob Rader Marcus* (ed.), Jacob Rader Marcus, Cincinnati, Ohio, AJA, 1958.
EAZ   *Essays in American Zionism, 1917–1948*, Melvin I. Urofsky (ed.), Herzl Year Book, vol. 8, New York, 1978.
JSS   *Jewish Social Studies*
PAJHS   *Publications of the American Jewish Historical Society*
YA   *YIVO Annual of Jewish Social Science*

The number of printed sources is so voluminous that, for the reader's convenience, only a selected sample has been included. A full bibliography is available in volume II of the author's doctoral dissertation, entitled "The Role of the Emergency Committee for Zionist Affairs as the Political Arm of American Zionism 1938–1944" (Hebrew University, Jerusalem, 1979)—upon which this work is largely based.

A. Speeches, Documents, Memoirs and Pamphlets

American Emergency Committee for Zionist Affairs. *The Balfour Declaration and American Interest in Palestine: Issued in Connection with the Twenty-Fifth Anniversary of the Balfour Declaration*, New York, 1942.

——. *Call to American Zionists*, New York, February 10, 1942.

——. *Zionism an Affirmation of Judaism: A Reply by 757 Orthodox, Conservative and Reform Rabbis of America to a Statement Issued by Ninety Members of the Reform, Charging that Zionism is Incompatible with the Teaching of Judaism*, New York, 1942.

——. *The Zionist Position: A Statement Submitted to the Delegates to the American Jewish Conference, August 29, 1943*, New York, 1943.

American Jewish Committee. *Palestine, Your Questions Answered*, New York, 1946.

——. *Statement of Withdrawal from the American Jewish Conference*, New York, 1943.

——. *Proposed Plans on the Future of Palestine*, New York, 1944.

——. *The American Jewish Year Book*, vols. XXIX–LVIII, Philadelphia, 1927–50.

American Jewish Conference (Alexander S. Kohanski [ed.]). *Organization and Proceedings of the First and Second Sessions*, New York, 1943, 1944.

——. *The Jewish Position at the United Nations Conference on International Organization, A Report to the Delegates*, New York, 1945.

——. *Report of the Interim Committee and the Commissions on Rescue, Palestine, Post-War, to the Delegates*, New York, November, 1944.

——. *Rules of Election for the American Jewish Conference, National Board of Elections*, New York, April, 1943.

——. *Statement of the Organization of the Conference and a Summary of Resolutions Adopted at the First Session*, New York, 1943.

——. *Statement on the Withdrawal of the American Jewish Committee, Adopted by the Interim Committee*, New York, November 7, 1943.

——. *Committee on Preliminary Studies. A Survey of Facts and Opinions on Problems of Post-War Jewry in Europe and Palestine*, New York, 1943.

American Palestine Committee. *The American Palestine Committee—What It Is*, New York, n.d. (c. 1941).

——. *A Christian Point of View on Palestine*, New York, 1946.

———. *"The Common Purpose of Civilized Mankind," A Declaration by 68 Members of the Senate and 198 Members of the House of Representatives of the Seventy-Seventh Congress on the Occasion of the Twenty-Fifth Anniversary of the Balfour Declaration*, New York, November 2, 1942.

American Zionist Emergency Council. *After the Victory: A Blue-print for the Rehabilitation of European Jewry*, New York, n.d. (c. 1944).

———. *American Speaks on Palestine*, New York, n.d. (c. 1944).

———. *Press Book on the 1939 British White Paper on Palestine*, New York, n.d. (c. 1943).

———. *Press Book on Palestine Jewry's Contribution to the War Against the Axis*, New York, n.d. (c. 1944).

———. *A Report of Activities, 1940–1946*, New York, 1946.

Anti-Defamation league of B'nai B'rith. *Previewing the Jewish State*, Chicago, 1937.

Browder, Earl. *Zionism*, New York, 1936.

The Committee for a Jewish Army of Stateless and Palestinian Jews. *From Evian to Bermuda*, New York, 1943.

The Committee of Christian Leaders, Clergymen and Laymen. *Memorandum on Behalf of Jewish Immigration into Palestine*, New York, n.d. (c. 1942).

Emergency Committee for Zionist Affairs. *Revisionism: A Destructive Force*, New York, 1940.

Emergency Committee to Save the Jewish People of Europe. *Memorandum on the Finding of the Emergency Conference to Save the Jewish People of Europe, July 20, 1943*, New York, 1943.

ESCO Foundation for Palestine Inc. *Palestine: A Study of Jewish, Arab, and British Policies*, New Haven, 1947.

Fertig, M. Maldwin. *The Pittsburgh Conference*, New York, 1943.

Foreign Relations of the United States (FRUS). Diplomatic Papers, Washington, 1940 vol. III (1958); 1941 vol. III (1959); 1942 vol. IV (1963); 1943 vol. IV (1964); 1944 vol. V (1965); 1945 vol. VIII (1969).

———. *The Conference at Washington and Quebec, 1943* (1970).

Fortune magazine. *Jews in America*, New York, 1936.

Ginzberg, Eli. *Report to American Jews on Overseas Relief, Palestine and Refugees in the United States*, New York, 1942.

Goldman, Solomon. *Undefeated*, Washington, 1940.

Hull, Cordell. *The Memoirs of Cordell Hull*, vol. II, New York, 1948.

Hurewitz, J. C. *The Struggle for Palestine*, New York, 1950.

Ickes, Harold L. *Cycles of Darkness*, New York, 1938.

———. *Palestine and the Destiny of the Jewish People*, New York, 1936.

Jabotinsky, Vladimir Z. *The War and the Jew*, New York, 1942.

Linfield, Harry S. *The Communal Organization of the Jews in the United States*, New York, 1930.

Niebuhr, Reinhold. *Jews After the War*, reprint from *Nation*, February 21 and 28, 1942.

Palestine Year Book, Sophie A. Udin (ed.), vol. I, Washington D.C., 1945.

Polier, Justine W., and James Wise. *The Personal Letters of Stephen Wise,* Boston, 1956.

Proskauer, Joseph. *A Segment of My Times,* New York, 1950.

Saltzman, Rubin. *The American Jewish Conference, Facts and Documents Which Should be Known to the Jewish Public,* New York, 1943.

Silver, Abba H. *"Advance on All Fronts!"* New York, 1943.

———. *The World Crisis and Jewish Survival: A Group of Essays,* New York, 1941.

———. *Vision and Victory: A Collection of Addresses, 1942–1948,* New York, 1949.

———. *A Year's Advance: A Political Report Submitted to the Convention of the Zionist Organizations of America, October 15, 1944,* New York, 1944.

———. *Zionism—What It Is—What It Is Not,* Cleveland, n.d.

Ulitzur, A. *Foundations: A Survey of Twenty-Five Years of Activity of the Palestine Foundation Fund—Keren Hayesod,* Jerusalem, 1946.

Urofsky, Melvin I., and David W. Levy. *Letters of Louis D. Brandeis,* 5 vols., Albany, 1971–1976.

U.S. House of Representatives, Committee on Foreign Affairs. *Hearings before the . . . The Jewish National Home in Palestine.* Seventy-eighth Congress, second session on H. Res. 418 and H. Res. 419: February 8, 9, 15, 16, 1944, Washington D.C., 1944.

Weisgal, Meyer. *. . . So Far an Autobiography,* Jerusalem, 1971.

Wise, Stephen S. *As I See It,* New York, 1944.

———. *Challenging Years,* London, 1951.

World Zionist Organization. *Report of the Executive of the . . . Submitted to the Sixteenth, Seventeenth, Eighteenth, Nineteenth Zionist Congresses at Zurich, Basel, Prague, Lucerne,* London, 1929, 1931, 1933, 1935.

Jewish Agency for Palestine. *Report of the Executives of the . . . submitted to the Twentieth, Twenty-First, Twenty-Second Zionist Congress and the Fifth, Sixth Session of the Council of the Jewish Agency at Zurich, Geneva, Basle,* Jerusalem, 1937, 1939, 1946.

Zionist Organization of America. *Report to the Annual Convention, Thirtieth-Fifty-Third Conventions,* New York-Washington, 1937–45.

B. Monographs and Studies

Adler, Cyrus, and Aaron Margalith. *With Firmness in the Right: American Diplomatic Action Affecting Jews, 1940–1945,* New York, 1946.

Adler, Selig. *The Isolationist Impulse,* New York, 1957.

———. *The Palestine Question in the Wilson Era,* New York, 1948.

Agus, Jacob B. *Guideposts in Modern Judaism: An Analysis of Current Trends in Jewish Thought,* New York, 1954.

Almond, E. A. *The American People and Foreign Policy,* New York, 1960.

Arlosoroff, Chaim. *Surveying American Zionism,* New York, 1929.

Bailey, Thomas A. *The Man in the Street: The Impact of American Public Opinion on Foreign Policy*, New York, 1948.

Bar Zohar, Michael. *Ben Gurion*, vol. I, Tel Aviv, 1975 (Hebrew).

Baram, Philip J. *The Department of State in the Middle East 1919–1945*, Philadelphia, 1978.

Bauer, Yehuda. *American Jewry and the Holocaust: The American Jewish Joint Distribution Committee, 1939–1945*, Detroit, 1981.

——. *From Diplomacy to Resistance: A History of Jewish Palestine, 1939–1945*, Philadelphia, 1970.

——. *The Jewish Emergence from Powerlessness*, Toronto, 1979.

——. *My Brother's Keeper: A History of the American Jewish Joint Distribution Committee 1929–1939*, Philadelphia, 1974.

Belth, Nathan C. *A Promise to Keep: A Narrative of the American Encounter with Anti-Semitism*, New York, 1979.

——. Harold Braverman and Morton Puner (eds.). *Barriers: Patterns of Discrimination Against Jews*, New York, 1958.

Bemis, Samuel F. *A Diplomatic History of the United States*, New York, 1965.

Ben-Gurion, David. *Letters to Paula and the Children*, London, 1971.

——. *Meetings with Arab Leaders*, Tel Aviv, 1957.

Berben, Paul. *Dachau: The Official History 1933–1945*, London, 1975.

Berlin, Isaiah. *Chaim Weizmann*, New York, 1974.

Bernard, Jesse. *American Community Behavior*, New York, 1949.

Bishop, Jim. *F.D.R.'s Last Years*, New York, 1975.

Brandeis, Louis D. *The Jewish Problem—How to Solve It*, New York, n.d.

Brinkly, Alan. *Voices of Protest: Huey Long, Father Coughlin and the Great Depression*, New York, 1983.

Brown, Frances J., and Joseph Roncek (eds.). *One America: The History, Contributions, and Present Problems of Our Racial and National Minorities*, New York, 1952.

Burms, James M. *Roosevelt, The Soldier of Freedom*, New York, 1970.

Carlson, John R. *Under Cover*, New York, 1968.

Cellar, Emanuel. *You Never Leave Brooklyn*, New York, 1953.

Cohen, Elliot E. *Commentary on the American Scene; Portraits of Jewish Life in America*, New York, 1953.

Cohen, Gabriel. *Churchill and Palestine, 1939–1942*, Jerusalem, 1976.

Cohen, Israel. *Contemporary Jewry*, London, 1950.

——. *A Short History of Zionism*, London, 1951.

——. *The Zionist Movement*, New York, 1946.

Cohen, Michael J. *Palestine: Retreat from the Mandate. The Making of British Policy, 1936–1945*, New York, 1978.

Cohen, Naomi W. *American Jews and the Zionist Idea*, New York, 1975.

——. *Not Free to Desist: The American Jewish Committee 1906–1966*, Phildelphia, 1972.

Craig, Gordon, A., and Felix Gilbert. *The Diplomats 1919–1939*, Princeton, 1953.

Dallek, Robert. *Franklin D. Roosevelt and American Foreign Policy 1932–1945*, New York, 1979.

DeNovo, John A. *American Interests and Policies in the Middle East 1900–1939*, Minnesota, 1963.

Diamond, Sander. *The Nazi Movement in the United States, 1924–1941*, Ithaca, 1974.

Dinnerstein, Leonard. *Uneasy at Home. Antisemitism and the American Jewish Experience*, New York, 1987.

Divine, Robert A. *Second Chance: The Trials of Internationalism in America During World War II*, New York, 1967.

Dobkowski, Michael N. *The Tarnished Dream. The Basis of American Anti-Semitism*, Westport, Conn., 1979.

Duker, Abraham G. *The American Jewish Community: Its History and Development*, New York, 1953.

Edidin, Ben M. *Jewish Community Life in America*, New York, 1947.

Elath, Eliahu. *San Francisco Diary*, Tel Aviv, 1971 (Hebrew).

Elazar, Daniel J. *Community and Polity. The Organizational Dynamics of American Jewry*, Philadelphia, 1976.

Epstein, Melech. *Jewish Labor in U.S.A. 1882–1952*, New York, 1950.

Feingold, Henry L. *The Politics of Rescue. The Roosevelt Administration and the Holocaust, 1938–1945*, New Brunswick, 1970.

Feinstein, Marnin. *American Zionism 1884–1904*, New York, 1965.

Fink, Reuben. (ed.). *America and Palestine: The Attitude of Official America and of the American People Toward the Rebuilding of Palestine as a Free and Democratic Jewish Commonwealth*, New York, 1944.

———. *The American War Congress and Zionism: Statements by Members of the American War Congress on the Jewish National Movement*, New York, 1919.

Fishman, Hertzel. *American Protestantism and the Jewish State*, Detroit, 1973.

Fox, Maier B. *American Zionism in the 1920s*, unpublished Ph.D. dissertation, George Washington University, 1979.

Friedman, Theodore, and Robert Gordin (eds.). *Jewish Life in America*, New York, 1955.

Friedlander, Saul. *Prelude to Downfall—Hitler and the U.S., 1939–1941*, London, 1967.

Friedman, Saul S. *No Haven for the Oppressed: United States Policy Toward Jewish Refugees, 1938–1945*, Detroit, 1973.

Friesel, Evyatar. *The Zionist Movement in the United States 1897–1914*, Tel Aviv, 1970 (Hebrew).

———. *Zionist Policy After the Balfour Declaration, 1917–1922*, Tel Aviv, 1977.

Fuchs, Lawrence H. *The Political Behavior of American Jews*, Glencoe, Ill., 1956.

Fuss, Samuel. *A Comparative Analysis of the American Jewish Conference Resolution on Palestine and Consideration of the Dissent Therefrom*, Pittsburgh, 1943.

Gal, Alon. *Brandeis of Boston*, Cambridge, Mass., 1980.

———. *David Ben Gurion—Preparing for a Jewish State: Political Alignment in Response to the White Paper and the Outbreak of World War II 1938–1941*, Sde Boker, 1985 (Hebrew).

Ganin, Zvi. *Truman, American Jewry and Israel 1945–1948*, New York, 1979.

Gelber, Yoav. *Jewish Palestinian Volunteering in the British Army During the Second World War*, vol. II, *The Struggle for a Jewish Army*, Jerusalem, 1981 (Hebrew).

Gerber, David A. *Anti-Semitism in American History*, Urbana, Chicago, 1980.

Ginzburg, Eli. *Agenda for American Jews*, New York, 1950.

Glanz, Rudolf. *Studies in Judaica Americana*, New York, 1970.

Glazer, Nathan. *American Judaism*, Chicago, 1957.

———. *Social Characteristics of American Jews 1654–1954*, New York, 1955.

Goldstein, Israel. *My World as a Jew*, New York, 1984.

Gordis, Robert. *Judism for the Modern Age*, New York, 1955.

Goren, Arthur A. *Dissenter in Zion. From the Writings of Judah L. Magnes*, Cambridge, Mass. and London, England, 1982.

Gorni, Yosef. *Partnership and Conflict. Chaim Weizmann and the Jewish Labor Movement in Palestine*, Tel Aviv, 1976 (Hebrew).

Gottheil, Richard J. H. *Zionism*, Philadelphia, 1941.

Graeber, Isacque, and Steuart H. Britt (eds.). *Jews in a Gentile World*, New York, 1942.

Grand, Samuel. *A History of Zionist Youth Organizations in the United States from their Inception in 1940*, unpublished Ph.D. dissertation, Columbia University, 1958.

Grose Peter. *Israel in the Mind of America*, New York, 1983.

Gurock, Jonathan. *American Jewish History—A Bibliographical Guide*, New York, 1983.

Halperin, Samuel. *The Political World of American Zionism*, Detroit, 1961.

Halpern, Ben. *The American Jew—A Zionist Analysis*, New York, 1956.

———. *A Clash of Heroes: Brandeis, Weizmann and American Zionism*, New York-Oxford, 1987.

———. *The Idea of the Jewish State*, Cambridge, Mass., 1969.

Hanna, Paul L. *British Policy in Palestine*, Washington D.C., 1942.

Harris, Leon. *The Merchant Princes: An Intimate History of Jewish Families who Built Great Department Stores*, New York, 1979.

Hattis, Susan L. *The Bi-National Idea in Palestine During Mandatory Times*, Tel Aviv, 1970.

Heller, Joseph. *The Zionist Idea*, London, 1947.

Herberg, Will. *Protestant–Catholic–Jew*, New York, 1956.

Hertzberg, Arthur. *The Zionist Idea: A Historical Analysis and Reader*, Garden City, New York, 1959.

Hilberg, Raul. *The Destruction of the European Jews*, New York, 1973.

Hoffer, Eric. *The True Believer*, New York, 1958.

Hull, Cordell. *Memoirs*, New York, 1948.

Ilan, Amitzur. *America, Britain and Palestine: The Origin and Development of America's Intervention in Britain's Palestine Policy, 1938–1947*, Jerusalem, 1979 (Hebrew).

Jabotinsky, Vladimir Z. *The War and the Jew*, New York, 1942.

Janowsky, Oscar (ed.). *The American Jew: A Composite Portrait*, New York-London, 1942.

Jonas, Manfred. *Isolationism in America 1935–1941*, Ithaca, New York, 1966.

Kallen, Horace. *Judaism at Bay: Essays Towards the Adjustment of Judaism to Modernity*, New York, 1932.

Karpf, Maurice J. *Jewish Community Organization in the United States*, New York, 1938.

Kaufman, Menahem. *Non-Zionists in America and the Struggle for Jewish Statehood 1939–1948*, Jerusalem, 1984 (Hebrew).

Kenen, Isaiah. *Israel's Defense Line: Her Friends and Foes in Washington*, Buffalo, N.Y., 1981.

Key, Vladimir O. *Politics, Parties and Pressure Groups*, New York, 1958.

King, C. Wendell. *Social Movements in the U.S.*, New York, 1956.

Kiplinger, William M. *Washington is Like That*, New York-London, 1942.

Klapperman, Gilbert. *The Story of Yeshiva University*, London, 1969.

Knee, Stuart E. *The Concept of Zionist Dissent in the American Mind 1917–1941*, New York, 1979.

Korn, Bertram W. *Eventful Years and Experience*, Cincinnati, 1954.

Kubowitzki, A. Leon. *Unity in Dispersion: A History of the World Jewish Congress*, New York, 1948.

Kutscher, C. B. *The Role of Hadassah in the American Zionist Movement 1912–1922*, unpublished Ph.D. dissertation, Brandeis University, 1975.

Langer, William L., and S. Evert Gleason. *The Challenge of Isolationism*, New York, 1962.

———. *The Undeclared War 1940–1941*, New York, 1953.

Laqueur, Walter. *The Terrible Secret*, London, 1980.

Lee, Albert. *Henry Ford and the Jews*, New York, 1980.

Lowdermilk, Walter C. *Palestine, Land of Promise*, London, 1944.

Machover, Jonah M. *Toward Rescue—The Story of Australian Jewry's Stand for the Jewish Cause, 1940–48*, Jerusalem, 1972.

Manuel, Frank E. *The Realities of American–Palestine Relations*, Washington, 1949.

Marcus, Sheldon. *Father Coughlin: The Tumultuous Life of the Priest of the Little Flower*, Boston, 1973.

Mardor, Meir. *Shlihut Alumah*, Tel Aviv, 1957.

McWilliams, Carey. *A Mask for Privilege: Anti-Semitism in America*, Boston, 1948.

Meyer, Isidore S. (ed.). *Early History of Zionism in America*, New York, 1958.

Miller, Donald H. *A History of Hadassah 1912–1935*, unpublished Ph.D. dissertation, New York University, 1968.

Moore, Deborah Dash. *At Home in America: Second Generation New York Jews*, New York, 1981.

——. *B'nai B'rith and the Challenge of Ethnic Leadership*, Albany, 1981.

Namier, Louis B. *Diplomatic Prelude, 1938–1939*, London, 1948.

——. *Conflicts. Studies in Contemporary History*, London, 1942.

Neumann, Emanuel. *In the Arena: An Autobiographical Memoir*, New York, 1976.

Neustadt-Noy, Isaac. *The Unending Task: Efforts to Unite American Jewry from American Jewish Congress to the American Jewish Conference*, Ph.D. dissertation, Brandeis University, 1976.

Niv, David. *Battle for Freedom. The Irgun Zvai Leumi*, Tel Aviv, 1965 (Hebrew).

Nutter, Harley A. *Postwar Foreign Preparation 1939–1945*, Washington D.C., 1959.

Oder, Irving. *The United States and the Palestine Mandate 1920–1948. A Study of the Impact of Interest Groups on Foreign Policy*, unpublished Ph.D. dissertation, Columbia University, 1956.

Ofer, Dalia. *Illegal Immigration During the Holocaust*, Jerusalem, 1988 (Hebrew).

Orian, Noah. *The Leadership of Rabbi Abba Hillel Silver on the American Jewish Scene 1939–1949*, unpublished Ph.D. dissertation, Tel Aviv University, 1983 (Hebrew).

Penkower, Monty N. *The Jews Were Expendable. Free World Diplomacy and the Holocaust*, Urbana, Chicago, 1983.

Pilat, Oliver. *Drew Pearson: An Unauthorized Biography*, New York, 1973.

Quinley, Harold E., and Charles Y. Glock. *Anti-Semitism in America*, New York, 1979.

Rabinowitz, Ezekiel. *Justice Louis D. Brandeis: The Zionist Chapter of his Life*, New York, 1968.

Rauch, Basil. *Roosevelt from Munich to Pearl Harbor*, New York, 1950.

Rose, Norman. *Chaim Weizmann: A Biography*, London, 1986.

Rosenblatt, Samuel. *The History of the Mizrachi Movement*, New York, 1951.

Ross, Robert W. *So It Was True: The American Protestant Press and the Nazi Persecution of the Jews*, Minneapolis, 1981.

Sacher, Leon. *The Redemption of the Unwanted: From the Liberation of the Death Camps to the Founding of Israel*, New York, 1983.

Savord, Ruth. *American Agencies Interested in International Affairs*, New York, 1942.

Schachner, Nathan. *The Price of Liberty*, New York, 1948.

Schechtman, Joseph B. *The United States and the Jewish State Movement*, New York, 1966.

Schwadron, Benjamin. *The Middle East Oil and the Great Powers*, Jerusalem, 1974.

Shapiro, Jonathan. *Leadership of the American Zionist Organization 1897–1930*, Urbana, Ill., 1971.

Sherman, C. Bezalel. *The Jew Within American Society: A Study in Ethnic Individuality*, Detroit, 1961.

——. *Labor Zionism in America*, New York, 1957.

Silverberg, Robert. *If I Forget Thee O Jerusalem: American Jews and the State of Israel*, New York, 1970.

Sington, Derek. *Belsen Uncovered*, London, 1946.

Sklare, Marshall. *America's Jews*, New York, 1971.

———. *Conservative Judaism: An American Religious Movement*, Glencoe, Ill., 1955, rev. 1972.

———. (ed.). *The Jew in American Society*, New York, 1974.

———. (ed.). *The Jewish Community in America*, New York, 1974.

———. (ed.). *The Jews: Social Patterns of an American Group*, Glencoe, Ill., 1958.

Slutsky, Yehuda. *History of the Hagana*, vol. 3, *From Resistance to War*, Tel Aviv, 1972 (Hebrew).

Smith, Gaddis. *American Diplomacy During the Second World War*, New York, 1970.

Soltes, Mordecai. *The Yiddish Press: An Americanizing Agency*, New York, 1950.

Spivak, John L. *Plotting America's Pogroms: A Documented Expose of Organized Anti-Semitism in the United States*, New York, 1934.

Stark, Freya. *Dust in the Lion's Paw*, autobiography 1939–1946, London, 1961.

Stark, Rodney et al. *Wayward Shepherds, Prejudice and the Protestant Clergy*, New York, 1971.

Stein, Leonard. *Weizmann and England*, London, 1964.

Stember, Charles et al. (eds.). *Jews in the Mind of America*, New York, 1966.

Strong, Donald S. *Organized Anti-Semitism in America. The Rise of Group Prejudice During the Decade 1930–1940*, Washington D.C., 1941.

Taylor, Alan R. *Prelude to Israel: An Analysis of Zionist Diplomacy 1897–1947*, New York, 1959.

Teller, Judd L. *Strangers and Natives*, New York, 1968.

Tevet, Shabtai. *"Kinat David": The Life of David Ben Gurion (parts A–C)*, Jerusalem-Tel Aviv, 1976–1987 (Hebrew).

Tillard, Paul. *Mauthausen*, Paris, 1945.

Truman, David. *The Governmental Process*, New York, 1951.

Tull, Charles J. *Father Coughlin and the New Deal*, Syracuse, 1965.

Urofsky, Melvin I. *American Zionism from Herzl to the Holocaust*, New York, 1975.

———. *Louis D. Brandeis and the Progressive Tradition*, Boston-Toronto, 1981.

———. *A Mind of One Piece. Brandeis and American Reform*, New York, 1971.

———. *A Voice that Spoke for Justice: The Life and Times of Stephen S. Wise*, Albany, 1982.

———. *We Are One. American Jewry and Israel*, New York, 1978.

Voss, Carl H. (ed.). *Stephen S. Wise: Servant of the People*, Philadelphia, 1969.

Weinstein, Jacob J. *Solomon Goldman—A Rabbi's Rabbi*, New York, 1973.

Welles, Sumner. *We Need Not Fail*, Cambridge, Mass., 1948.

Wischnitzer, Mark. *To Dwell in Safety: The Story of Jewish Migration Since 1800*, Philadelphia, 1948.

Woocher, Jonathan, S. *Sacred Survival. The Civil Religion of American Jews,* Bloomington-Indianapolis, 1986.

Woodwar, Sir Evelyn L. *British Foreign Policy in the Second World War,* vol. IV, London, 1975.

Wyman, David S. *The Abandonment of the Jews,* New York, 1984.

———. *Paper Walls: America and the Refugee Crisis, 1938–1941,* Massachusetts, 1968.

Zaar, Isaac. *Rescue and Liberation. America's Part in the Birth of Israel,* New York, 1954.

Zait, David. *Zionism and Peace. The Ideological–Political Road of "Hashomer Hatzair," 1927–1947,* Givat Haviva, 1985 (Hebrew).

C. Periodicals and Newspapers

American Zionist (ZOA)
Answer (Irgun Zvai Leumi delegation)
B'nai B'rith Magazine
Commentary (American Jewish Committee)
Conference Record (American Jewish Conference)
Congress Bulletin (American Jewish Congress)
Congress Weekly (American Jewish Congress)
Contemporary Jewish Record (American Jewish Committee)
Davar (daily Hebrew newspaper of the Histadrut)
Hadassah Newsletter
Independent Jewish Press Service
Jewish Frontier (Labor Zionist Organization of America)
Jewish Horizon (Hapoel Hamizrachi of America)
Jewish Outlook (Mizrachi organization of America)
Jewish Social Studies
JTA Daily News Bulletin (Jewish Telegraphic Agency)
Menorah Journal
National Jewish Monthly (B'nai B'rith)
New Judea (London)
New Palestine (ZOA)
New York Times
Opinion, A Journal of Jewish Life and Letters
Palcor News Agency Cables
Palestine (American Zionist Emergency Council)
Palestine and Zionism
Pro-Palestine Herald
Publications of the American Jewish Historical Society
Unity for Palestine
Voice of the Unconquered (Jewish Labor Committee)
Young Israel Viewpoint

Young Judean
Youth and Nation (Hashomer Hatzair)
Zionews (New Zionist Organization of America)
Zionist (New York region of the ZOA)
ZOA Program and Education Bulletin (ZOA)

D. Articles

Adler, Selig, "Franklin D. Roosevelt and Zionism: The Wartime Record," *Judaism* (Summer 1972), pp. 265–77.
——. "The Palestine Question in the Wilson Era," *JSS* (October 1948), pp. 303–35.
——. "The Roosevelt Administration and Zionism," in *EAZ*, pp. 132–48.
——. "The United States and the Holocaust," *AJHQ* (September 1974), pp. 14–24.
Baram, Philip J., "A Tradition of Anti-Zionism: The Department of State's Middle Managers," in *EAZ*, pp. 178–94.
Bauer, Yehuda, "When Did They Know," *Midstream* (April 1968), pp. 51–8.
Berlin, George L., "The Brandeis–Weizmann Dispute," *AJHQ* (September 1970), pp. 37–69.
——. "The Jewish Labor Committee and American Immigration Policy in the 1930's," in *Studies in Jewish Bibliography, History and Literature in Honor of I Edward Kiev*, New York, 1971, pp. 45–73.
Bernstein, Philip S., "A Jew Looks at the Christian Problem," in Voss, Carl H. (ed.), *The World Jewish Crisis and Palestine Today*, Rochester, N.Y., 1940.
Bierbrier, Doreen, "The American Zionist Emergency Council: An Analysis of a Pressure Group," *AJHQ* (September 1970), pp. 82–106.
Brody, David, "American Jewry, The Refugees and Immigration Restriction, 1932–1942," *PAJHS* (June 1956), pp. 219–48.
Carosso, Vincent, "A Financial Elite: New York's German-Jewish Investment Bankers," *AJHQ* (September 1976), pp. 67–89.
Cohen, Naomi W., "Anti-Semitism in the Gilded Age: The Jewish View," *JSS* (Summer/Fall 1979), pp. 187–211.
——. "The Maccabean's Message: A Study in American Zionism Until World War I," *JSS* (July 1956), pp. 163–78.
——. "The Reaction of Reform Judaism in America to Political Zionism (1897–1922)," *JSS* (July 1956), pp. 163–78.
——. "The Specter of Zionism: American Opinions, 1917–1922," in *EAZ*, pp. 96–116.
Dinnerstein, Leonard, "Jews and the New Deal," *AJH* (June 1983), pp. 461–75.
Feingold, Henry L., " 'Courage First and Intelligence Second': The American Jewish Secular Elite, Roosevelt and the Failure to Resist," *AJH* (June 1983), pp. 424–61.

——. "Who Shall Bear the Guilt for the Holocaust: The Human Dilemma," *AJH* (March 1979), pp. 261–83.

Feuer, Leon, "Abba Hillel Silver: A Personal Memoir," *AJA* (November 1967), pp. 107–26.

Freeman, Howard E., and Morris Showel, "Differential Political Influence of Voluntary Associations," *Public Opinion Quarterly* (Winter 1951/52), pp. 703–14.

Friesel, Evyatar, "American Zionism and American Jewry, An Ideological Communal Encounter," *AJA* (April 1988), pp. 5–23.

——. "Brandeis' Role in American Zionism Historically Reconsidered," *AJH* (September 1979), pp. 34–65.

Gal, Alon, "American Zionism Between the World Wars—Ideological Characteristics," *Yahadut Zemanenu Year Book*, 1989, pp. 79–90.

Glanz, Rudolf, "The German Jewish Mass Migration: 1820–1880," *AJA* (April 1970), pp. 49–66.

Goldblatt, Charles I., "The Impact of the Balfour Declaration in America," *AJHQ* (June 1968), pp. 455–515.

Gottlieb, Moshe, "The Anti-Nazi Boycott Movement in the United States: An Ideological and Sociological Appreciation," *JSS* (July–October 1973), pp. 198–228.

Grobman, Alex, "What Did They Know? The American Jewish Press and the Holocaust, 1 September, 1939–17 December, 1942," *AJH* (March 1979), pp. 283–305.

Halpern, Ben, "The Americanization of Zionism, 1880–1930," *AJH* (September 1979), pp. 15–33.

——. "Brandeis' Way to Zionism," *Midstream* (October 1971), pp. 3–13.

Kagedan, Allan J., "American Jews and the Soviet Experiment: The Agro-Joint Project, 1924–1937, *JSS* (Spring 1981), pp. 165–78.

Kaufman, Menahem, "From Neutrality to Involvement: Zionists, non-Zionists and the Struggle for a Jewish State," in *EAZ*, pp. 263–83.

Kober, Adolf, "Jewish Emigration from Würtemburg to the United States of America," *PAJHS* (March 1952), pp. 225–73.

Lerner, Natan, "World Jewish Congress," in *Encyclopedia Judaica*, vol. 16, Jerusalem, 1972, pp. 637f.

Lipstadt, Deborah E., "Louis Lipsky and the Emergence of Opposition to Brandeis, 1917–1920," in *EAZ*, pp. 37–60.

——. "The New York *Times* and the News about the Holocaust: A Quantified Study," *Proceedings of the Seventh World Congress of Jewish Studies*, Jerusalem, 1980.

Mandel, Irving, "Attitude of the American Jewish Community Toward East European Immigration," *AJA* (June 1950), pp. 11–36.

Mashberg, Michael, "American Diplomacy and the Jewish Refugee 1938–1939," *YA* (1974), pp. 339–65.

Maslow, Will, "Jewish Political Power: An Assessment," *AJHQ* (December 1976), pp. 349–62.

Matz, Eliahu, "Political Actions vs. Personal Relations," *Midstream* (April 1981), pp. 41–9.

Muzik, Edward J., "Victor L. Berger: Congress and the Red Scare," *Wisconsin Magazine of History* (Summer 1964), pp. 309–18.

Neustadt-Noy, Isaac, "Towards Unity: Zionist and Non-Zionist Cooperation, 1941–1942," in *EAZ*, pp. 149–65.

O'Brien, David J., "American Catholics and Anti-Semitism in the 1930's," *The Catholic World* (February 1967), pp. 270–6.

Panitz, Esther, "Washington Versus Pinsk: The Brandeis–Weizmann Dispute," in *EAZ*, pp. 77–131.

Parzen, Herbert, "The Lodge-Fish Resolution," *AJHQ* (September 1970), pp. 69–82.

——. "The Roosevelt Palestine Policy 1943–1945," *AJA* (April 1974), pp. 31–66.

Penkower, Monty N., "Ben Gurion, Silver and the 1941 UPA National Conference for Palestine: A Turning Point in American Zionist History," *AJH* (September 1979), pp. 66–78.

——. "In Dramatic Dissent: The Bergson Boys," *AJH* (March 1981).

——. "Jewish Organizations and the Creation of the U.S. War Refugee Board," *Annals of the American Academy of Political and Social Science* (July 1980), pp. 122–30.

——. "The 1943 Joint Anglo-American Statement on Palestine," in *EAZ*, pp. 212–41.

Pinsky, Edward, "American Jewish Unity During the Holocaust—The Joint Emergency Committee, 1943," *AJH* (June 1983), pp. 477–94.

Ribuffo, Leo P., "Henry Ford and *The International Jew*," *AJH* (June 1980), pp. 497–505.

Rosenstock, Morton, "Are There Too Many Jews at Harvard?" in L. Dinnerstein (ed.), *Antisemitism in the United States*, New York, 1971.

Schmidt, Sarah, "Horace M. Kallen and the 'Americanization' of Zionism—In Memoriam," *AJA* (April 1976), pp. 59–73.

——. "The Zionist Conversion of Louis D. Brandeis," *JSS* (January 1975), pp. 18–34.

Shafir, Shlomo, "American Jewish Leaders and the Emerging Nazi Threat, 1928–January, 1933," *AJA* (November 1979), pp. 150–83.

Shpiro, David H., "American Zionist Leaders and the Rescue of European Jews—November–December 1942," *Yad Vashem Studies* (1984), pp. 363–79.

——. "Decision at Biltmore," *The Jerusalem Quarterly* (Winter 1987), pp. 112–22.

——. "The Political Background of the 1942 Biltmore Resolution," in *EAZ*, pp. 166–77.

Singerman, Robert, "The American Career of the *Protocols of the Elders of Zion*," *AJH* (September 1981), pp. 48–78.

Stern-Taeubler, Selma, "The Motivation of the German-Jewish Emigration to America in the Post-Mendelssohnian Era," in *EAJ*, pp. 247–63.

Szajkowski, Zosa, "The Attitude of American Jews to East European Jewish Immigration, 1881–1893," *PAJHS* (March 1951), pp. 221–80.

——. "The Attitude of American Jews to Refugees from Germany in the 1930s," *AJHQ* (December 1971), pp. 101–44.

——. "A Note on the American Jewish Struggle Against Nazism and Communism in the 1930s," *AJHQ* (March 1970), pp. 272–90.

——. "The Yehudi and the Immigrant: A Reappraisal," *AJHQ* (September 1973), pp. 13–45.

Tenenbaum, Jospeh, "The Anti-Nazi Boycott Movement in the United States," *Yad Vashem Studies on the European Jewish Catastrophe and Resistance* (1959), pp. 141–61.

Urofsky, Melvin I., "Rifts in the Movement: Zionist Fissures, 1942–1945," in *EAZ*, pp. 195–211.

Voss, Carl Hermann, "The American Christian Palestine Committee," in *EAZ*, pp. 242–62.

Index

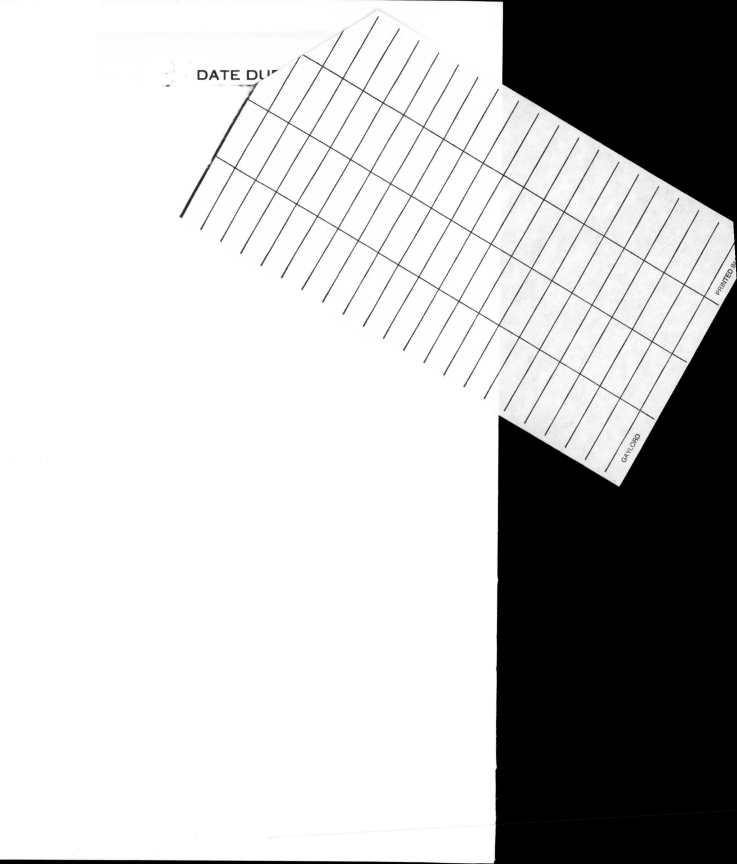

DATE DUE